BARBECUE

BARBECUE

Smoked & Grilled Recipes From Across the Globe

HUGH MANGUM

WITH SHANA LIEBMAN

CONTENTS

LEGENDS

Vegan	Grilled
V	

Vegetarian	Smoked
VG	

Gluten free	Cooking time longer than 10 hours
GF	

Dairy free	Direct heat
DF	

Nut free	Indirect heat
NF	

5 ingredients or fewer	Complex
5	

INTRODUCTION

Barbecue

(1) To cook, most often meat, through the use of wood fire or smoke.

(2) A celebratory event revolving around friends, family, food, and fire.

—Hugh Mangum

Lighting the Fire

In 1975, about a half mile north of Sunset Boulevard on Doheny Drive in West Hollywood, California, a stocky Texan who looked a bit like Orson Welles, smoked meat, producing faint bluish plumes with the sweetest smell. I can't remember what particular cuts of meat my father, Hugh Mangum III, used to smoke, but I do remember that smell. It was my introduction to the world of barbecue.

When my father suddenly passed away in 1999, I realized that I had taken for granted all that we shared, and at the top of that list was food. Inspired to honor my father and our relationship, I decided to take some time off from my career as a musician and enroll in culinary school. I thought it might be a meaningful way to posthumously connect to him.

I packed a van and moved from Los Angeles to New York City's East Village with my dog, Clyde, to attend the French Culinary Institute, where I absorbed every possible morsel of information. I felt inspired and purposeful. I dug into classical French cooking with the exuberance of a child learning to ride a bike and became obsessed with learning technique after technique. I had never tackled anything like this before, and my beginner's mind was on fire.

While attending culinary school in 2000, I was making my way to my kitchen classroom, and I was struck by a bolt of lightning when I saw a woman walking down the stairs. She was Laura Malone—whom I was lucky enough to marry and now share our three incredible children: Quinn, Lucas, and Henry.

After culinary school, I was determined to capture the heart of Laura's family, who were from North Carolina, a place with a rich barbecue culture that was very different from that of Texas. In North Carolina, whole hog barbecue reigns supreme, and pulled pork is the go-to main. I grew up with brisket, spareribs, and sausage, so to learn how to make pulled pork, I dove into a multitude of recipes and notes my father had left behind. I purchased a barrel smoker that weighed a couple hundred pounds. I was giddy at the prospect of getting to know my new toy and started smoking pork butts with the oak wood and apple wood that was abundant in Bucks County, Pennsylvania, where we had recently moved.

I learned that although barbecue presents as bold, assertive, and primal, what separates good barbecue from truly great barbecue is the nuanced details: the burn rate of the fire, the amount of coals below the burning wood. Barbecue perfection exists in consistency. It exists only if the cook is fully present.

Barbecue is a meditation that begins with tending a proper fire. Fire is a dance, and it requires attention, affection, and the ability to react to subtle changes. Forget about special rubs and sauces—if your fire is a mess, then all else will be a mess. All the sauce in the world can't cover up what a poorly tended fire will do to your food.

I learned to tend a fire by cooking pork butts. I cooked a lot of pork butts, and I messed up a lot of pork butts. I began by undercooking them because I had not learned trust and patience. Then I overcooked them because I was overcompensating.

I also learned that a four-inch probe in a three-foot-diameter pit can't possibly give a true read on the actual temperature of a smoker. I learned about hot spots and airflow and that 225°F/107°C is absolutely not the catch-all temperature to smoke meat. I learned to quit lifting the lid of the smoker, which not only causes you to lose temperature but also decreases humidity. I learned how to gauge temperature by touch and to trust the process. I learned about the stall, when the meat's temperature plateaus. I learned about which tools and gadgets actually work and which ones are useless. I learned that as the sun rises on a crisp fall morning, drinking a fresh cup of coffee while tending a fire is a religious experience for me.

I learned to differentiate between white smoke, which overwhelms food and is a sign of improper combustion, and blue smoke, which kisses the food it encounters and is a sign of proper combustion.

The thing about barbecue is that by doing it often, you also tend to learn a lot about yourself. You spend a lot of quiet hours alone. You must practice extreme patience. You must pay attention to very small details (wind direction, temperature, humidity, etc.), and you must be open to making mistakes and learning from them. If you learn to barbecue, you will eat well, feed friends and family, and ultimately make people happy. It's really simple.

The Making of Mighty Quinn's

After seven years of smoking meat as a hobby (albeit a very dedicated hobby), Laura and I applied to be a vendor at the Brooklyn Flea, at the urging of her cousin Adam Johnson. The Brooklyn Flea is a very successful, very busy outdoor flea market in Brooklyn that attracts thousands every weekend. The prospect of becoming a vendor there was massive. At the time, our family was struggling: We had been caught up in the housing crisis of 2008 and lost just about everything. We were on fumes, and the potential of selling at this market seemed like it could be the lifeline we needed.

We smoked brisket, spareribs, and lamb and brought them warm from New Jersey to Brooklyn for a meeting with Eric Demby and Jonathan Butler, the founders of the Brooklyn Flea. While they seemed to thoroughly enjoy the barbecue, they let us know that the Flea already had a barbecue vendor and they were loyal to their vendors; thus, there was no room for us. But they were in the process of launching a new food-only market called Smorgasburg.

The market was set to launch in Williamsburg, Brooklyn, that spring, and we hustled to get all the minutiae handled: permits, smallwares, serving equipment, coolers, etc. Laura, who is one of the most creative humans I've ever known and has the greatest handwriting on the planet, created a chalkboard sign with a large Q (and pinstripes across the Q) that read "Mighty Quinn's." Fourteen years later, we still use that hand-drawn logo.

We smoked five briskets, six pork butts, and twelve racks of ribs, which at the time seemed like a lot. We ended up selling out in an hour and a half, and that was the real birth of Mighty Quinn's. Smorgasburg turned out to be the epicenter of New York City's creative food movement; it's like the food version of Woodstock—a juggernaut, where thousands gather on Saturdays to consume so many kinds of dishes. We became family with vendors like Anarchy in a Jar, Slant Shack, Blue Bottle, and Dough Doughnuts. We all looked forward to our weekend hangs and the energy of Brooklyn. It sounds like a cliche, but things were so wonderfully simple at that time.

Our success at Smorgasburg led to the opening of Mighty Quinn's first brick-and-mortar in the East Village in 2012. We were relatively busy from the day we opened. Then, in 2013, Pete Wells of the *New York Times* gave Mighty Quinn's a glowing review, and it was like winning an Academy Award. Suddenly, we were busting-at-the-seams busy. The floodgates had opened. There was no turning back. We had officially made it.

A year later, Mighty Quinn's had become bigger than we ever expected, and I was spending around five hours a day commuting in and out of New York City. Business was growing, and I was making regular television appearances and traveling to open more Mighty Quinn's locations.

As the business grew, I found myself less connected to the everyday cooking at the restaurants. I had worked tirelessly on Mighty Quinn's and put in more than the proverbial 10,000 hours. Yet when I was no longer in the kitchen, being a part of the business wasn't fulfilling in the way I had hoped.

When I was approached about helming this book, something in me woke up.

A Book on Barbecue

Often, customers would walk into Mighty Quinn's and declare their hometown and its barbecue heritage. I would make it my mission to hit them over the head with everything we had. The goal was not only to wow them but to return them to that sense of family and home that barbecue can conjure.

Barbecue transcends the fork and knife. It's so much bigger than what's in your rub or at what temperature you smoke your meat. It's about connecting. It's about nourishing—including nourishing your soul. It's about community. Although my fellow Americans like to argue about which regional barbecue is superior, the truth is that regardless of the sauce, protein, or technique, every barbecue provides a place for people to gather, eat, and connect.

And we're not just talking about Texas brisket versus North Carolina pulled pork. It's *lechon* in the Philippines and *char siu* in China. It's *barbacoa* in Mexico and *churrasco* in South America. It's pork satay on the streets of Indonesia, smoky pits filled with goat leg in Ghana, and ash-cooked root vegetables in Spain. A tradition of barbecue is present all over the world. For thousands of years, people have been using fire and smoke to cook their food.

For this book, I scoured the world for great food cooked with fire and/or smoke. I dove into barbecue's international heritage and the ways in which cultures from Ireland to Iran celebrate food and life around the fire. I spoke to both professional chefs and home cooks to discover the best barbecue around the globe and then whittled it down to around 280 dishes, from Cedar Plank Salmon (page 264) to Tea-Smoked Duck (page 244).

The dishes in this book differ dramatically because of indigenous ingredients and traditional methods, but they also have many commonalities. Many are festive dishes, lovingly served at informal celebratory gatherings, which showcase local flavors, embody the culture that they come from, and continue the tradition that started them.

These are also dishes that make people happy.

When I was a little kid in 1975, my father taught me that barbecue made him happy. It made my mother happy, it made our neighbors happy, and without my realizing it at the time, that happiness I also felt set my path in motion to becoming a chef some twenty-five years later.

This book is a love letter to fire and smoke and an opportunity to connect with others who experience that same passion.

There will always be the latest and greatest gear for barbecue enthusiasts, including shiny, expensive versions of every tool imaginable: custom aprons, fancy spatulas, luxe oven mitts. This section is not that.

Instead, these are recommendations for tools that make barbecuing a more efficient and enjoyable experience. Some items on the list are not cheap, but some more expensive items are worth the cost in the long run. Also, please keep in mind that you don't need every item on this list. This is simply a handy guide as you pursue your journey into the world of barbecue.

Aluminum foil
Heavy-duty preferred.

Ash can
Or galvanized can with a lid.

Bus tubs
These are an easy way to transport meat to and from the grill/smoker and to transport loose items like pepper mills, tools, plates, etc.

Butcher paper
Peach butcher paper is ideal for wrapping brisket; used butcher paper makes a wonderful fire starter.

Chimney starter
Every grill set-up should have one.

Click lighters
It's best to have at least a couple handy.

Cooler
Any heavy-duty sealing cooler works. It's best to have two, one for cold beverages and one for wrapped briskets. A well-sealed cooler is a great way to hot-hold meats after they are removed from the grill/smoker.

Disposable gloves
The most sanitary way to handle raw meats and colorful spices; also handy for serving food.

Fire extinguisher
Hopefully, it will never be needed.

Folding table
Ideally, a 6-foot/1.8-meter table to work on.

Gloves
Inexpensive, hardware store–style gloves are a must for preventing splinters while gathering wood, and they double as great heat protection while you're managing your smoker, moving shelves, cleaning, etc.

Grill brush
A clean grill is imperative.

Grill hoe or rake
The most efficient way to move around coals or small logs.

Hotel pans
6-inch/15-cm-deep pans work for collecting water and holding meats. They will last forever and are preferable to disposable ones.

Instant-read thermometer
The ThermoWorks Thermapen is my favorite battle-tested probe.

Kindling
These small, dry pieces of wood ignite fast and are essential to easily building a proper fire.

Lawn chair
It's going to be a long day, so you may as well be comfortable.

Newspaper
For helping to start the fire.

Nitrile gloves
These are the best disposable gloves for dealing with hot/warm food because they last longer than regular disposable gloves.

Portable Grill and Smoker
For small spaces and traveling, these sturdy mini units, like the well-constructed Nomad Portable Grill/Smoker, can deliver great results.

Pizza peel

A wooden peel is the absolute best way to move, rearrange, or remove large cuts of meat from the grill/smoker. Cut the handle down to about 8 inches/20 cm for best leverage.

Plastic wrap

Heavy-duty plastic wrap is perfect for wrapping and covering meats, sides, and salads. Use the largest and most durable wrap available.

Pop-up tent

It may seem like overkill, but a 10-foot/3-meter pop-up tent is useful if you live in an area prone to poor weather conditions. A tent is a relatively inexpensive way to protect yourself from being stuck in the rain for a long time.

Propane camping torch

This is better than a click lighter for starting fires.

Sheet trays

Both full- and half-sized.

Shovel

This is probably the item I use most to arrange coals, clean ash, move wood, etc.

Skewers

Use either metal or wooden (which need to soak in warm water for 20–30 minutes before they hit the grill).

Small hand-held mop

For basting.

Smoker thermometer

A great tool when you are getting to know your smoker and its temperature gauge. Set it up in multiple zones, and adjust your load accordingly. I prefer the ThermoWorks Smoke.

Spray bottles

For spritzing meat. For example, apple cider on ribs and apple cider vinegar on brisket.

Tarp

To cover your wood during rain.

Tongs

Stainless steel ones are best.

PANTRY LIST

Although specialty ingredients are required for a handful of recipes in this book, the following catch-all pantry list will set you up for success and create a solid foundation for building your barbecue house. Barbecue is intentionally low maintenance, so most of these items are relatively inexpensive, easy to source, and may already be regulars in your home pantry.

Dry Goods

Aleppo pepper
ancho chili powder
bay leaves
black pepper (cracked, whole, and ground)
cayenne pepper
celery seeds
coriander (whole)
cumin (ground)
curing salt (for sausages)
dark brown sugar
dark chili powder
dried chiles (ancho, arbol, guajillo, pequiín)
granulated garlic
granulated sugar
kosher salt
mustard powder
mustard seeds (yellow)
onion powder
paprika
smoked paprika (pimenton)

Produce, Liquids, and Canned Goods

apple cider
apple cider vinegar
bacon
butter
canola oil
chipotle peppers in adobo
Dijon mustard
extra-virgin olive oil
fish sauce
garlic
hot sauce
ketchup
lemons
limes
maple syrup
mayonnaise
molasses
pickle relish
pure vanilla extract
red onions
red wine vinegar
scallions (spring onions)
soy sauce
Spanish onions
vanilla paste
Vidalia (sweet) onions
Worcestershire sauce

FIRE PRIMER

Building and tending a fire is one of the most important skills for barbecue. It takes time, patience, and many mistakes. You must turn away from technology and focus in the opposite direction: Fire is basic, analog, and primal. A fire requires your attention—and this primer will help you become an expert.

Wood

Apple produces a mild, somewhat sweet, and fruity smoke. It is best when tempered with oak. It shines on pork and poultry, specifically spareribs, baby back ribs, and half chickens.

Cherry has a mild, sweet smoke that is best blended with oak. (Use about 75% oak and 25% cherry or apple.) It works with pork and poultry, as well as beef brisket and short ribs, and helps impart color to the bark.

Hardwood pellets are used in a pellet grill/smoker, which is fed into a firebox by an auger system. Most pellet smokers have a thermostat, which makes smoking easier than it is in an offset (horizontally oriented) smoker. A pellet smoker is a good entry point for a beginner or someone with limited space, but it won't achieve the same depth of flavor that a wood-burning smoker can deliver.

Hickory has a strong, assertive flavor and burns like oak.

Mesquite has a strong flavor best suited for red meat. It is one of the hottest burning woods and thus not as conducive to a balanced, low, slow, and steady smoke.

Oak (post, red, white) is the stalwart of cooking woods. It burns long and clean with a medium smoke profile. It pairs well with every protein and plays well with other woods, usually apple and/or cherry.

Peach has a subtle, sweet flavor and mild smoke. It is especially suited for shorter smokes and works best with poultry, smaller cuts of pork (like thick pork chops or baby back ribs), and seafood.

Pecan belongs to the hickory family and is nutty and mild. It smells like Texas. It is what every road trip with my father smelled like as we approached our next barbecue pit stop. If pecan were local to me in the Northeast United States, I would use it with the other woods I've come to love. However, it feels wrong to ship wood from thousands of miles away when great local options are available.

Wood chunks and chips work well with charcoal, though the best wood to use for a smoker is local logs. Wood chunks will help impart smoke to your cook, but they also burn down to embers, which will help the coals stay hot for four hours or longer. For shorter cooks or smaller vessels, use wood chips, which create bursts of smoke.

Charcoal

Binchotan is a Japanese-style charcoal made from Japanese oak trees that are not logged (branches are selectively cut, leaving the tree alive). The branches are then placed in kilns and burned at a low temperature until they become charcoal—a process that can take weeks to complete. Binchotan charcoal excels at high-heat grilling and doesn't produce odor or smoke. The downside is that it is expensive, but it may be worth the cost, especially for Japanese dishes like yakitori.

Briquettes are readily available and easy to use. They produce even heat and generally burn at a slower rate than natural wood. Briquettes are produced by compressing wood scraps and sawdust together using binders. Choose a briquette that is 100% natural; some products contain additives that are bad for the environment and for consumption. Choose **hardwood briquettes**, which are essentially the same as standard briquettes but contain a higher percentage of hardwood, which makes them burn longer.

Coconut shell briquettes are made using the shells and husks of coconuts, plus water and cornstarch. The briquettes are usually cut into honeycomb logs or cubes. Coconut briquettes last longer than almost all other charcoal, but they can be a little finicky to light and are expensive.

Lump charcoal is pure charcoal made from real wood (which is slowly burned until all the moisture, natural chemicals, and sap are removed). Unlike briquettes, which use molds, lump charcoal comes in different shapes and sizes. Although it doesn't burn as evenly or hold heat as long as briquettes, lump charcoal produces a pure, additive-free burn that responds to oxygen like a real wood fire.

Which is better: charcoal or gas?
Use whichever grill is easiest to operate and/or most cost-effective. Gas grills are great because they turn on with a click, but you get a better flavor from using charcoal and real wood.

For grilling, what is high, medium, and low heat?
High heat is anything 450°F/230°C and higher; medium heat is 350°F/180°C; low is 300°F/150°C.

High heat means you have white hot or glowing coals. If you put a hand over the grate, you can barely hold it there for one or two seconds without having to pull it away. Medium heat: You can hold a hand over the coals for three to four seconds. Low heat: You can hold a hand there indefinitely, but the grill still has heat.

What does direct versus indirect heat mean?
Direct: Sitting directly above the heat source.
Indirect: The food is not placed directly above the heat source, so is cooked by the smoke or ambient temperature.

Direct heat can be great for poultry and steak, but many proteins, like pork shoulder and brisket, benefit from indirect heat, which will slowly melt away the intermuscular fat and thereby increase tenderness. Sausages benefit from both indirect and direct heat. Finishing a smoked sausage, rib roast, or chicken over direct heat is also useful to get the benefit of the smoke and the slower cook, but also crispy skin and snap.

Some cuts of meat, like a whole lamb, suckling pig, or lamb leg, benefit from more ambient direct heat, which can be on a spit or open fire.

Should I oil the grill/smoker or the food?
A well-seasoned smoker does not have to be oiled. A clean grill—and you should clean the grates with a grill brush while hot—doesn't need to be oiled if the food is fatty. However, it can't hurt to swipe the grates (before they get too hot) with a towel dipped in vegetable or canola oil.

How long will preheating the grill/smoker take?
This depends on size. My smoker, which is 7,000 pounds (3,200 kg) and 18-feet (5.5-meters) long, needs 1 hour to get up to temperature. In the winter, that might be 75 minutes, and in the summer, it might be 45 minutes. A small smoker takes about 30 minutes. More importantly, you want to stabilize the temperature throughout the cook by adding small amounts of wood to keep the initial embers burning. If you lose your embers and you're playing catch up, the temperature will dip or rise too high.

If you're using charcoal, use a chimney starter, which, according to an old motto, will be properly hot in the time it takes to drink a beer (or at least within 20 minutes).

Can I smoke food without a smoker?
Yes, although there's a learning curve to using a grill to smoke food, and it won't be identical to an offset smoker. You can create a smoker out of a charcoal grill by banking the fire to one side and continually adding hot coals (from a chimney starter) as well as wood chips/chunks. This would not be ideal for something like a brisket, because you will have to lift the lid every 30 minutes to add coals, but it will work for a chicken or a rack of ribs.

Do I need lighter fluid?
Never. Nothing chemical should ever touch the inside of a grill or smoker. Also, always use charcoal that is additive-free.

What should I do if the food catches on fire?
Always have a spray bottle of water nearby. If your spray bottle is already filled with apple cider or apple cider vinegar, then use that to put out the fire.

What is the best way to gauge the temperature of the grill, the smoker, and the food?
If you have a small smoker, the thermometer will be pretty accurate, but if you're dealing with a barrel smoker, it's a very nearsighted view, so you will have to learn how to read the temperature beyond the factory-provided probe.

Get to know your grill/smoker until you can just feel the outside to know its internal temperature. Before then, use a thermometer (such as the ThermoWorks Smoke) that has two probes, to use in different quadrants or areas of the grill/smoker. It connects to a thermometer outside the grill/smoker, as well as a wireless unit. It also comes with a probe for large cuts of meat. Until you can tell by feel, stick this probe into a large cut like a brisket before you start smoking (so the protein seals around the probe) and monitor it until it reaches 201°F/94°C. That's when a brisket is perfectly moist and almost gelatinous, yet sliceable.

SKEWERS

&

SAUSAGES

CONGOLESE BEEF SKEWERS

Central Africa's barbecue tradition, called *coupé-coupé* (from the French word *couper*, meaning "to slice"), uses tough cuts of beef marinated in ginger, beef bouillon, and cayenne pepper, then cooked over charcoal and served with a baguette. In urban parts of the Democratic Republic of Congo, vendors start grilling beef skewers early in the morning so they will be ready for the lunchtime crowds.

PREPARATION TIME 10 minutes, plus overnight marinating
COOKING TIME 10 minutes
SERVES 4

2 beef bouillon cubes
4 cloves garlic, crushed
4 tablespoons yellow mustard
2 teaspoons grated ginger
½ teaspoon cayenne pepper
Juice of 1 lemon
1 (2¼-lb/1-kg) sirloin steak, trimmed of fat and cut into 2-inch/5-cm cubes
4 tablespoons olive oil
1 sliced baguette, to serve

In a large bowl, combine the bouillon, garlic, mustard, ginger, cayenne pepper, and lemon juice and mix well. Stir in the beef. Cover and refrigerate overnight.

Preheat a grill to high heat.

Thread the beef cubes onto skewers and brush them with the olive oil. Place the skewers on the grill and cook for 3 minutes on each side, or until browned and cooked through. Transfer to a serving dish.

Serve hot with the baguette.

Thousands of Cambodians who fled their homes after the overthrow of the Khmer Rouge landed in Stockton, California, where, on weekends, many gather at Angel Cruz Park to hang out and share food. These Cambodian beef kabobs, named after the California park, are marinated in lemongrass, makrut lime, and fish sauce and are usually cooked on a charcoal grill.

PREPARATION TIME 15 minutes, plus 3 hours marinating
COOKING TIME 10 minutes
SERVES 6–8

6 stalks lemongrass, outer leaves removed
and thinly sliced
6 makrut lime leaves, finely chopped,
or 1 teaspoon lime zest
6 cloves garlic
2 shallots, finely chopped
½ tablespoon grated ginger
1 teaspoon ground turmeric
3 lb/1.3 kg beef chuck, cut into ½-inch/1-cm cubes
Generous ½ cup (4½ fl oz/130 ml) honey
6 tablespoons canola oil
6 tablespoons fish sauce
6 tablespoons oyster sauce
1½ tablespoons sweet paprika

In a food processor, combine the lemongrass, makrut lime leaves or lime zest, garlic, shallots, ginger, and turmeric. Blend into a smooth paste. Transfer the paste to a large bowl, then add the remaining ingredients. Cover with plastic wrap (clingfilm) and refrigerate for 3 hours.

Preheat a grill to high heat.

Thread the beef onto skewers. Place them on the grill and cook for 8 minutes, turning frequently, until charred and cooked through. Transfer to a serving dish.

Serve hot.

Seasoned with lemongrass, makrut lime, and fresh turmeric, these beef skewers, or *sach ko ang*, are a classic early evening snack in Cambodia. Most recipes call for the addition of pork fat (these skewers use pork belly), which drips into the charcoal and produces a smoky richness. The meat is typically eaten with pickled vegetables on a buttered baguette.

PREPARATION TIME 15 minutes, plus 1 hour marinating
COOKING TIME 5–10 minutes
SERVES 4

FOR THE SPICE PASTE

5 cloves garlic, minced
2 shallots, minced
7 oz/200 g stalks lemongrass, outer leaves removed
1 tablespoon galangal, peeled and finely chopped
1 teaspoon turmeric root, peeled and finely chopped
8 makrut lime leaves or 1 teaspoon lime zest

FOR THE BEEF SKEWERS

4 tablespoons spice paste (see above)
4 tablespoons fish sauce
2 tablespoons palm sugar
1 tablespoon peanuts roasted, finely chopped, then pounded
1 (14-oz/400-g) sirloin steak, cut into ½-inch/1-cm cubes
2 oz/55 g skinless pork belly, cut into ½-inch/1-cm cubes

FOR SERVING

Vietnamese Pickles (page 300)
1 baguette, buttered and sliced

FOR THE SPICE PASTE In a food processor, combine all the ingredients and blend into a smooth paste. (Some fibers from the lemongrass may remain, which is fine.)

FOR THE BEEF SKEWERS In a medium bowl, combine the spice paste, fish sauce, palm sugar, and peanuts. Add the beef and pork and marinate at room temperature for 1 hour.

Preheat a grill to high heat.

Thread the beef onto skewers, alternating with the pork cubes. Place the skewers on the grill and cook for 5–10 minutes, turning frequently and brushing with the leftover marinade, until the meat is cooked. Transfer to a serving dish.

Serve immediately with pickled vegetables and buttered baguette.

GRILLED BEEF HEARTS

Anticuchos, or chargrilled beef skewers, date back to the Incas in the early sixteenth century. They were originally made with the hearts of llamas or white-tailed deer, but the more modern versions use beef hearts marinated with ají panca chiles and achiote paste. Serve with potatoes, corn, and hot sauce.

PREPARATION TIME 25 minutes,
plus at least 1 hour marinating
COOKING TIME 10 minutes
SERVES 4

6 dried ají panca, pasilla, or ancho chiles
4 cloves garlic, minced
1 tablespoon achiote paste
1 teaspoon black pepper
1 teaspoon ground cumin
½ cup (4 fl oz/120 ml) red wine vinegar
3 tablespoons vegetable oil
1 teaspoon salt, plus extra to taste
1 lb/450 g beef hearts or other meat,
trimmed and cut into 2-inch/5-cm cubes

Put the dried chiles in a small bowl, then add enough boiling water to cover them. Set aside for 20 minutes, then drain the chilies.

In a blender or food processor, combine the drained chilies with all remaining ingredients except the meat and blend until smooth. Transfer the marinade to a large bowl, then add the beef. Cover and refrigerate for at least 1 hour and up to 1 day.

Preheat a grill to high heat.

Thread the meat onto skewers, reserving the extra marinade. Place the skewers on the grill and cook for 3 minutes on each side, occasionally basting with the extra marinade, until they are charred and cooked through. Transfer to a serving dish.

Serve hot.

Anticuchos are traditionally made with beef hearts (page 26), but these skewers made with sirloin, and flavored with smoky ají Amarillo, are a staple across South America. They are especially popular at restaurants and street vendors in Peru.

PREPARATION TIME 10 minutes,
plus at least 1 hour marinating
COOKING TIME 10 minutes
SERVES 4

4 cloves garlic, minced
2 teaspoons dried oregano
1 teaspoon ground cumin
½ teaspoon salt
½ teaspoon black pepper
4 tablespoons Ají Amarillo Paste (page 336)
4 tablespoons red wine vinegar
4 tablespoons olive oil
1 (2-lb/900-g) sirloin steak, cut into 2-inch/5-cm cubes
6 boiled new potatoes, chopped, to serve

In a large bowl, combine all the ingredients except the beef. Stir in the beef. Cover and refrigerate for at least 1 hour but, preferably, overnight.

Preheat a grill to high heat.

Thread the beef onto skewers. Place the skewers on the grill and cook for 3 minutes on each side, or until browned and cooked through. Transfer to a serving dish.

Serve hot with boiled potatoes.

JAPANESE BEEF SKEWERS

Japanese barbecue, or *yakiniku*, is so beloved in Japan that, in 1993, the Japan Yakiniku Association declared August 29 to be Yakiniku Day (the date is a form of numerical wordplay). Like Korean barbecue, *yakiniku* involves non-marinated, bite-sized pieces of beef, pork, chicken, and shellfish grilled on small fireproof clay grills called *konro* using charcoal called *binchotan*. The meat can be either *ami-yaki* (grilled on a net) or *teppanyaki* (grilled on an iron plate). This recipe uses a standard grill to cook the thinly sliced beef tenderloin.

PREPARATION TIME 15 minutes
COOKING TIME 10 minutes
SERVES 4

FOR THE YAKINIKU SAUCE

1 clove garlic, minced	
3 tablespoons sugar	
4 tablespoons soy sauce	
2 tablespoons mirin	
2 teaspoons sesame oil	
1 tablespoon sesame seeds, toasted	

FOR THE BEEF

1 lb/450 g beef tenderloin, thinly sliced	
1 tablespoon canola oil	
Salt and pepper	

FOR THE YAKINIKU SAUCE In a small saucepan, whisk together all the ingredients except the sesame seeds. Bring it to a boil over high heat, then reduce the heat to medium-low and simmer for 3 minutes. Set the sauce aside to cool, then strain it. Stir in the sesame seeds.

FOR THE BEEF Preheat a grill to medium-high heat.
Brush the beef with oil and season with salt and pepper. Place it on the grill and cook for 3–4 minutes, turning once. Transfer the beef to a serving dish.

Serve hot with a small bowl of the yakiniku sauce.

A popular street food in Nigeria, these charred beef skewers, or beef *suya*, are coated in *yajin kuli* (a blend of chiles, ginger, garlic, onions, and dehydrated peanut butter). In this recipe, powdered peanut butter imparts a nutty, mildly sweet flavor to the spice blend. To serve, the spicy meat is sprinkled with more *yajin kuli* and accompanied with tomatoes, red onions, and lime.

PREPARATION TIME 45 minutes,
plus at least 2 hours marinating
COOKING TIME 10 minutes
SERVES 4

FOR THE SKEWERS

1 (1-lb/450-g) beef flank or sirloin steak

3 tablespoons canola oil

FOR THE SPICE MIX (YAJIN KULI)

½ cup (1½ oz/40 g) powdered peanut butter
or unsweetened peanut butter

1 tablespoon ground ginger

1 tablespoon sweet paprika

1 tablespoon onion powder

1 tablespoon salt

1 teaspoon garlic powder

1 teaspoon cayenne pepper

½ teaspoon black pepper

¼ teaspoon ground cloves

FOR SERVING

4 limes, halved

2 red onions, thinly sliced

2 tomatoes, thinly sliced

Bunch of cilantro (coriander), chopped

FOR THE SKEWERS Wrap the steak in plastic wrap (clingfilm) and freeze for 15–30 minutes. Slice the steak into 2-inch/5-cm-long strips.

FOR THE SPICE MIX Combine all the ingredients in a medium bowl and mix well.

In a large bowl, combine the steak, oil, and ½ cup (1½ oz/40 g) of spice mixture. Refrigerate for 2–8 hours.

Preheat a grill to high heat.

Thread the steak onto skewers, bunching the pieces tightly together. Place the skewers on the hot side of the grill and cook for 8 minutes, turning frequently, until cooked through. Transfer to a serving dish.

Serve hot with a small bowl of spice mix for sprinkling and a plate of limes, red onions, tomatoes, and cilantro (coriander).

Espetadas Madeira, from the Portuguese island of Madeira, is made with chunks of seasoned sirloin skewered on bay branches and cooked over an open fire. The bay infuses the smoky beef with a delightful hint of menthol.

PREPARATION TIME 15 minutes
COOKING TIME 5 minutes
SERVES 6

1 tablespoon garlic powder

1 teaspoon salt

1 teaspoon black pepper

3 strip steaks, cut into 2-inch/5-cm chunks

20 bay leaves

2 tablespoons olive oil

In a large bowl, combine the garlic powder, salt, and pepper. Add the steak and toss to coat. Press the seasoning into the steak.

Preheat a grill to high heat.

Thread the steak chunks onto skewers, alternating them with the bay leaves. Brush each skewer with oil. Place the skewers on the grill and cook for 2 minutes on each side, or until the meat reaches an internal temperature of 135°F/57°C. Transfer the skewers to a serving dish.

Serve hot.

Gola kabobs are one of many traditional kabobs in Pakistan. The name *gola*, meaning "round," comes from their oval shape. They are commonly made with ground (minced) beef or lamb, seasoned with warm spices such as nutmeg and cumin, and grilled over charcoal. They are similar to Turkish Beef Kabobs (page 31) but softer in texture and spicier.

PREPARATION TIME 20 minutes, plus 4 hours marinating
COOKING TIME 15 minutes
SERVES 6–8

1 tablespoon canola oil
1 large onion, thinly sliced
3 Thai green chiles, chopped
1½ lb/675 g ground (minced) beef
3 tablespoons all-purpose (plain) flour
3 tablespoons cilantro (coriander) leaves
1 tablespoon kachri powder
2 teaspoons garam masala
1½ teaspoons red pepper flakes
1 teaspoon ground nutmeg
1 teaspoon mace
1 teaspoon ground cumin
3 tablespoons plain yogurt
2 tablespoons ginger-garlic paste
1 tablespoon lemon juice
Salt and black pepper, to taste

FOR SERVING
Indian Yogurt Sauce (page 352)
Grilled Naan (page 329)

Heat the oil in a large skillet over medium-high heat. Add the onion and sauté for 7 minutes, until they are golden brown. Transfer them to a paper towel–lined plate to drain.

In a food processor, combine the onion and remaining ingredients. Pulse to blend. Season to taste with salt and pepper. Refrigerate for 4 hours.

Preheat a grill to high heat for indirect grilling.

Divide the mixture into 16–18 balls, then roll each ball into a sausage shape. Thread the centers of each kabob through a metal or wooden skewer.

Place the kabobs over the hot part of the grill and cook for 2 minutes. Flip and cook for another 3–5 minutes, until the other side is charred. Transfer to a serving dish and set aside to rest for 5 minutes.

Serve hot with Indian yogurt sauce and grilled naan.

ARMENIAN BEEF SKEWERS

Armenians take grilling meats, or *khorovats*, very seriously. Skewered chunks of beef grilled over charcoal (or wood from an apricot or grape tree) are served with lavash or pita, which can act as an oven mitt. In this recipe, the skewers are suspended over the fire via a brick to help the meat cook more evenly.

PREPARATION TIME 15 minutes,
plus at least 4 hours marinating
COOKING TIME 10 minutes
SERVES 4–6

FOR THE SKEWERS

1 yellow onion, grated	
1 tablespoon salt, plus extra to taste	
½ teaspoon black pepper	
4 tablespoons canola oil	
4 tablespoons tomato paste (purée)	
4 tablespoons red wine	
1 (2-lb/900-g) boneless beef flap meat (bottom sirloin butt), trimmed and cut into 1-inch/2.5-cm cubes	
Salt, to taste	

FOR SERVING

4–6 pita breads	
Armenian Salad (page 288)	

FOR THE SKEWERS In a medium bowl, combine all the ingredients except the beef and whisk to combine. In a zip-top bag, combine the meat and the marinade. Seal and refrigerate for 4–24 hours.

Preheat a grill to high heat.

Thread the meat tightly onto skewers. Use foil-covered bricks to set up a prop for the skewers on the grill (one at each end of the skewer). Balance the skewers over the bricks and cook for 10 minutes, turning frequently, until the meat is lightly charred and reaches an internal temperature of 135°F/57°C.

Using tongs or a pita, slide the meat off the skewers. Season with salt, then cover with aluminum foil and set aside to rest for 2 minutes. Transfer to a serving dish.

Serve immediately with the pita breads and Armenian salad.

TURKISH BEEF KABOBS

In Turkey, there are almost 300 types of *köfte*, which comes from the Farsi word *küfta* (meaning "to beat" or "to grind"). While cuts, spices, and cooking techniques can differ, *köfte* is usually made with ground (minced) beef or lamb (or a combination of both). It can be in the shape of meatballs or formed into a log along a skewer.

PREPARATION TIME 20 minutes
COOKING TIME 10 minutes
SERVES 4

FOR THE KABOBS
2 lb/900 g ground (minced) beef
2 cloves garlic, minced
1 (2-inch/5-cm) piece ginger, peeled and grated
1 small onion, grated
1 cup (2¼ oz/60 g) finely chopped mint or parsley leaves
2 tablespoons harissa paste
1 tablespoon red pepper flakes
2 teaspoons ground cumin
1 teaspoon ground coriander
¼ teaspoon ground cinnamon
Salt and black pepper, to taste

FOR SERVING
Grilled Naan (page 329)
Tzatziki (page 348)
1 lemon, cut into wedges
1 onion, thinly sliced

FOR THE KABOBS Preheat a grill to high heat for indirect grilling.

Combine all the ingredients in a large bowl and mix well using your hands. Divide the mixture into 12 balls, then roll each ball into a sausage shape. Thread the center of each kabob through skewers.

Place the kabobs over the hot part of the grill and cook for 2 minutes. Flip and cook for another 3–5 minutes, until the other side is charred. Move the kabobs to the cooler side of the grill and cook for another 2 minutes. Transfer to a serving dish and set aside to rest for 5 minutes.

Serve hot with naan, tzatziki, lemon wedges, and onions.

RUSSIAN LAMB KABOBS

Shashlik, meaning "kabob" in Russian, is beloved throughout Russia, the Middle East, and Siberia. In southern Russia, the most popular version of *shashlik* is a uniquely sweet and tart lamb kabob. This version is traditionally marinated overnight in onions, garlic, and pomegranate juice, then cooked on a *mangal*—a long, narrow charcoal grill with slots for the skewers.

PREPARATION TIME 20 minutes, plus overnight marinating
COOKING TIME 15 minutes
SERVES 4

1 (1½-lb/680-g) lamb shoulder or leg,
cut into 2-inch/5-cm cubes

1 onion, chopped

2 cloves garlic, minced

2 teaspoons salt

¼ teaspoon cayenne pepper

2 tablespoons canola oil

1¼ cups (10 fl oz/300 ml) pomegranate juice

In a large bowl, combine all the ingredients and mix well. Cover and refrigerate overnight.

Preheat a grill to high heat.

Thread the lamb onto skewers with the fat positioned towards the outside. Place the skewers on the grill and cook for 15 minutes, or until the lamb is cooked through. Transfer to a serving dish, then set aside to rest for 5 minutes.

Serve hot.

The Armenian version of *shashlik* (page 37) is traditionally made with a vinegar-marinated lamb cooked on a *mangal*—an open, grateless charcoal grill with indentations for the kabob sticks. In Armenia, these slightly tart kabobs are sold on the street and served at outdoor gatherings.

PREPARATION TIME 15 minutes,
plus at least 4 hours marinating
COOKING TIME 10–15 minutes
SERVES 4–6

1 (1-lb/450-g) boneless lamb leg,
cut into 2-inch/5-cm cubes
3 cloves garlic, minced
1 onion, sliced
1 cup (2¼ oz/60 g) chopped parsley
½ teaspoon ground coriander
½ teaspoon salt
½ teaspoon black pepper
¼ teaspoon red pepper flakes
5 tablespoons red wine vinegar
5 tablespoons dry red wine
4 tablespoons vegetable oil

FOR SERVING
Jordanian Flatbread (page 322) or pita
Armenian Salad (page 288)

Combine all the ingredients in a large bowl. Cover and refrigerate for at least 4 hours but, preferably, overnight.

Preheat a grill to high heat.

Thread the lamb onto skewers with the fat positioned towards the outside. Place the skewers on the grill and cook for 10–15 minutes, until the lamb is cooked through. Transfer to a serving dish, then set aside to rest for 5 minutes.

Serve with flatbread and Armenian Salad.

CHINESE LAMB SKEWERS

Xinjiang lamb is an iconic street snack in northern China. The lamb is cut into small pieces and marinated with cumin, white pepper, chili powder, and Sichuan peppercorns. Chunks of fat are then placed between each piece of meat, or the lamb skewer is dipped in fat. When the skewers hit the grill, the fat melts away and leaves behind caramelized, crispy bits and juicy meat.

PREPARATION TIME 20 minutes, plus at least 30 minutes marinating
COOKING TIME 10 minutes
SERVES 2–4

2 tablespoons vegetable oil
2 tablespoons soy sauce
2 teaspoons cornstarch (cornflour)
2 teaspoons ground cumin, plus extra for grilling
½ teaspoon chili powder, plus extra for grilling
½ teaspoon salt
¼ teaspoon Sichuan pepper powder
1 lb/450 g lamb meat with fat cap, trimmed

In a small bowl, combine all the ingredients except the lamb and mix well.

Cut the lean part of the lamb into ½-inch/1-cm cubes. Cut the fat into thin pieces half the size of the lean pieces. Thread the lamb cubes onto skewers, alternating with the fat.

In a zip-top bag, combine the lamb skewers and marinade and massage the bag so that everything is evenly coated. Seal and marinate for 30 minutes at room temperature or overnight in the refrigerator.

Preheat a grill to high heat for indirect grilling.

Place the lamb skewers, 1 inch/2.5 cm apart, onto the hot part of the grill and cook for 5–7 minutes, turning frequently, until browned on all sides. Transfer the skewers to the cooler side of the grill. Generously sprinkle each skewer with a layer of cumin and chili powder. Flip, then sprinkle over another layer of cumin. Grill for 3–5 minutes, until the meat is cooked through. Transfer to a serving dish.

Serve hot.

These curried lamb skewers from Cape Malay are called *sosaties*—which comes from the Afrikaans words *sate* and *saus*, meaning "skewered meat" and "spicy sauce," respectively. This dish, however, is less spicy and sweeter, smokier, and more succulent. The marinade usually includes apricot jam, curry powder, and garlic, and the skewers interweave the meat with chunks of onions, peppers, apricots, prunes, or mushrooms.

PREPARATION TIME 30 minutes, plus overnight marinating
COOKING TIME 20–25 minutes
SERVES 4

FOR THE MARINADE

1 tablespoon canola oil
½ onion, finely chopped
1 clove garlic, minced
1 teaspoon grated ginger
3 tablespoons white wine vinegar
3 tablespoons apricot jam
1 tablespoon curry powder
2 teaspoons ground cumin
1 teaspoon salt

FOR THE SKEWERS

1 (1-lb/450-g) lamb leg or shoulder, cut into 2-inch/5-cm cubes
16 apricots
½ onion, cut into 1-inch/2.5-cm pieces
1 tablespoon canola oil
Tzatziki (page 348), to serve (optional)

FOR THE MARINADE Heat the oil in a medium skillet over medium-high heat. Add the onion and sauté for 7 minutes, until it's translucent. Add the garlic and ginger and cook for another minute. Add the remaining ingredients and stir to mix. Set the marinade aside to cool.

FOR THE SKEWERS In a large bowl, combine the lamb and the cooled marinade. Cover and refrigerate overnight.

Preheat a grill to medium-high heat.

Remove the lamb from the refrigerator and bring to room temperature. Soak the apricots in hot water for 15–20 minutes. Thread the lamb onto skewers, alternating with the soaked apricots and onion. Brush with oil.

Cook the skewers for 10–15 minutes, turning occasionally, until they are caramelized on the outside but still slightly pink in the middle. Transfer to a serving dish.

Serve hot with tzatziki on the side, if desired.

MOROCCAN LAMB SKEWERS

Many Moroccans grill year-round, but these lamb skewers are often reserved for special occasions. They are seasoned with onions, herbs, paprika, and cumin and served with rice or the Moroccan version of pita bread called *batbout*. A tender cut of lamb, such as the leg, produces the juiciest skewers.

PREPARATION TIME 30 minutes,
plus at least 2 hours marinating
COOKING TIME 10 minutes
SERVES 6

1 (2 lb 4-oz/1-kg) leg of lamb, cut into ¾-inch/2-cm cubes
1 large onion, finely chopped
3 tablespoons coarsely chopped parsley
3 tablespoons coarsely chopped cilantro (coriander)
1 tablespoon vegetable oil
1 tablespoon lemon juice
2 teaspoons paprika
2 teaspoons salt, or to taste
1 teaspoon ground cumin
1 teaspoon black pepper

In a large bowl, combine all the ingredients and mix well using your hands. Cover and refrigerate for at least 2 hours but, preferably, overnight.

Preheat a grill to medium heat.

Thread the meat onto metal skewers. Place the skewers on the grill and cook for 10 minutes, turning 2 or 3 times, until cooked through. Transfer to a serving dish.

Serve hot.

ITALIAN LAMB SKEWERS

These simple mutton skewers known as *arrosticini Abruzzesi* originated in Italy's Abruzzo Apennine mountains. Small pieces of meat—in this case, lamb—are interspersed with squares of fat to ensure a juicy skewer. You can use foil-wrapped bricks to build a suspended platform for the skewers or just place the skewers directly on the grate. Aim for a charred exterior and a slightly pink interior.

PREPARATION TIME 20 minutes
COOKING TIME 10 minutes
SERVES 6

1 (2-lb/900-g) boneless lamb shoulder with fat cap
2 tablespoons extra-virgin olive oil
Salt and black pepper, to taste

Cut off the fat cap from the lamb shoulder, then cut the fat into ¾- x ¼-inch/2- x 0.5-cm-thick pieces. Remove the silver skin and sinew from the lamb shoulder and cut the meat into ¾- x ½-inch/2- x 1-cm-thick pieces. For each skewer, alternate 2 pieces of meat with 1 piece of the fat.

Preheat a grill to high heat.

Brush the lamb with the olive oil, then season with salt and pepper. Place the lamb on the grill and cook for 6–8 minutes, turning frequently, until the lamb is lightly charred. Transfer the skewers to a serving dish, then season with salt. Set aside to rest for 1–2 minutes.

Serve immediately.

This popular Persian dish is called *kabob koobideh*. *Koobideh* means "to smash" in Farsi, and this kabob is made with a mixture of lamb, herbs, onions, and garlic, which is crushed into a paste so it sticks to the skewers. The lamb kabobs are suspended on bricks over the fire and served with rice, flatbread, and fresh herbs.

PREPARATION TIME 20 minutes, plus 1 hour marinating
COOKING TIME 10 minutes
SERVES 4–6

1½ yellow onions, quartered
2 lb 4 oz/1 kg ground (minced) lamb
3 cloves garlic, minced
1 egg
1 teaspoon salt
1 teaspoon sumac
½ teaspoon black pepper
½ teaspoon ground turmeric
4 tablespoons melted butter

FOR SERVING
Rice
Grilled Naan (page 329)
Fresh herbs

Add the onions to a food processor and finely chop. Strain the juice out of the processed onions.

In a medium bowl, combine the onion pulp and the remaining ingredients except the butter.

Knead the mixture for 3 minutes, until it forms a sticky paste that holds together. Cover and refrigerate for 1 hour.

Preheat a grill to medium-high heat.

Divide the mixture into 10 balls. Using wet hands, squeeze a meatball around the middle of a skewer. Shape it into a 6-inch/15-cm length, leaving the top and bottom clear. Place the skewer on a baking sheet. Repeat with the remaining balls.

Use foil-covered bricks to set up a prop for the skewers on the grill (one at each end of the skewer). Balance the skewers over the bricks and cook for 5–8 minutes, turning frequently, until the meat browns but remains pink inside. Transfer to a serving dish, then brush with the melted butter.

Serve hot with rice, naan, and fresh herbs.

TURKISH LAMB KABOBS

Adana kabobs are the specialty of Adana, the fifth largest city in Turkey. Ground (minced) lamb is seasoned with sumac and pepper, then molded around flat metal skewers. The skewers are typically cooked over a pit of smoldering coals, then served with rice and salad or wrapped with lavash, red onions, and parsley.

PREPARATION TIME 30 minutes, plus 2 hours marinating
COOKING TIME 15 minutes
SERVES 6

FOR THE LAMB
1 lb/450 g ground (minced) lamb
2 teaspoons salt
1 teaspoon ground cumin
2 teaspoons sumac
1 teaspoon Aleppo pepper
1 teaspoon smoked paprika
2 tablespoons canola oil

FOR THE SEASONING
1 teaspoon ground cumin
2 teaspoons sumac
1 teaspoon Aleppo pepper
1 teaspoon smoked paprika
2 teaspoons salt

FOR THE SUMAC ONIONS
1 red onion, thinly sliced
2 teaspoons sumac
1 teaspoon salt

FOR SERVING
6 warm lavashes or pita breads
1 cup (2¼ oz/60 g) chopped parsley

FOR THE LAMB In a large bowl, combine all the ingredients except the oil. Knead until the mixture becomes sticky and add 1–2 teaspoons of cold water as you knead. Refrigerate for 2 hours.

FOR THE SEASONING In a small bowl, combine all the ingredients and mix well.

FOR THE SUMAC ONIONS In a small bowl, combine the red onions, sumac, and salt. Refrigerate until needed.

Preheat a grill to high heat for indirect grilling.

Form the lamb mixture into 12 balls. Wrap 2 balls onto 1 skewer, flattening the meat against the skewer. Repeat with the remaining 5 skewers. Place the kabobs over the hot side of the grill and cook for 12 minutes, turning occasionally and sprinkling over the seasoning, until cooked through. Transfer to a serving dish.

Serve hot with warm lavash, sumac onions, and parsley.

GHANAIAN GOAT KABOBS

These street food kabobs, which are similar to Nigerian Beef Skewers (page 30), are called *chichinga* (a transliteration of the Ghanaian word *kyinkyinga*, meaning "kabob"). While they are traditionally made with goat, the spicy peanut marinade works with almost any kind of meat, so feel free to substitute chicken or beef.

PREPARATION TIME 15 minutes, plus at least 1 hour marinating
COOKING TIME 10 minutes
SERVES 4

FOR THE SPICE RUB

Scant 1 cup (4¼ oz/125 g) roasted peanuts
3 cloves garlic, minced
1 (2-inch/5-cm) piece ginger, peeled and grated
1 teaspoon cayenne pepper or red pepper flakes
1 teaspoon smoked paprika
½ teaspoon salt
1 teaspoon black pepper
2 tablespoons groundnut or vegetable oil

FOR THE GOAT

1 (1-lb/450-g) boneless leg of kid goat, diced
1 large red onion, quartered
2 red bell peppers, seeded, deveined, and cut into chunks
1 tablespoon vegetable oil
Salt and black pepper, to taste

FOR SERVING

4 tablespoons cilantro (coriander), chopped
Jollof rice
Citrus salad

FOR THE SPICE RUB Using a mortar and pestle or a food processor, grind the peanuts to a coarse paste. In a large bowl, combine the peanut paste, garlic, ginger, cayenne pepper, paprika, salt, pepper, and oil.

FOR THE GOAT Add the goat to the bowl with the spice rub and massage the rub into the goat meat. Thread the onion, peppers, and goat onto skewers. Refrigerate for at least 1 hour or, preferably, overnight.

Preheat a grill to high heat.

Remove the skewers from the refrigerator and bring to room temperature. Brush the skewers with oil, then season with salt and pepper. Place the skewers on the grill and cook for 10 minutes, turning every 2 minutes, until cooked through. Transfer the skewers to a serving dish and set aside to rest for 2 minutes. Sprinkle with cilantro (coriander) on top.

Serve immediately with jollof rice and a bright citrus salad.

46   SKEWERS & SAUSAGES

PORK SATAY WITH PEANUT SAUCE

This recipe for *sate babi* is a complex and satisfying version of *satay*, meaning "small chunks of meat on a stick." Fatty pork shoulder is marinated with lemongrass and pasilla chiles, and the sweet soy glaze insulates the meat from the flames. The result is juicy, powerfully spiced pork served with a rich and umami-forward peanut sauce.

PREPARATION TIME 25 minutes, plus at least 45 minutes marinating
COOKING TIME 15–20 minutes
SERVES 4–6

FOR THE SPICE PASTE
6 cloves garlic, sliced
3 pasilla chiles, stemmed, seeded, and coarsely chopped
2 stalks lemongrass, outer leaves removed
2 small shallots, sliced
2 tablespoons brown sugar
1 tablespoon black peppercorns
2 teaspoons coriander seeds
2 teaspoons salt
1 teaspoon ground turmeric

FOR THE MARINATED PORK
1 (2-lb/900-g) boneless pork shoulder, cut into ¾-inch/2-cm cubes
⅓ quantity Spice Paste (see above)

FOR THE GLAZE
4 cloves garlic, coarsely chopped
1 (2-inch/5-cm) piece ginger, peeled and grated
¾ cup (6 fl oz/175 ml) soy sauce
½ cup (3½ oz/100 g) sugar
⅓ quantity Spice Paste (see above)

FOR COOKING AND SERVING
2 tablespoons olive oil, plus extra for brushing
⅓ quantity Spice Paste (see above)
Indonesian Peanut Sauce (page 346)

FOR THE SPICE PASTE Combine all the ingredients in a food processor and process into a paste. Divide the paste into 3 portions.

FOR THE MARINATED PORK In a large bowl, mix the pork with one portion of the spice paste. Cover and refrigerate for at least 45 minutes or, preferably, overnight.

FOR THE GLAZE In a small saucepan, combine the garlic, ginger, soy sauce, and sugar. Bring to a simmer over medium-low heat and simmer for 3–5 minutes, until the glaze has thickened. Stir in the second portion of spice paste. Strain the mixture.

Preheat a grill to high heat for indirect grilling.

Heat the oil in a medium skillet over medium-high heat. Stir in the remaining portion of spice paste and cook for 1 minute.

Thread the pork onto skewers, then brush with the oil. Place the skewers over the hot side of the grill and cook for 6–8 minutes, turning frequently. Brush the pork with the glaze and cook for another 2 minutes, or until sticky. Add another layer of glaze, then transfer the satay to a serving dish.

Serve hot with peanut sauce on the side.

THAI PORK SKEWERS

A popular Bangkok street food and night market staple, *moo ping* consists of small skewers of pork tenderized in coconut milk and caramelized on the grill. It's a lively, sweet, and salty dish usually served with a Thai Dipping Sauce (page 338).

PREPARATION TIME 20 minutes, plus at least 2 hours marinating
COOKING TIME 10 minutes
SERVES 4–6

6 cloves garlic
1 stalk lemongrass, outer layer removed and coarsely chopped
½ teaspoon salt
3 tablespoons coconut milk
2 tablespoons fish sauce
2 tablespoons sugar
1 tablespoon finely chopped cilantro (coriander)
1 tablespoon light soy sauce
2 teaspoons vegetable oil
1 (1 lb 5-oz/600-g) pork shoulder, cut into thin strips
Thai Dipping Sauce (page 338), to serve

In a food processor, combine the garlic, lemongrass, and salt and process into a paste. Add the remaining ingredients except the pork and blend until smooth. In a zip-top bag or bowl, combine the pork and marinade. Seal or cover and refrigerate for at least 2 hours but, preferably, overnight.

Preheat a grill to high heat.

Thread the pork onto skewers. Place the skewers on the grill and cook for 10 minutes, turning frequently, until cooked through. Transfer to a serving dish.

Serve with Thai dipping sauce.

Ihaw-ihaw, sweet and sticky skewers of grilled pork or chicken that are often made with soda and banana ketchup, is the most popular Filipino street food. In the Philippines, the skewers are cooked on makeshift grill carts and then dipped into spicy vinegar. They are often accompanied with white rice cooked in coconut leaves.

PREPARATION TIME 30 minutes, plus overnight marinating
COOKING TIME 20 minutes
SERVES 6–8

FOR THE SPICED VINEGAR DIP

3 bird's eye chiles, chopped
3 cloves garlic, minced
½ onion, finely chopped
¼ teaspoon salt
⅛ teaspoon black pepper
1 cup (8 fl oz/240 ml) white vinegar

FOR THE MARINADE

5 cloves garlic, minced
1 onion, finely chopped
1 cup (7¾ oz/220 g) packed brown sugar
1 tablespoon salt
1 tablespoon black pepper
1 teaspoon red pepper flakes
1 cup (8 fl oz/240 ml) lemon-lime soda
½ cup (4 fl oz/120 ml) soy sauce
½ cup (4 fl oz/120 ml) apple cider vinegar
4 tablespoons orange juice
4 tablespoons ketchup
3 tablespoons oyster sauce
2 tablespoons lemon juice

FOR THE PORK

1 (4-lb/1.8-kg) pork shoulder, cut into 1-inch/2.5-cm cubes

FOR THE SPICED VINEGAR DIP Combine all the ingredients in a large bowl. Refrigerate until needed.

FOR THE MARINADE In a medium saucepan, combine all the ingredients and whisk. Bring the marinade to a boil, then reduce the heat to low and simmer for 5 minutes. Set aside at room temperature.

In a large zip-top bag or bowl, combine the pork and marinade. Seal or cover and refrigerate overnight.

Preheat a grill to high heat.

FOR THE PORK Thread the pork onto skewers so they touch but are not overcrowded. Place the skewers on the grill and cook for 5–7 minutes, turning every 2 minutes, until browned and cooked through. Transfer to a serving dish.

Serve hot with the spiced vinegar dip.

CROATIAN PORK SKEWERS CROATIA

GF DF NF 5 ◖◗ ◎

There are many variations of *ražnjići* (pork skewers), a popular party dish in the Croatian countryside. This one is made with bacon and onions and then grilled over high heat.

PREPARATION TIME 15 minutes
COOKING TIME 10 minutes
SERVES 3–4

6–8 small onions, such as cipollini (4 oz/115 g)
2 thick strips bacon, sliced into ½-inch/1-cm strips
2 red bell pepper, seeded, deveined, and sliced into ½-inch/1-cm strips
1 (1-lb/450-g) pork loin, cut into 1-inch/2.5-cm cubes
Olive oil, for brushing
1 tablespoon finely chopped parsley
Salt and black pepper, to taste

Preheat a grill to high heat.
　　Thread the ingredients onto 3–4 skewers, alternating onions, bacon, pepper, and pork. Brush each skewer with olive oil. Place the skewers on the grill and cook for 3–4 minutes on each side, until charred and cooked through. Transfer to a serving dish.
　　Sprinkle with parsley, season with salt and pepper, and serve hot.

PORK TAPAS SPAIN

GF DF NF ◖◗ ◎

These grilled pork skewers, or *pinchos morunos*, use a blend of spices that dates to the eighth century. Feel free to substitute lamb or chicken and play around with the spice blend. The Spanish serve these as tapas or small plates, but the dish could easily be the centerpiece of a barbecue.

PREPARATION TIME 15 minutes, plus overnight marinating
COOKING TIME 10 minutes
SERVES 6

5 cloves garlic, minced
1 tablespoon ground cumin
1 tablespoon sweet Spanish paprika
1 teaspoon ground coriander
1 teaspoon ground turmeric
1 teaspoon dried oregano
1 teaspoon salt
½ teaspoon black pepper
¼ teaspoon ground cinnamon
4 tablespoons extra-virgin olive oil
Juice of ½ lemon
1 (2-lb/900-g) pork tenderloin, trimmed and cut into 1½-inch/4-cm cubes
6 lemon wedges, to serve

In a large bowl, combine all the ingredients except the pork. Add the pork, then massage the marinade into the meat. Cover and refrigerate overnight.
　　Preheat a grill to high heat.
　　Thread the pork onto skewers. Place the skewers on the grill and cook for 10 minutes, or until the meat reaches an internal temperature of 145°F/63°C. Transfer to a serving plate, then set aside to rest for 5 minutes.
　　Serve hot with lemon wedges.

SOUVLAKI

Souvlaki (*souvla* meaning "spit") is often regarded as fast food in Greece, even though most souvlaki shops marinate the pork, lamb, or chicken in high-quality olive oil and a blend of spices. The grilled meat is usually served with yogurt sauce, pita, and tomato wedges.

PREPARATION TIME 10 minutes, plus at least 5 hours marinating

COOKING TIME 10 minutes

SERVES 6

FOR THE SKEWERS

1 (2-lb/900-g) boneless pork shoulder, trimmed and cut into 2-inch/5-cm cubes

3 cloves garlic, minced

1 onion, grated

1 teaspoon dried oregano, plus extra for sprinkling

1 teaspoon salt, plus extra to season

1 teaspoon black pepper

4 tablespoons olive oil

Lemon juice, for sprinkling

FOR SERVING

6 pita breads

1 cup (8 fl oz/240 ml) Tzatziki (page 348)

2 large tomatoes, cut into wedges

FOR THE SKEWERS Combine all the ingredients in a large bowl. Cover and refrigerate for at least 5 hours but, preferably, overnight.

Preheat a grill to medium heat.

Remove the marinated pork from the refrigerator and bring it to room temperature. Thread the pork onto skewers. Place the skewers on the grill and cook for 3–4 minutes on each side, until the pork is cooked but still slightly pink inside. Sprinkle the grilled souvlaki with lemon juice, salt, and oregano. Transfer the skewers to a serving dish.

Serve the pork inside (or alongside) the pita bread with the tzatziki and tomatoes on the side.

SPIEDIES

Spiedies, from the Italian word *spiedino*, or "skewer," are grilled meat sandwiches made with long-marinated meat (traditionally lamb) served without toppings on Italian bread. They are beloved in Binghamton, in New York, and celebrated by thousands at Binghamton's annual Spiedie Festival and other large gatherings. This easy recipe, which feeds a crowd, uses juicy chicken thighs in place of lamb.

PREPARATION TIME 15 minutes, plus 24 hours marinating
COOKING TIME 15 minutes
SERVES 16

5 cloves garlic, minced
3 tablespoons crushed dried mint
2 tablespoons dried basil
1 tablespoon garlic powder
2 teaspoons dried oregano
1 teaspoon salt
1 teaspoon black pepper
2 cups (16 fl oz/475 ml) olive oil
1 cup (8 fl oz/240 ml) white vinegar
2 tablespoons lemon juice
4 lb/1.8 kg skinless, boneless chicken thighs, cubed
16 Italian hoagie rolls

In a large bowl, combine all the ingredients except the chicken and hoagies. Add the chicken, then cover and refrigerate for 24 hours.

Preheat a grill to medium-high heat.

Skewer the chicken, shaking off excess marinade. Place the skewers on the grill and cook for 15 minutes, turning every 3 minutes, until the internal temperature reaches 165°F/74°C.

Use the hoagies to pull the chicken off the skewers and eat it as a sandwich.

LEBANESE CHICKEN SKEWERS

This Lebanese dish, *shish tawook*, was named by the Turks who ruled Lebanon during the Ottoman Empire. (The Turkish word *şiş* means "skewer" and the Arabic word *tawook* means "chicken.") It is traditionally made with boneless chicken breast marinated in a mixture of yogurt, lemon, garlic, and spices, then skewered and grilled until the exterior is slightly charred. In Lebanon, the chicken is served as a pita sandwich or as a platter with pita and Lebanese Garlic Sauce (page 352).

PREPARATION TIME 20 minutes,
plus at least 4 hours marinating
COOKING TIME 10–15 minutes
SERVES 4–6

FOR THE MARINATED CHICKEN
15 cloves garlic, crushed
2 teaspoons salt, or to taste
1 teaspoon white pepper
1 teaspoon ground thyme
1 teaspoon paprika
1 teaspoon tomato paste (purée)
½ teaspoon ground ginger
1 cup (8 fl oz/240 ml) lemon juice
½ cup (3½ oz/100 g) plain yogurt
½ cup (4 fl oz/120 ml) olive oil
2 tablespoons apple cider vinegar
2 lb/900 g boneless chicken breasts, cut into 2-inch/5-cm cubes

FOR SERVING
4–6 pita breads
Lebanese Garlic Sauce (page 352)

FOR THE MARINATED CHICKEN In a medium bowl, combine all the ingredients except the chicken. Add the chicken and mix well. Cover and refrigerate for at least 4 hours but, preferably, overnight.

Preheat a grill to medium heat.

Thread the chicken onto skewers. Place the skewers on the grill and cook for 10–12 minutes, turning frequently. Transfer the chicken to a serving dish, then tent with aluminum foil and rest for 5 minutes. Transfer to a serving dish.

Serve hot with pita bread and a small bowl of Lebanese garlic sauce.

CHICKEN SKEWERS WITH SCALLIONS

In Japan, *yakitori* (chicken grilled on skewers) is served in *yakitori* restaurants or *izakaya* (small plate) restaurants, where hundreds of variations exist. Some *yakitori* are seasoned with salt, some with *yakitori* sauce, and others with sake, soy sauce, and sweetener. The easiest and perhaps most popular version is *negima yakitori*, or chicken thighs with scallions (spring onions).

PREPARATION TIME 15 minutes
COOKING TIME 10 minutes
SERVES 4–6

FOR THE CHICKEN

6 boneless, skinless chicken thighs, cut into 1-inch/2.5-cm cubes

2 teaspoons salt, plus extra to season

½ teaspoon black pepper, plus extra to season

Bunch of scallions (spring onions), cut into 1-inch/2.5-cm segments

FOR THE YAKITORI SAUCE

3 cloves garlic, minced

½ cup (4 fl oz/120 ml) mirin

½ cup (4 fl oz/120 ml) soy sauce

4 tablespoons sake

3 tablespoons honey

2 teaspoons grated ginger

Preheat a grill to medium-high heat for indirect grilling.

FOR THE CHICKEN In a bowl, combine the chicken, salt, and pepper. Thread the chicken onto skewers, alternating it with a scallion (spring onion) segment. You should have 3 pieces of each on the skewer.

FOR THE YAKITORI SAUCE Whisk all the ingredients in a medium bowl.

Place the skewers directly over the hot part of the grill and cook for 10 minutes, turning frequently, until the chicken reaches an internal temperature of 165°F/74°C. Once the chicken reaches temperature, brush one side of the skewers with the sauce, then 30 seconds later, brush the other side. Transfer to a serving dish, then set aside to rest for 2 minutes.

Serve hot.

TURKISH CHICKEN KABOBS

These spicy chicken kabobs, *tavuk şiş*, are a staple of Turkish cuisine and often served with rice, salad, and Tzatziki (page 348) on special occasions and at celebrations. In this simple yet authentic recipe, chicken thighs are coated in mint, Aleppo pepper, and Turkish sweet red pepper paste *(biber salçası)*—which caramelizes beautifully when grilled.

PREPARATION TIME 20 minutes, plus 30 minutes marinating
COOKING TIME 15 minutes
SERVES 4

FOR THE MARINATED CHICKEN

2 tablespoons dried mint

1 tablespoon red pepper flakes

1 tablespoon finely chopped thyme

1 tablespoon Aleppo pepper

1 teaspoon black pepper

1 teaspoon salt

½ cup (4 fl oz/120 ml) extra-virgin olive oil

1 tablespoon tomato paste (purée)

1 tablespoon Turkish sweet red pepper paste
(biber salçası) or another tablespoon of tomato paste)

3–4 boneless, skinless chicken thighs,
cut into 1-inch/2.5-cm pieces

FOR SERVING

Tzatziki (page 348)

Steamed rice

FOR THE MARINATED CHICKEN In a large bowl, combine all the ingredients except the chicken. Add the chicken and mix well. Cover, then set aside at room temperature for 30 minutes.

Preheat a grill over high heat.

Thread the chicken onto skewers. Place the skewers on the grill and cook for 12 minutes, turning occasionally, until charred. Transfer to a serving dish.

Serve hot with tzatziki and rice.

MALAYSIAN CHICKEN SKEWERS

Satay Kajang, from the small Malaysian town of Kajang, is popular across Southeast Asia and sold in both restaurants and street stalls. The chicken is flavored with lemongrass, shallots, and galangal, then grilled over an open flame. The ingredients come together quickly in a food processor.

PREPARATION TIME 20 minutes,
plus at least 3 hours marinating
COOKING TIME 10 minutes
SERVES 6

FOR THE SPICE PASTE

12 cloves garlic
3–4 shallots (5 oz/140 g), chopped
1 (2-inch/5-cm) piece galangal
1 stalk lemongrass, chopped
1 tablespoon *belacan* (Malaysian shrimp paste)
1 teaspoon salt

FOR THE MARINATED CHICKEN

½ cup (3½ oz/100 g) palm sugar
1 tablespoon ground coriander
1 tablespoon ground cumin
2 teaspoons white pepper
1 teaspoon fennel powder
1 teaspoon salt
1 quantity Spice Paste (see above)
½ cup (4 fl oz/120 ml) canola oil, plus extra for brushing
1 tablespoon sweet soy sauce
6 boneless chicken thighs, cut into ½-inch/1-cm cubes

FOR THE SPICE PASTE Combine all the ingredients in a food processor and process until almost smooth.

FOR THE MARINATED CHICKEN In a medium bowl, combine all the ingredients except the chicken. Add the chicken and mix well to coat. Cover and refrigerate for at least 3 hours or, preferably, overnight.

Preheat a grill to medium heat.

Thread 4–5 pieces of chicken onto each skewer, then brush the chicken with oil. Place the skewers on the grill and cook for 2–3 minutes on each side, until the chicken is charred and cooked through. Transfer to a serving dish.

Serve hot.

This popular Balinese dish called *sate lilit* (*lilit* meaning "to wrap around") is made with chicken, spices, and coconut, then molded onto bamboo or lemongrass skewers and grilled.

PREPARATION TIME 20 minutes
COOKING TIME 15 minutes
SERVES 4

1 tablespoon vegetable oil, plus extra for brushing
3 shallots, minced
4 cloves garlic, minced
2 small Thai red chiles, finely chopped
4 tablespoons grated ginger
½ teaspoon ground turmeric
½ teaspoon white pepper
½ teaspoon ground coriander
¼ teaspoon ground nutmeg
Pinch of ground cloves
2 makrut lime leaves, cut into thin strips with scissors (optional)
1 tablespoon unsweetened dried shredded (desiccated) coconut
1 tablespoon salt
1 lb/450 g ground (minced) chicken
12 stalks lemongrass or wooden skewers

Preheat a grill to high heat.

Heat the oil in a skillet over low heat. Add the shallots, garlic, chiles, and ginger and sauté for 1–2 minutes, until the shallots have softened. Stir in 2 tablespoons of water. Add the turmeric, white pepper, coriander, nutmeg, and cloves. Cook for another 1 minute. Set aside to cool to room temperature.

Transfer the cooled mixture to a food processor and process into a paste. Add the makrut lime leaves (if using), coconut, salt, and chicken and pulse to combine. The texture should be slightly rough not smooth.

Scoop up a walnut-sized amount of the spiced chicken mixture and flatten it into a round. Lay a lemongrass stalk or skewer in the center of the round, then mold the mixture around the stalk or skewer. Repeat with the remaining skewers, then brush them with oil. Place the skewers on the grill and cook for 8–10 minutes, turning frequently, until cooked through. Transfer to a serving dish.

Serve hot.

Ground (minced) fish is mixed with a traditional Balinese spice paste, then molded around lemongrass stalks and grilled in the traditional version of this Indonesian classic. This version substitutes wooden or metal skewers for the lemongrass.

PREPARATION TIME 20 minutes
COOKING TIME 10 minutes
SERVES 4

FOR THE SPICE PASTE

5 small shallots, chopped
4 macadamia nuts, chopped
3 cloves garlic, minced
2 small Thai red chiles, seeded and chopped
1 stalk lemongrass, chopped
1 (3-inch/7.5-cm) slice ginger, peeled and chopped
1 (3-inch/7.5-cm) slice turmeric root, chopped
1 (1-inch/2.5-cm) piece galangal, peeled and chopped
½ teaspoon coriander seeds
½ teaspoon white pepper
½ teaspoon black pepper

FOR THE FISH SKEWERS

2 lb/900 g white fish, such as cod,
snapper, or grouper, coarsely chopped
½ cup (1½ oz/40 g) unsweetened dried shredded
(desiccated) coconut
5 tablespoons spice paste (see above)
1½ tablespoons brown sugar
1½ tablespoons chopped celery
1¼ teaspoons salt
4 tablespoons canola oil

Preheat a grill over medium heat.

FOR THE SPICE PASTE Combine all the ingredients in a food processor and process into a paste.

Heat a large skillet over medium-high heat. Add the spice paste and 3 tablespoons of water to loosen the paste into a sauce. Cook for 5 minutes, then set aside to cool.

FOR THE FISH SKEWERS In a food processor, combine the fish, coconut, spice paste, brown sugar, celery, and salt. Process until almost smooth.

Using wet hands, take a small scoop of the fish mixture and mold into an oval shape around a skewer. Repeat with the remaining fish mixture. Brush the fish skewers with the oil. Place the skewers on the grill and cook for 2 minutes on each side, until cooked through. Transfer to a serving dish.

Serve hot.

SINGAPORE SHRIMP SKEWERS

Satay udang is one of Singapore's most beloved dishes. A popular street food, it features skewered shrimp marinated in lime, coconut milk, ginger, chiles, and ground nuts. The shrimp are grilled until succulent, almost creamy, slightly sweet, and nutty with a hint of heat.

PREPARATION TIME 20 minutes, plus at least 2 hours marinating
COOKING TIME 10 minutes
SERVES 4

FOR THE SHRIMP SKEWERS

1½ lb/680 g medium shrimp, peeled and deveined

1 tablespoon lime juice

1 teaspoon lime zest

5 macadamia nuts

3 cloves garlic, chopped

3 red bird's eye chiles, stemmed

2 shallots, chopped

1 (3-inch/7.5-cm) piece ginger, peeled and chopped

1½ tablespoons brown sugar

1 teaspoon salt

3 tablespoons peanut oil

⅓ cup (2¾ fl oz/80 ml) coconut milk

FOR SERVING

2 scallions (spring onions), chopped

¼ cucumber, chopped

4 tablespoons chopped pineapple

FOR THE SHRIMP SKEWERS In a bowl, combine the shrimp, lime juice, and zest and mix well.

In a food processor, combine the nuts, garlic, chiles, shallots, ginger, brown sugar, and salt and blend until smooth.

Heat the oil in a skillet over high heat. Add the spice paste and cook for 3–4 minutes, until the oil separates. Stir in the coconut milk, then set aside to cool.

Add the marinade to the bowl of shrimp and mix well. Cover and refrigerate for 2–4 hours.

Preheat a grill over high heat.

Thread the shrimp onto skewers so the shrimp lay flat. Place the skewers on the grill and cook for 3–5 minutes, turning occasionally and basting with the sauce, until charred. Transfer the shrimp to a serving dish.

Serve hot with chopped scallions (spring onions), cucumber, and pineapple.

INDIAN VEGETABLE SKEWERS

Vegetable skewers, often called "tikka vegetables," are popular in northern India, where tandoori cooking originated. Peppers, onions, tomatoes, mushrooms, and paneer, a soft non-melting cheese, marinated in a mixture of yogurt and spices, are skewered and then grilled or roasted in a tandoor oven. Serve this dish as an appetizer or main course, along with chutney, Indian Yogurt Sauce (page 352), and Grilled Naan (page 329).

PREPARATION TIME 15 minutes,
plus at least 1 hour marinating
COOKING TIME 20 minutes
SERVES 4-6

FOR THE MARINADE

1 cup (8 oz/225 g) plain yogurt
1 (1-inch/2.5-cm) piece ginger, grated
2 cloves garlic, minced
½ cup (½ oz/15 g) mint leaves, finely chopped
1 tablespoon lemon juice
1 tablespoon canola oil
1 teaspoon garam masala
1 teaspoon ground cumin
1 teaspoon ground turmeric
1 teaspoon Kashmiri red chili powder (or paprika)
1 teaspoon salt

FOR THE VEGETABLES

2 red bell peppers, cut into 1-inch/2.5 cm squares
2 green bell peppers, cut into 1-inch/2.5cm squares
2 yellow onions, cut into 1-inch/2.5 cm cubes
8oz/225 g cherry tomatoes
1 lb/450 g button mushrooms, stemmed
10 oz/300 g paneer, cut into 1-inch/2.5 cm cubes

FOR SERVING

Chutney
Indian Yogurt Sauce (page 352)
Grilled Naan (page 329)

FOR THE MARINADE In a large bowl, whisk together the marinade ingredients.

FOR THE VEGETABLES Add the vegetables and paneer to the marinade. Stir to coat evenly. Cover the bowl and refrigerate for at least 1 hour, preferably overnight.

Heat a grill to medium-high heat. Thread the marinated vegetables and paneer onto skewers, alternating between different types of vegetables.

Grill the skewers until the vegetables are soft and slightly charred, 10-15 minutes. Remove from the grill and rest for 5 minutes. Serve hot with chutney, Indian yogurt sauce, and grilled naan.

OYSTER MUSHROOM SATAY

In *sate jamur*, a vegan street food dish from the island of Java, oyster mushrooms are bathed in an umami-rich marinade of miso paste, dried porcini, and peanut sauce, then charred over high heat.

PREPARATION TIME 15 minutes, plus 1 hour marinating
COOKING TIME 10 minutes
SERVES 6

3 cloves garlic
3 macadamia nuts
2 small shallots, chopped
1 tablespoon coriander seeds
½ teaspoon salt
2 tablespoons porcini mushroom powder
2 tablespoons sweet soy sauce
2 tablespoons canola oil, plus extra for oiling
1 tablespoon red miso
¼ teaspoon black pepper
14 oz/400 g oyster mushrooms, cut into strips
2 tablespoons Indonesian Peanut Sauce (page 346), plus extra to serve

In a food processor, combine the garlic, candlenuts or macadamia nuts, shallots, coriander seeds, and salt. Add the porcini mushroom powder, sweet soy sauce, oil, miso, and pepper and blend well.

Preheat a grill to medium-high heat for indirect grilling.

In a large bowl, combine the mushrooms and marinade and marinate for 1 hour. Add the peanut sauce, then thread the mushrooms onto skewers. Place the skewers on the hot side of the grill and cook for 6 minutes, until the mushrooms are charred on both sides. Transfer to a serving dish.

Serve immediately with the peanut sauce.

A staple at Australian barbecues, beef or pork sausages, known colloquially as "snags," are usually served on white bread and topped with caramelized onions and tomato or barbecue sauce. Adding chutneys to these sandwiches is also common.

PREPARATION TIME 10 minutes
COOKING TIME 10 minutes
SERVES 6

2 tablespoons vegetable oil
2 yellow onions, thinly sliced
2 lb 4 oz/1 kg beef and/or pork sausages
6 slices white bread
1 cup (8 fl oz/240 ml) barbecue sauce or tomato sauce

Preheat a grill to high heat.

Heat the oil in a large skillet over medium heat. Add the onions and sauté for 10 minutes, or until golden brown.

Place the sausages on the grill and fry for 10 minutes, or until cooked through and browned.

Place the bread slices on a serving dish. Place a sausage diagonally over each bread slice, then top with sautéed onions and a drizzle of sauce.

Serve immediately.

Danish hot dogs—long, bright-red sausages topped with spicy remoulade, fried shallots, and sweet pickles—are a big part of Nordic street food culture in major cities like Copenhagen.

PREPARATION TIME 10 minutes
COOKING TIME 10 minutes
SERVES 6

FOR THE REMOULADE

1 cup (8 fl oz/240 ml) mayonnaise

4 tablespoons Icelandic yogurt

3 tablespoons chopped sweet pickles

2 tablespoons finely chopped shallots

2 tablespoons finely chopped parsley

1 tablespoon finely chopped capers

1 tablespoon whole-grain mustard

1 teaspoon curry powder

Salt and black pepper, to taste

FOR THE HOT DOGS

6 Danish red sausages (*røde pølser*)
or high-quality hot dogs

6 hot dog buns

15–20 sweet pickles

1 yellow onion, finely chopped

½ cup (3¼ oz/90 g) fried shallots or fried onions

Preheat a grill over high heat.

FOR THE REMOULADE Combine all the ingredients in a small bowl and mix well.

FOR THE HOT DOGS Place the sausages or hot dogs on the grill and cook for 10 minutes, or until cooked through and browned.

Place a hot dog inside each bun. Top each hot dog with a drizzle of remoulade, sweet pickles, onion, and fried shallots or fried onions. Serve warm with any extra remoulade alongside.

Isterband sausages—*ister* means "lard" and *band* comes from *att binda*, meaning "to bind"—are made with coarsely ground (minced) pork, pearl barley (barley groats), pork fat, and spices, including white pepper and ginger. Because these sausages ferment while they cure, they tend to taste slightly sour. They are traditionally fried, broiled, or grilled and served with potatoes or cabbage in a creamy white sauce.

PREPARATION TIME 40 minutes,
plus overnight soaking and 4 days curing
COOKING TIME 1 hour 10 minutes
SERVES 8

1½ cups (10½ oz/300 g) pearl barley

8½ cups (68 fl oz/2 L) beef stock or water

2 lb/900 g lean pork

2 lb/900 g lard (no rind)

2 tablespoons salt

½ teaspoon white pepper

½ teaspoon ground ginger

20 feet/6 meter (26-mm) hog casing, presoaked and rinsed

Canola oil, for grilling

In a large saucepan, combine the barley and stock or water. Set aside to soak overnight.

The next day, bring the saucepan of barley to a boil. Reduce the heat to medium-low, partially cover, and simmer for 1 hour. Drain the barley, then set aside to cool.

Using a meat grinder with a ⅜-inch/8-mm plate, grind the meat and lard. Repeat. In a large bowl, combine the meat, cooked barley, and the remaining ingredients.

Loosely stuff the mixture into the casing, making 10-inch/25-cm links. Tie every second sausage with kitchen string, then cut in between these, forming pairs. Let the sausages dry in a cool place for 4 days.

Preheat a grill to medium-high heat.

Lightly brush the sausages with canola oil and place them on the grill. Cook for 8–10 minutes, turning occasionally, until evenly charred.

Serve warm.

Cervelat, the national sausage of Switzerland, is a staple at Swiss barbecues and soccer matches. It is named after the Italian word for cow or pig "brain," *cervello*, an ingredient in the original recipe dating back to 1749. One hundred million *cervelats* are eaten in Switzerland every year. Most are made with both pork and beef, then wrapped in a piece of bread or bürli roll with mustard and ketchup.

PREPARATION TIME 20 minutes,
plus 1 hour freezing, 1 hour drying, and 24 hours refrigeration
COOKING TIME 20 minutes
SERVES 8–10

1 (2-lb/900-g) pork shoulder, cut into 1-inch/2.5-cm chunks

1 (1-lb/450-g) beef chuck, cut into 1-inch/2.5-cm chunks

½ cup (2½ oz/70 g) crushed ice

4 tablespoons non-fat milk powder

2 tablespoons salt

1 tablespoon dextrose

1 tablespoon white pepper

1 tablespoon garlic powder

1 teaspoon mace

½ teaspoon pink curing salt

½ teaspoon ground coriander

½ teaspoon ground nutmeg

¼ teaspoon ground cardamom

10 feet/3 meter (28–32-mm) hog casing, presoaked and rinsed

Freeze the pork and beef for 1 hour. Using a meat grinder with a ¼-inch/6-mm plate, grind the semi-frozen meat.

In a large bowl over ice, combine the ground (minced) meat and the remaining ingredients except the hog casing. Mix until sticky. Stuff the mixture into the casing, making 6-inch/15-cm links. Prick the sausages to eliminate air pockets.

Dry the sausages at room temperature for 1 hour. Leave uncovered, then refrigerate them for 24 hours. Steam or boil the sausages for 10-15 minutes, or until the internal temperature reaches 155°F/68°C. Finish on a hot grill for a few minutes on each side, until browned and crispy.

Transfer to a serving dish and serve immediately.

LINCOLNSHIRE SAUSAGES

DF NF

This famous sausage from the county of Lincolnshire, England likely created in the nineteenth century, is a simple, unctuous, chunky pork sausage powerfully flavored with sage. Every year, the city of Lincoln (in Lincolnshire) holds a local competition for the best homemade sausage.

PREPARATION TIME 10 minutes, plus 2 days refrigeration
COOKING TIME 20 minutes
SERVES 6

5 oz/140 g stale bread
1½ lb/680 g pork shoulder or ground (minced) pork
2 tablespoons chopped sage
1½ tablespoons salt
2 teaspoons white pepper
4 feet/1.2 meter (36-mm) hog casing, presoaked and rinsed

FOR SERVING
Mustard
Mashed potatoes

In a large bowl, combine the bread and ⅔ cup (5 fl oz/150 ml) water and set aside to soak.

If using pork shoulder, grind the pork through a meat grinder with a ⅜-inch/10-mm plate. In a large bowl, combine the pork, the soaked bread, sage, salt, and pepper.

Stuff the mixture into the casing, making 4-inch/10-cm links. Transfer to a large plate, cover, and refrigerate for 2 days.

When ready to cook, heat a skillet over medium heat. Add sausages and cook, turning frequently, 15-20 minutes, until golden brown and cooked through.

Serve hot with mustard and/or mashed potatoes.

CUMBERLAND SAUSAGES

DF NF

The traditionally long and coiled sausage from Cumberland, England is made from coarsely ground (or roughly chopped) pork and seasoned with dried spices like mace, thyme, and pepper but rarely fresh herbs—unlike England's other famous "banger," Lincolnshire Sausage (left), which relies heavily on fresh sage.

PREPARATION TIME 1 hour
COOKING TIME 30-40 minutes
SERVES 6-8

2 lb/900 g pork shoulder, coarsely ground
8 oz/225 g pork belly, coarsely ground
½ cup (1 oz/25 g) breadcrumbs
2 teaspoons salt
1 teaspoon white pepper
1 teaspoon black pepper
1 teaspoon ground nutmeg
½ teaspoon ground mace
1 teaspoon dried sage
1 teaspoon dried thyme
½ teaspoon dried marjoram
½ teaspoon dried rosemary
¼ teaspoon ground ginger
¼ teaspoon ground coriander
¼ teaspoon cayenne pepper
¼ cup cold water
5-6½ feet/1.5-2 meter hog casing, presoaked and rinsed

In a large bowl, combine the ground pork shoulder and pork belly. Add the breadcrumbs, salt, white pepper, black pepper, nutmeg, mace, sage, thyme, marjoram, rosemary, ginger, coriander, and cayenne pepper to the meat mixture. Mix thoroughly until the seasonings are evenly distributed.

Gradually add ¼ cup (2 fl oz/60 ml) cold water to the mixture, ensuring it is fully absorbed and the mixture becomes slightly sticky.

Stuff the sausage mixture into the casings. As you stuff, gently twist the casing to form a continuous coil.

Lay the sausage on a clean surface and shape it into a large, even coil. Use small skewers or toothpicks to keep the shape.

Preheat a grill to medium-high. Lightly oil the sausage coil and place it on the grill. Cook, turning every 5 minutes, for 20-25 minutes until golden brown and cooked through. Alternatively, heat an oven to 350°F/180°C and place the sausage coil on a baking sheet lined with parchment paper. Bake the sausage for about 30–40 minutes, or until it is golden brown and cooked through.

Remove the sausage from the grill or oven and let it rest for 5 minutes. Slice and serve hot.

Knack d'Alsace are smoked pork and beef sausages from France's Alsace region. Similar to German frankfurters, but with a darker pink hue that comes from smoking with beechwood, these sausages get their name from the distinct "knack" sound when bitten into. Traditionally, they are served in pairs with boiled potatoes, mustard, and sauerkraut.

PREPARATION TIME 30 minutes,
plus 1 hour curing and overnight refrigeration
COOKING TIME 70–80 minutes
SERVES 8

1 (2-lb/900-g) pork butt (pork shoulder) cut into 1-inch/2.5-cm cubes

1 (8-oz/225-g) beef shoulder, cut into 1-inch/2.5-cm cubes

1 tablespoon salt

½ teaspoon pink curing salt

2 cloves garlic, chopped

1½ teaspoons white pepper

1 teaspoon sweet paprika

10 feet/3.1 meter (26-mm) sheep casing, presoaked and rinsed

Beechwood, for smoking

FOR SERVING

Mustard

Boiled potatoes

Sauerkraut

In a large bowl, combine the pork, beef, salt, and curing salt and mix well. Cover and refrigerate for at least 1 hour.

Using a meat grinder with a ⅜-inch/8-mm plate, grind the pork and beef. Using a food processor or stand mixer, process the meat, garlic, pepper, paprika, and ⅓ cup (2¾ fl oz/80 ml) ice water until the mixture turns sticky. Stuff the mixture into the casing, making 6-inch/15-cm links. Cover and refrigerate overnight.

Preheat a smoker to 130°F/55°C.

Place the sausages in the smoker and smoke for 45 minutes.

Heat a large saucepan of water to 165°F/74°C. Carefully lower the sausages into the water and boil for 25–35 minutes, until the sausage reaches an internal temperature of 158°F/70°C.

Fill a large bowl with ice water. Using a slotted spoon, transfer the sausages into the ice bath to cool. Dry, then refrigerate for 24 hours.

Serve warm with mustard, boiled potatoes and sauerkraut.

Chorizo criollo is made with *culantro*, a cousin of cilantro (coriander); garlic; and the Ecuadorian criollo chile, with its tropical fruit notes and earthy undertones. In Panama, the sausage is usually sold fresh, in casings, and then pan-fried or grilled.

PREPARATION TIME 30 minutes, plus 1 hour freezing, overnight marinating, overnight drying, and 4 hours standing
COOKING TIME 6 hours
SERVES 8

1 lb 9 oz/700 g lean pork, cubed
10½ oz/300 g pork back fat, cubed
2 tablespoons salt
2 teaspoons black pepper
4–6 criollo peppers or jalapeños (2¾ oz/80 g)
⅓ cup (¾ oz/20 g) finely chopped cilantro (coriander)
⅓ cup (2¾ oz/80 g) minced garlic
½ teaspoon pink curing salt
3 tablespoons non-fat milk powder
5 feet/1.5 meter hog casing, presoaked and rinsed
Your favorite wood, for smoking

In a large bowl, combine all the ingredients except the milk powder. Cover and refrigerate overnight.

Freeze the mixture for 1 hour. Using a meat grinder with a ¼-inch/6-mm plate, grind the mixture. In a large bowl, combine the ground meat, milk powder, and 4 tablespoons ice-cold water. Stuff the mixture into the casing, making 5-inch/12-cm links. Cover and refrigerate overnight.

Preheat a smoker with your favorite wood to 120°F/48°C.

Place the sausages in the smoker and smoke for 1½ hours. Increase the temperature to 125°F/52°C and smoke for 1 hour. Increase the temperature to 135°F/57°C for another 1 hour. Increase the smoker to 155°F/68°C and smoke for 1½ hours. Finally, increase the smoker to 175°F/80°C, until the sausage reaches an internal temperature of 145°F/63°C, about 30 minutes to 1 hour.

Cool in an ice water bath, then let the sausages sit at room temperature for 4 hours.

When ready to eat, heat the sausages in a skillet for 8-10 minutes. Serve hot.

Käsekrainer is a lightly smoked pork sausage stuffed with Swiss cheese (*käse* means "cheese" in German) and was reportedly invented in the 1980s. It is usually served with mustard and horseradish and sprinkled with curry powder. It can also be made into a *bosna* sandwich, in which the sausage is wrapped in white bread with onions and a blend of mustard, ketchup, and curry powder, then grilled.

PREPARATION TIME 1 hour,
plus at least 8 hours refrigeration and 30 minutes drying
COOKING TIME 1½ hours
SERVES 8-10

2 lb/900 g pork belly, rind removed and
cut into 1-inch/2.5-cm cubes

1½ lb/750 g beef shoulder, cut into 1-inch/2.5-cm cubes

2 tablespoons pink curing salt

9 oz/250 g boiled pork rind
(cut pork rind into small pieces and boil for 2 hours)

3 cloves garlic, minced

10½ oz/300 g Swiss cheese, cut into ¼-inch/5-mm cubes

2 teaspoons white pepper

1½ teaspoons ground allspice

1½ teaspoons sugar

1 teaspoon freshly grated nutmeg

½ cup (4 fl oz/120 ml) whole (full-fat) milk

5 feet/1.5 meter hog casing, presoaked and rinsed

Hickory wood, for smoking

Mustard, to serve

Place the pork and beef into 2 separate bowls. Sprinkle both with half the curing salt. Refrigerate for 8–12 hours.

Using a meat grinder with a ⅛-inch/3-mm perforated plate, grind the beef twice. Replace the plate with a 1/16-inch/2-mm plate, then grind the pork belly, prepared rind, and garlic.

In a food processor, combine the meat mixtures, cheese, pepper, allspice, sugar, nutmeg, and milk. Blend for 5 minutes.

Stuff the mixture into the casing, making 8-inch/20-cm links. Set aside to dry at room temperature for 30 minutes.

Preheat a smoker with hickory to 140°F/60°C.

Place the sausages in the smoker and smoke for 1 hour.

Bring a saucepan of water to a boil. Add the sausages and boil for 30 minutes.

Fill a large bowl with ice water. Using tongs, place the sausages into the ice bath to cool. Transfer them to a plate, then pat dry with paper towels.

Serve warm with mustard.

Store the cooled sausages in the refrigerator for 5 days.

POLISH SAUSAGES

The most well-known traditional sausage in Poland is probably the *wiejska* (meaning "rural"). This pork sausage is relatively simple to make, though it requires a few days to dry and cure. This is best when smoked but can also be cooked in a pan or oven.

PREPARATION TIME 30 minutes, plus 3 days curing and 3 hours drying
COOKING TIME 3–4 hours
SERVES 4–6

1 (5-lb/2.25-kg) pork shoulder, cut into 1-inch/2.5-cm chunks
12–15 cloves garlic, crushed
2 tablespoons mustard seeds
4 teaspoons salt
1 tablespoon marjoram
1 tablespoon black pepper
1 teaspoon pink curing salt
10 feet/3 meter hog casings casing, presoaked and rinsed
Oak or apple wood, for smoking

FOR SERVING
Mustard
Sauerkraut

Using a meat grinder with a ¼-inch/6-mm plate, grind the pork and garlic. In a large bowl, combine the ground (minced) pork mixture, mustard seeds, salt, marjoram, pepper, and curing salt. Stir, then add 1 cup (8 fl oz/240 ml) ice-cold water. Using your hands, mix well.

Stuff the mixture into the casing, making 5-inch/12.7-cm links. Refrigerate for 3 days, turning every day to dry and cure the sausages.

Preheat a smoker to 160°F/71°C.

Place the sausages in the smoker and smoke for 3–4 hours, until they reach an internal temperature of 152°F/67°C. Fill a large bowl with ice water. Using tongs, transfer the sausages into the ice bath, then set aside to cool until the internal temperature is 120°F/49°C. Dry the sausages at room temperature for 3 hours.

Grill or fry the sausages for 10–15 minutes until cooked through, with a good color and a nice crust, and serve with mustard and sauerkraut. Store the sausages in the refrigerator for 4 days or in the freezer for up to 3 months.

Variations of this mild sausage abound but most contain a combination of pork, marjoram, coriander, nutmeg, and pepper. The sausages are typically grilled and served on a hard roll with sauerkraut. German immigrants brought "brats" to the American Midwest, where the sausages are often smoked or boiled in beer (page 84) and served in a soft bun with mustard.

PREPARATION TIME 30 minutes,
plus at least 2 hours refrigeration and overnight chilling
COOKING TIME 25 minutes
SERVES 6–8

1 (3-lb/1.3-kg) pork shoulder, cut into 2-inch/5-cm cubes
1 (2-lb/900-g) top round beef, cut into 2-inch/5-cm cubes
2 eggs
1 cup (8 fl oz/240 ml) beer, plus extra, if desired, for poaching
1 tablespoon salt
1 tablespoon ground mustard
1 tablespoon ground coriander
2 teaspoons sugar
2 teaspoons onion powder
1 teaspoon ground sage
1 teaspoon black pepper
1 teaspoon cayenne pepper
1 teaspoon smoked paprika
½ teaspoon ground nutmeg
10 feet/3 meter hog casing, presoaked and rinsed

Using a meat grinder with a ¼-inch/6-mm plate, grind the pork and beef.

In a large bowl, whisk the eggs and beer until combined. Mix in the remaining ingredients, then add in the ground (minced) meat. Cover and refrigerate for 2–24 hours.

Stuff the mixture into the casing, making 6-inch/15-cm links. Chill overnight.

To cook the sausages, gently poach in beer or lightly salted water for 20-25 minutes, until cooked through. Alternatively, fry or grill over medium-high heat for 20 minutes, until the skins are crispy.

The cooked sausages will keep in the refrigerator for a week.

BEER BRATWURST

"Beer brats," as they are known in Wisconsin, were first introduced in 1954 at a Milwaukee Brewers baseball game. Bratwurst or German Sausages (page 83) are boiled in beer, then grilled and served on a long, split roll with mustard, onions, and sauerkraut.

Beer brats are the epitome of celebratory barbecues where food is the centerpiece, and they continue to be a staple at American football tailgate parties.

PREPARATION TIME 10 minutes
COOKING TIME 15–20 minutes
SERVES 12

3 large Spanish onions, cut into ¼-inch/5-mm-thick slices
1 head garlic, unpeeled and sliced in half crosswise
12 raw Bratwurst (page 83)
6 (12-fl oz/350-ml) cans IPA or lager beer
12 hot dog or hoagie rolls, sliced or split
1 cup (8 fl oz/240 ml) brown mustard
2 cups (11 oz/315 g) sauerkraut

Preheat a grill to medium-high heat.

In a large saucepan, combine the onions, garlic, and sausages. Pour in enough beer to cover and bring to a boil. Reduce the heat to medium-low and simmer for 10 minutes, or until the sausages are cooked through. Using tongs, transfer the sausages to a baking sheet and set aside.

Cook the onions and garlic in the beer for another 5–10 minute, until softened. Transfer the onions to a plate.

Meanwhile, grill the sausages for 5–10 minutes, until grill marks appear on all sides. Transfer them to a large plate.

Place a sausage in each roll, then top with mustard, sauerkraut, and beer-cooked onions. Serve warm.

SLOVENIAN SAUSAGES

Kranjska klobasa has its roots in the nineteenth century, when the sausage became a favorite among the people of the Carniola region in Austria, now part of Slovenia. Originally, it was a hearty meal for shepherds and farmers working in the rugged mountains. Today, it's commonly eaten at feasts and family gatherings, typically served on platters with sauerkraut and mustard.

PREPARATION TIME 30 minutes,
plus 1 hour refrigeration and 20 minutes freezing
COOKING TIME 25–30 minutes
SERVES 8

2 lb/900 g pork shoulder, cut into 1-inch/2.5-cm cubes
8 oz/225 g pork fatback, cut into 1-inch/2.5-cm cubes
8 thick strips bacon, cut into 1-inch/2.5-cm cubes
1 tablespoon salt
4 cloves garlic, pressed
2 teaspoons sweet paprika
1½ teaspoons black pepper
1 teaspoon mustard seeds, ground
1 cup (8 fl oz/240 ml) ice water
10 feet/3 meters (28–32-mm) hog casing, presoaked and rinsed

In a large bowl, combine the pork, bacon, and salt. Cover and refrigerate for at least 1 hour. Transfer the mixture to the freezer and set aside for 20 minutes.

Preheat a grill to high heat.

Using a meat grinder with a ¼-inch/6-mm plate, grind the pork mixture.

In a food processor or stand mixer, combine the ground (minced) pork mixture and the remaining ingredients except for the casing. Pour in 1 cup (8 fl oz/240 ml) of ice water and process until the mixture turns sticky.

Stuff the mixture into the casing, making 6-inch/15-cm links. Bring a large saucepan of water to a simmer. Add the sausages and cook for 15–20 minutes, until the internal temperature reaches 160°F/71°C.

Place the sausages on the grill and cook for 10 minutes, or until browned and cooked through. Transfer to a serving dish.

Serve hot.

SERBIAN SAUSAGES

Although uncased sausages hail from Serbia, their origin is often disputed because they are so popular in the Balkans and southeastern Europe. *Ćevapi* are similar to Romania's *mici* (page 88), Turkey's *köfte* (page 31), and Bulgaria's *kebapche* (page 91). Serve them with sliced sweet onions, flatbread, Red Pepper-Eggplant Sauce (page 347), and Serbian Cheese Spread (page 354).

PREPARATION TIME 1 hour, plus at least 1 hour refrigeration
COOKING TIME 10 minutes
SERVES 6

FOR THE SAUSAGES

1 lb/450 g ground (minced) beef

8 oz/225 g ground (minced) pork

3 cloves garlic, minced

1¼ teaspoons salt

1 teaspoon black pepper

1 teaspoon paprika

¾ teaspoon baking soda (bicarbonate of soda)

FOR SERVING

Sliced onions

Balkan Flatbread (page 323)

Red Pepper-Eggplant Sauce (page 347)

Serbian Cheese Spread (page 354)

FOR THE SAUSAGES Combine all the ingredients in a large bowl and mix well.

Take 1 tablespoon of the mixture and form it into a small sausage shape, about 3 inches/7.5 cm long and ¾ inch/2 cm in diameter. Transfer to a baking sheet. Repeat with the remaining mixture. Cover and refrigerate for at least 1 hour but, preferably, overnight.

Preheat a grill to medium heat.

Place the sausages on the grill and cook for 4–5 minutes on each side, until golden and springy. Transfer to serving dish.

Serve hot with onions, flatbread, red pepper-eggplant sauce, and Serbian cheese spread.

SERBIAN MEAT PATTIES

Like *ćevapi* (see left), the Serbian *pljeskavica* comes from the word *pljesak*, "to clap the hands," which is how these thin meat patties are formed. Made with beef, pork, lamb, or a combination, the patties are often served with a hard roll and a Serbian Cheese Spread (page 354) and/or Red Pepper-Eggplant Sauce (page 347).

PREPARATION TIME 30 minutes, plus at least 2 hours marinating
COOKING TIME 15 minutes
SERVES 6

FOR THE PATTIES

1 lb/450 g ground (minced) beef chuck

8 oz/225 g lean ground (minced) pork

8 oz/225 g lean ground (minced) lamb

2 cloves garlic, minced

1 small onion, finely chopped

1½ teaspoons salt

1 tablespoon paprika

FOR SERVING

6 hard rolls

Serbian Cheese Spread (page 354)

Red Pepper-Eggplant Sauce (page 347)

FOR THE PATTIES In a large bowl, combine all the ingredients and mix well. Cover and refrigerate for 2–4 hours.

Preheat a grill to high heat.

Using wet hands, divide the meat mixture into 6 portions. Form thin 9-inch/23-cm-wide patties. Grill the patties for 7 minutes on each side, flipping once.

Serve in hard rolls with Serbian cheese spread and/or red pepper-eggplant sauce.

ROMANIAN SAUSAGES

These small, uncased sausages called *mititei* or *mici* (meaning "little ones") are a popular street food in Romania. Made with a combination of ground meat, garlic, and warm spices, they are a close cousin to the Serbian *ćevapi* (page 87), Bulgarian *kebapche* (page 91), and Turkish *köfte* (page 31).

PREPARATION TIME 20 minutes,
plus at least 2 hours refrigeration
COOKING TIME 10 minutes
SERVES 6

2 lb/900 g ground (minced) meat (50% beef/50% pork or equal parts pork, lamb, and beef)

6–8 cloves garlic, minced

1 tablespoon salt

1 tablespoon black pepper

½ tablespoon ground coriander

1 teaspoon ground cumin

1 teaspoon dried thyme

1 teaspoon baking soda (bicarbonate of soda)

4 tablespoons sparkling water

In a food processor, combine the meat, garlic, and spices and blend until smooth.

In a small bowl, dissolve the baking soda (bicarbonate of soda) in the sparkling water. Add it to the meat mixture and mix well.

With damp hands, shape a handful of the mixture into a sausage, about 4 inches/10 cm long by 1-inch/2.5-cm in diameter. Transfer the sausage to a baking sheet. Repeat with the remaining mixture. Cover and refrigerate for at least 2 hours but, preferably, overnight.

Preheat a grill to high heat.

Place the sausages on the grill and cook for 8 minutes, turning once, until cooked through.

Spišské párky was created over 100 years ago for the Hungarian nobility when they visited Slovakia's Spiš Castle. The sausage is made with beef, pork, and both sweet and hot paprika, then smoked and generally cooked in hot (but not boiling) water so the natural casing doesn't burst.

PREPARATION TIME 20 minutes, plus 12 hours marinating
COOKING TIME 2 hours
SERVES 8

¾ cup (3½ oz/100 g) salt

⅓ cup (1½ oz/40 g) sweet paprika

4 tablespoons hot paprika

6 lb/2.8 kg lean pork leg and shoulder, cut into 1-inch/2.5-cm cubes

5 lb/2.25 kg fatty pork belly and shoulder, cut into 1-inch/2.5-cm cubes

Scant 3 cups (24 fl oz/700 ml) pork stock

10-15 feet/3-5 meters sheep casing, presoaked and rinsed

Apple or cherry wood, for smoking

FOR SERVING

Bread

Mustard

In a small bowl, combine the salt and both paprikas.

In a large bowl, combine the lean pork and half of the paprika salt. In another large bowl, combine the fatty pork and the remaining half of the paprika salt. Cover both bowls and refrigerate for 12 hours.

Preheat the smoker to 225°F/107°C.

Using a meat grinder with a ⅛-inch/3-mm plate, grind the lean and fatty pork into a large bowl. Add the stock and mix thoroughly.

Stuff the mixture into the casing, making 6-inch/15-cm links. Place the sausages in the smoker and smoke for 1 hour. Reduce the heat to 180°F/82°C and smoke the sausage for another 1 hour.

Serve hot with bread and mustard.

BULGARIAN SAUSAGES

Kebapche, meaning "little kabob" in Bulgarian, are small, uncased sausages made with beef, pork, cumin, black pepper, and an aerator—such as soda water, beer, or baking soda (bicarbonate of soda)—to lighten the mixture. They are typically served with a Red Pepper–Eggplant Sauce known as *ajvar* (page 347) and French fries smothered in cheese.

PREPARATION TIME 15 minutes,
plus at least 1 hour marinating
COOKING TIME 10 minutes
SERVES 4

1 lb/450 g ground (minced) pork
5½ oz/150 g ground (minced) beef
1½ teaspoons ground cumin
1 teaspoon salt
½ teaspoon black pepper
4 tablespoons beer
1 egg, beaten

FOR SERVING
Red Pepper-Eggplant Sauce (page 347)
French fries

In a large bowl, combine the pork and beef, cumin, salt, pepper, and beer. Stir in the egg and mix until homogeneous. Cover and refrigerate for at least 1 hour or, preferably 24 hours.

Preheat a grill to high heat.

Using your hands, roll the meat mixture into sausages, about 6 inches/15 cm long and 1½ inches/ 4 cm in diameter. Place the sausages on the grill and cook for 7–10 minutes, turning at least twice, until browned and cooked through.

Serve hot with red pepper-eggplant sauce and French fries.

Kupati is a Georgian sausage made with pork, onions, black pepper, cinnamon, garlic, cilantro (coriander), and often pomegranate seeds. Each region has its own version, with some using beef or even chopped organ meat. This recipe eliminates the casing and turns the meat mixture into patties.

PREPARATION TIME 10 minutes
COOKING TIME 8 minutes
SERVES 4

1½ lb/680 g ground (minced) pork
2 cloves garlic, minced
1 pomegranate, seeded
2 tablespoons chopped dill or 1 tablespoon dried
2 tablespoons cilantro (coriander), chopped
1½ teaspoons salt, plus extra to taste
1 teaspoon black pepper
¼ teaspoon ground cinnamon
1–2 tablespoons canola oil, for brushing

In a large bowl, combine all the ingredients except the oil. Using your hands, knead for 3–4 minutes, until blended. Divide the mixture into 8 equal portions.

Preheat a grill to high heat.

Using wet hands, shape each portion into a 3-inch/7.5-cm patty, about ½ inch/1 cm thick. Lightly brush them with oil. Place the sausages on the grill and cook for 4 minutes on each side, turning occasionally, until the patties are cooked through. Transfer to a serving dish.

Serve immediately.

MEXICAN CHORIZO

Chorizo originated centuries ago in Spain as a firm, dry-cured, paprika-flavored sausage. When it arrived in Mexico after the Spanish conquered the Aztecs, chorizo transformed into an uncased sausage seasoned with vinegar and chili powder. It is traditionally served with tortillas or with a fried egg and sautéed potatoes.

PREPARATION TIME 15 minutes
COOKING TIME 10 minutes
SERVES 6

1½ lb/680 g ground (minced) pork
2 tablespoons paprika
1 tablespoon cayenne pepper
1 tablespoon ancho powder
1 tablespoon guajillo powder
1 tablespoon garlic powder
1 teaspoon ground cumin
1 teaspoon dried oregano
1 teaspoon ground coriander
½ teaspoon ground cinnamon
½ teaspoon ground clove
2 tablespoons red wine vinegar
1 teaspoon salt
1 teaspoon black pepper
1 tablespoon vegetable oil
6 corn tortillas, to serve

In a large bowl, combine all the ingredients except the oil and mix well.

Heat the oil in a large skillet over medium heat. Add the chorizo and sauté for 8–10 minutes, breaking it up with a spoon, until cooked through. Transfer to a serving dish.

Serve hot with tortillas and taco fillings.

ARGENTINIAN CHORIZO

In Argentina, chorizo, which the *gauchos* (nomadic cowboys) grilled in the nineteenth century, is now served from carts on street corners and outside stadiums. Flavored with wine and paprika, it falls somewhere between Spanish chorizo, which uses garlic and paprika, and Mexican Chorizo (left), which is seasoned with vinegar and chili powder.

PREPARATION TIME 30 minutes, plus at least 1 hour marinating, 15 minutes freezing, and overnight refrigeration
COOKING TIME 10 minutes
SERVES 8–10

1 (1-lb/450-g) pork shoulder, cut into 1-inch/2.5-cm cubes
1 (8-oz/225-g) beef chuck, cut into 1-inch/2.5-cm cubes
1 (8-oz/225-g) pork back or pork belly, cut into 1-inch/2.5-cm cubes
4 cloves garlic
1½ tablespoons paprika
1 tablespoon cayenne pepper
2 teaspoons salt
2 teaspoons black pepper
½ cup (4 fl oz/120 ml) red wine
1 tablespoon vegetable oil
12 feet/3.6 meters (28–32-mm) hog casing, presoaked and rinsed

FOR SERVING
8–10 rolls
Chimichurri (page 340)

In a large bowl, combine all the ingredients except the casing. Cover and refrigerate for at least 1 hour or, preferably, overnight. Transfer the meat mixture to the freezer and freeze for 15 minutes.

Using a meat grinder with a ¼-inch/6-mm plate, grind the mixture. Using your hands mix for 2–3 minutes, until the mixture is sticky. Stuff the chorizo mixture into the casing, making 6-inch/15-cm links. Refrigerate overnight.

Preheat a grill to medium heat.

Place the chorizo on the grill and cook for 5–6 minutes on each side, until browned.

Serve in rolls with chimichurri.

The Argentinian sandwich *choripán* gets its name from the sausage *(chori)* and the baguette *(pan)* but owes its flavor to the chimichurri sauce. Sold at parks, soccer stadiums, outdoor markets, and street fairs, the simple sandwich has grilled Argentinian chorizo split lengthwise and cradled in a roll with chimichurri.

PREPARATION TIME 5 minutes
COOKING TIME 15 minutes
SERVES 4

4 raw Argentinian Chorizo (page 95)
4 (6-inch/15-cm) rolls, halved lengthwise
Chimichurri (page 340), to serve

Preheat a grill to medium heat.

Place the chorizo on the grill and cook for 10–12 minutes, turning occasionally, until seared and cooked through.

Warm the rolls on the grill.

Transfer the rolls to a serving dish, then add a sausage to each roll. Smear the rolls and sausages with chimichurri and serve immediately.

MAINS

ARGENTINIAN SHORT RIBS

Argentinian barbecue, or *asado*, traditionally features a wide selection of grilled meats cooked on a brick-built grill called *la parrilla*. The fire can either be made with charcoal *(parrilla a carbón)* or wood *(parrilla a leña)*. This popular Argentinian dish, *tira de asado*, uses short ribs cut flanken-style (crosswise against the bone). After a simple marinade (usually salt and pepper), the meat is grilled over charcoal and served with Chimichurri (page 340).

PREPARATION TIME 10 minutes
COOKING TIME 10 minutes
SERVES 6

4 lb/1.8 kg flanken-style short ribs
Salt and black pepper, to taste
Chimichurri (page 340), to serve

Preheat a grill to high heat.

Generously season the short ribs with salt and pepper. Place the ribs on the grill and cook for 8–10 minutes, turning frequently, until the ribs are charred on all sides. Transfer them to a serving dish, tent with aluminum foil, and rest for 5 minutes.

Serve with a side of chimichurri.

SMOKED SHORT RIBS

A full-plate short rib, weighing close to six pounds (2.75 kg), is a barbecue showstopper. When smoked at the right temperature, short ribs render their abundant fat and essentially self-baste, producing a deliciously rich dish that is hard to match, especially in presentation.

PREPARATION TIME 5 minutes,
plus at least 12 hours refrigeration
COOKING TIME 8–10 hours
SERVES 6

1 (5–6-lb/2.25–2.75-kg) bone-in, whole-plate beef short rib
Salt and black pepper, to taste
Oak, pecan or cherry wood, for smoking

Generously season the short ribs with salt and pepper. Cover and refrigerate for 12–24 hours.

Preheat a smoker to 225°F/107°C.

Bring the short ribs to room temperature. Put the short ribs in the smoker and smoke for 8–10 hours, until the meat is meltingly tender with a little spring to it. Transfer the rib to a cutting board. Remove the center bone and cut in half, creating two large ribs.

GF DF NF 5 ◗

Beef back ribs, which sit between the cow's shoulder and loin, are the ribs on a standing (prime) rib roast and often removed when the cut is made into rib-eye steaks. They tend to be less meaty than full-plate or chuck ribs, but they are cheaper and cook more quickly than brisket—making them a great entry point to smoking beef. They are delicious simply seasoned with salt and pepper but can stand up to a more complex marinade or rub as well.

PREPARATION TIME 5 minutes
COOKING TIME 5 hours
SERVES 4–6

2 (3–4-lb/1.3–1.8-kg) beef back rib racks
1 cup (7 oz/200 g) Beef Rub (page 360)
1 cup (8 fl oz/240 ml) apple cider vinegar, in a spritz bottle
Oak, pecan or cherry wood, for smoking

Preheat a smoker to 250°F/120°C. As the ribs require a moist cooking environment, use a water pan to create humidity.

Place the beef back ribs on a baking sheet, then generously season both sides with the beef rub. Set aside while the smoker reaches temperature.

Place the ribs in the smoker, bone side down, and smoke for 1 hour. Spritz the ribs with the vinegar every 30 minutes. After 5 hours, check the internal temperature of the ribs. If they are around 200°F/93°C, remove them from the smoker. If not, check again in 30 minutes. Transfer the ribs to a serving dish, then set aside to rest for 20 minutes.

Serve warm.

COLOMBIAN BEEF RIBS

These South American–style beef ribs are seasoned with salt and pepper and cooked on a hot grill or over an open fire. Be sure to get a good-quality rib rack or prime rib roast from a butcher shop. Colombians often serve these ribs with Chimichurri (page 340) or Ají Amarillo Sauce (page 336).

PREPARATION TIME 5 minutes
COOKING TIME 4 hours
SERVES 6

2 (6- or 7-bone) racks of prime ribs
Salt and black pepper, to taste
Chimichurri (page 340) or Ají Amarillo Sauce (page 336), to serve

Preheat a grill to low heat for indirect grilling.

Generously season the rib racks with salt and pepper. Place them over the cool part of the grill and cook for 4 hours, turning occasionally, until the ribs are charred on all sides and the fat has rendered. Transfer to a cutting board, tent with aluminum foil, and rest for 10 minutes.

Transfer the ribs to a serving dish, then serve hot with a bowl of chimichurri or ají amarillo sauce.

KOREAN SHORT RIBS

Korean *galbi* is prepared with flanken-style beef short ribs, meaning the rib is cut across and along the bone. This cut became popular among the Los Angeles Korean community and is often known locally in Korean markets and barbecue restaurants as "LA-style."

The beef is cut into strips and flavored with a sweet and savory soy-based marinade, then grilled and served with lettuce leaves and *ssamjang* (Korean barbecue sauce).

PREPARATION TIME 20 minutes, plus at least 1 hour marinating
COOKING TIME 10 minutes
SERVES 4–6

FOR THE MARINATED BEEF

4 cloves garlic
1 onion (7 oz/200 g), coarsely chopped
1 pear (5¾ oz/170 g), peeled and coarsely chopped
1 tablespoon grated ginger
1 cup (8 fl oz/240 ml) soy sauce
2 tablespoons mirin
2 tablespoons brown sugar
4 scallions (spring onions), thinly sliced
2 tablespoons toasted sesame seeds, crushed
2 tablespoons toasted sesame oil
3 lb/1.3 kg flanken-style beef short ribs, cut into ½-inch/1-cm-thick strips

FOR SERVING

Korean Barbecue Sauce (page 347)
Bibb lettuce
Steamed rice
Thinly sliced garlic
Thinly sliced scallions (spring onions)

FOR THE MARINATED BEEF In a food processor, combine the garlic, onion, pear, and ginger and blend for 30 seconds. Add the soy sauce, mirin, and brown sugar and blend again for 30 seconds. If the mixture seems too thick, add up to 4 tablespoons of water to loosen it up.

Transfer the mixture to a medium bowl, then stir in the scallions (spring onions), sesame seeds, and sesame oil.

In a zip-top bag or large bowl, combine the beef and marinade. Seal or cover and refrigerate for 1–24 hours.

Preheat a grill to high heat for direct grilling.

Place the beef on the grill and cook for 6–8 minutes, turning often. Using tongs, transfer the beef to a cutting board to rest for 2 minutes. Cut into bite-sized pieces, then transfer to a serving dish.

Serve with Korean barbecue sauce, lettuce, rice, garlic, and scallions (spring onions).

DF NF 5 ◖◗ ◎

The name of this dish, *bulgogi*, comes from the Korean words *bul*, meaning "fire," and *goki*, meaning "meat." Similar to Korean Short Ribs (page 106), it is usually made with thinly sliced beef. You can use a trimmed hanger steak or boneless short rib. The trick is to cut the meat very thin so it quickly absorbs the marinade flavors.

PREPARATION TIME 10 minutes,
plus at least 30 minutes marinating
COOKING TIME 10 minutes
SERVES 4

1 clove garlic, minced
¼ large pear, grated
1 tablespoon grated ginger
1 tablespoon brown sugar
1 teaspoon red pepper flakes
2 tablespoons soy sauce
1 tablespoon toasted sesame oil
1 (1-lb/450-g) trimmed hanger steak or boneless short rib, sliced into very thin strips
Salt, to taste
5 scallions (spring onions), thinly sliced, to serve

In a medium bowl, combine the garlic, pear, ginger, brown sugar, and red pepper flakes. Stir in the soy sauce and sesame oil. Add the beef, cover, and set aside to marinate at room temperature for 30 minutes or in the refrigerator for up to 8 hours.

Preheat a grill to medium-high heat.

Remove the beef from the marinade, then season lightly with salt. Place it on the grill and cook for 3 minutes, until lightly browned. Flip and cook for another 3 minutes, until browned. Transfer to a serving dish.

Serve hot with scallions (spring onions).

GRILLED STEAK WITH AVOCADO SAUCE

This steak basted with a garlicky marinade and served with a creamy avocado sauce is typical of Venezuelan barbecues. The meat called *punta trasera* in Venezuela is a top sirloin or tri-tip in the United States. In Brazil, it is called *picanha*; in Argentina and Uruguay, *tapa de cuadril;* in Mexico, *cuadril*; and in Colombia, *punta de anca*.

PREPARATION TIME 10 minutes
COOKING TIME 10 minutes
SERVES 4

FOR THE GUASACACA SAUCE
1 avocado, pitted and peeled
1 green bell pepper, seeded, deveined, and chopped
Bunch of cilantro (coriander), chopped
1 small white onion, chopped
2 tablespoons canola oil
Juice of 1 lemon
Salt and black pepper, to taste

FOR THE BASTING SAUCE
6 cloves garlic, minced
3 sprigs rosemary
4 tablespoons finely chopped parsley
½ cup (4 fl oz/120 ml) olive oil

FOR THE STEAK
1 (4-lb/1.8-kg) steak, preferably tri-tip

Preheat a grill to high heat.

FOR THE GUASACACA SAUCE In a food processor, combine all the ingredients and blend until almost smooth. Season to taste with salt and pepper.

FOR THE BASTING SAUCE In a small bowl, combine all the ingredients. Season to taste with salt and pepper.

FOR THE STEAK Season the steak with salt and pepper. Place it on the grill and cook for 8–10 minutes, turning frequently and brushing with the basting sauce, until browned on both sides. Transfer the steak to a serving dish, then set aside to rest for 5 minutes.
Serve hot with the guasacaca sauce.

The origins of this dish's name are mysterious. It features a platter of smoky steak and warm sticky rice with a dipping sauce made of fish sauce, lime, and cilantro (coriander) on the side. It is often served as a salad, with the sauce used as a dressing.

PREPARATION TIME 20 minutes,
plus at least 1 hour marinating
COOKING TIME 15 minutes
SERVES 4

FOR THE STEAK

2 tablespoons soy sauce

1 tablespoon oyster sauce

1 tablespoon vegetable oil

1 tablespoon brown sugar

4 (12-oz/350-g) rib-eye or New York strip steaks, about 1½ inches/4 cm thick

FOR THE DIPPING SAUCE

½ cup (4 fl oz/120 ml) lime juice

½ cup (4 fl oz/120 ml) fish sauce

1 teaspoon sugar

2 tablespoons finely chopped cilantro (coriander)

2 tablespoons finely chopped scallions (spring onions)

1½ tablespoons toasted rice powder (see Note)

1 tablespoon chili powder

NOTE Toasted rice powder can be purchased at Asian supermarkets. You can also toast white rice in a skillet (frying pan) for 5–10 minutes, until browned, then grind into a powder.

FOR THE STEAK In a large bowl, combine all the ingredients except the steaks. Add the steaks and coat them with the marinade. Set aside at room temperature for 1–2 hours.

FOR THE DIPPING SAUCE In a small bowl, combine the ingredients.

Preheat a grill to high heat.

Add the steaks to the grill and cook for 10 minutes, turning frequently, until they reach an internal temperature of 125°F/52°C for medium-rare. Transfer the steaks to a cutting board, then set aside to rest for 5 minutes.

Cut the meat into ¼-inch/5-mm slices, then arrange on a serving dish. Serve with a side of the dipping sauce.

FLORENTINE STEAK

Italy's popular *bistecca alla Fiorentina* is a thick steak simply seasoned with garlic and rosemary, then seared on a hot grill. (Traditionally, the dish is made with Tuscany's Chianina breed of cattle, known for its high-quality, flavorful meat.) Although porterhouse is the cut most often used, another tender cut, like rib eye, T-bone, or New York strip steak, will work just as well. Serve with roasted potatoes over a bed of dressed arugula.

PREPARATION TIME 10 minutes,
plus at least 1 hour marinating
COOKING TIME 20 minutes
SERVES 2

1 clove garlic, minced

2 teaspoons chopped rosemary

2 tablespoons extra-virgin olive oil,
plus 2 teaspoons for drizzling

1 (2½-lb/1.1-kg) rib-eye, T-bone, or porterhouse steak

2 tablespoons sea salt, plus 1 teaspoon

1 lemon, cut in half

¼ teaspoon black pepper

In a large bowl, combine the garlic, rosemary, and olive oil. Add the steak and coat in the marinade. Cover and refrigerate for at least 1 hour but, preferably, overnight.

Preheat a grill to 500°F/260°C.

Bring the steak to room temperature. Rub 2 tablespoons of salt over the steak, then place it on the grill and cook for 7–10 minutes.

While the steak cooks, place the lemon halves cut-side down on the grill and cook for 2–3 minutes or until lightly charred.

Flip the steak, then cook for another 10 minutes, until the internal temperature reaches 125°F/52°C for medium-rare. Set aside to rest for 5–10 minutes, then transfer to a serving dish. Sprinkle with 1 teaspoon of salt and the pepper, then drizzle with oil.

Serve immediately with the grilled lemon.

Picanha, which gets its name from the location where the cow is branded with an iron, is basically a hunk of beef with a C-shaped fat cap and popular at Brazilian barbecue restaurants known as *churrascarias*. American butchers often break this cut down into the rump, round, and loin—any of which will work for the following recipe, so long as its fat cap is left intact.

PREPARATION TIME 10 minutes
COOKING TIME 25 minutes
SERVES 4

1 (2-lb/900-g) beef roast (rump, round, or loin), including the fat cap
Salt, to taste

Preheat a grill to high heat.

Using a sharp knife, score the fat side of the meat in a crosshatch pattern. Cut the beef horizontally into 4 pieces and curve each piece to insert a skewer through it twice. Season with salt.

Use foil-covered bricks to set up a prop for the skewers on the grill (one at each end of the skewer). Balance the skewers over the bricks, with the fat side up, and cook for 10 minutes. Turn, then cook for another 15 minutes, or until the internal temperature reaches 125°F/52°C. Transfer the steak to a cutting board, then set aside to rest for 5 minutes.

Thinly slice the meat against the grain, then arrange on a serving dish and serve immediately.

COLOMBIAN BEEF TENDERLOIN

In this simple yet unique dish known as *lomo al trapo* ("beef loin in a towel"), a heavily salted tenderloin is wrapped in a wine-soaked dish towel and cooked directly over burning embers. (Colombians often use a fireplace.) The salt flavors the lean meat and seals in the juices.

Be sure to let the beef rest on a metal plate before serving. Then crack the salt crust to expose the smoky, tender meat and serve with Chimichurri (page 340).

PREPARATION TIME 10 minutes
COOKING TIME 20 minutes
SERVES 4–6

1 cup (8 fl oz/240 ml) red wine
5 cups (1 lb 14 oz/850 g) salt
1 teaspoon red pepper flakes
1 teaspoon black pepper
4 sprigs oregano
1 (2 lb 4-oz/1-kg) beef tenderloin
Chimichurri (page 340), to serve

Preheat a charcoal grill to medium heat.

Place a dish (tea) towel into a large bowl and soak it in red wine. Wring out the dish towel, then lay it flat on a work surface. On the damp dish towel, spread out the salt into a 16- x 12-inch (40- x 30-cm) rectangle. Add the remaining ingredients, except the beef, on top.

Place the tenderloin in the middle of the towel. Roll it up like a burrito, tucking in the ends as you roll. Tie the roll with kitchen string at 1-inch/2.5-cm intervals.

Once the flames have died down, place the rolled beef directly on the coals and cook for 10 minutes. Flip, then cook for another 10 minutes. Transfer the towel to a metal plate, then set aside to rest for 5 minutes.

Cut the towel away and crack the salt to remove. Transfer the beef to a cutting board, then set aside to rest for another 10 minutes. Slice, then arrange in a serving dish.

Serve immediately with chimichurri.

Beef brisket is the holy grail of Texas barbecue but also the most daunting cut of meat to smoke. This recipe will produce an impossibly juicy beef with a bark that is equal parts smoky and salty with a hint of sweetness. It requires consistency, patience, and calm—and it's worth the investment. Make sure you use a full packer brisket, which is thicker and has more marbling than the "first cut" brisket.

PREPARATION TIME 20 minutes,
plus at least 8 hours marinating and 3 hours standing
COOKING TIME 12 hours
SERVES 12

1 (12–16-lb/5–7-kg) full packer beef brisket,
with deckle or fat visible

Salt and black pepper, to taste

Flaky sea salt, for finishing

Oak or pecan wood, for smoking

Remove the silver skin on the bottom of the brisket, leaving some fat on the top. Aim for a ½-inch/1-cm girdle. Generously season the brisket with salt and pepper. Leave uncovered and refrigerate for 8–24 hours.

Set the brisket aside for 2 hours to bring to room temperature.

Preheat your smoker to 250°F/120°C.

Put the brisket in the smoker, with the fat side up and the lean side pointed away from the hot spot. Close the lid, leave untouched, and smoke for 12 hours, or until the internal temperature reaches 200°F/93°C. (By this time, you will encounter "the stall." The brisket will appear as though it's not cooking, and the temperature won't budge. Don't panic; this is normal.) Transfer it to a clean work surface and wrap it in butcher paper. Allow to rest for 1 hour, then slice across the grain. Serve warm.

Burnt ends hail from Kansas City, Missouri, and refer to the delicious bits of fatty meat cut from the point or deckle of the brisket. Originally, pitmasters would reserve these oddly shaped end pieces for snacks or to throw into stews. During the 1970s, barbecue fans realized these "scraps" were actually gold. Although many cooks use the brisket point for their burnt ends, this recipe calls for an entire smoked brisket to be cubed, sauced, and re-smoked. (If you are smoking a brisket, go ahead and smoke another one just for these burnt ends.)

PREPARATION TIME 10 minutes
COOKING TIME 1–1½ hours
SERVES 10–12

1 whole Smoked Brisket (page 116)
4 cups (37 fl oz/1.1 L) Texas Table Sauce (page 335)
Oak or cherry wood, for smoking

Preheat a smoker to 250°F/120°C.

Separate the flat and the point of the brisket, reserving the flat to slice. Cut the smoked brisket into 1-inch/2.5-cm cubes and place onto a perforated pan. Add the brisket to the smoker and smoke for 40–60 minutes. Transfer the diced brisket to a large bowl, then add the sauce and toss well. Return the brisket to the smoker and smoke for another 20–30 minutes to caramelize.

Transfer to a serving dish and serve immediately.

SMOKED BEEF SHOULDER

Similar to a whole brisket, a beef shoulder is a large, primal cut of beef. It is leaner and has fewer muscles than a brisket, which means it cooks faster but also tends to dry out if the heat is not consistent. Because beef shoulder is considerably less expensive than brisket, it's a good cut to use to hone your skills. Plus, it serves a crowd, so plan on inviting guests.

PREPARATION TIME 5 minutes, plus at least 2 hours refrigeration and 30 minutes resting
COOKING TIME 12 hours
SERVES 10–20

1 (12–15 lb/5–7 kg) beef shoulder
2 cups (14 oz/400 g) Beef Rub (page 360)
4¼ cups (34 fl oz/1 L) apple cider vinegar, in a spray bottle
Oak, pecan or cherry wood, for smoking
4¼ cups (34 fl oz/1 L) Texas Table Sauce (page 335), to serve

Season the beef shoulder with the beef rub, making sure to cover all sides and surfaces. Refrigerate for at least 2 hours but, preferably, overnight.

Preheat a smoker to 250°F/120°C.

Put the beef in the smoker, fat side up, and away from the hot spots. Smoke for 1 hour. Smoke for another 11 hours, spritzing it with apple cider vinegar every 30 minutes, until the internal temperature reaches 195°F/90°C. Transfer the beef to a cutting board, then set aside to rest for 30–60 minutes.

Slice the beef across the grain, arrange in a serving dish, and serve with a side of the Texas table sauce.

This kosher smoked meat dish, brought to Canada by eastern European Jews in the late nineteenth century, is similar to Pastrami (page 122). It is made with a more savory brine and smoked a little longer than pastrami, acquiring a pronounced smoky flavor. Montreal smoked meat can be served cold or steamed; it can also be warmed for hot sandwiches (preferably on rye with mustard).

PREPARATION TIME 1 hour,
plus 4 days curing and 2 hours soaking
COOKING TIME 7–8 hours
SERVES 12

FOR THE CURED BRISKET
1 cup (5 oz/140 g) salt
3 tablespoons black pepper
3 tablespoons ground coriander
1 tablespoon pink curing salt
1 tablespoon sugar
1 teaspoon ground bay leaf
1 teaspoon ground cloves
1 (12–14-lb/5–7-kg) whole brisket, fat cap trimmed

FOR THE RUB
3 tablespoons coarsely ground black pepper
1 tablespoon ground coriander
1 tablespoon paprika
1 tablespoon garlic powder
1 tablespoon onion powder
1 teaspoon dill weed
1 teaspoon ground mustard
1 teaspoon celery seeds
1 teaspoon red pepper flakes
Oak or hickory wood, for smoking

FOR THE CURE In a small bowl, combine all the ingredients except the brisket. Rub the cure all over the brisket, then place it in an extra-large zip-top bag. Seal and refrigerate for 4 days, flipping it twice a day.

Remove the brisket from the bag, then rinse off the cure. Place the brisket in a deep container or stockpot and add enough water to cover. Set aside for 2 hours, replenishing the water every 30 minutes. Remove the brisket from the water, then pat it dry with paper towels.

FOR THE RUB Preheat a smoker with 2–3 large handfuls of oak or hickory wood to 225°F/107°C.

Combine all the rub ingredients in a small bowl. Coat the brisket in the rub. Place the brisket in the smoker, fat side up, and smoke for 6 hours, until the internal temperature reaches 165°F/74°C.

Transfer the brisket to a large roasting pan with a V-rack. Place the roasting pan over 2 burners on the stove and fill it with 1 inch/2.5 cm of water. Bring the water to a boil over high heat, then reduce the heat to medium. Cover the pan with aluminum foil, then steam the brisket for 1–2 hours, until the internal temperature reaches 180°F/82°C. If necessary, add more hot water. Transfer the brisket to a cutting board, then set aside to cool.

Slice and serve.

Pastrami, which likely originated in Romania and Turkey, is classically made using beef navel, beef brisket, or even beef cheek. (It can also be made with turkey, page 243.) The meat is brined, dried, smoked, and steamed, a process that was intended to preserve it (before refrigeration was possible). Pastrami first made its way to New York City around 1872 in a wave of Jewish immigration. In 1887, a Manhattan butcher named Sussman Volk made a pastrami sandwich. It became so popular that Volk turned his butcher shop into a sandwich shop. Thinly sliced pastrami on rye bread remains an iconic taste of New York.

PREPARATION TIME 15 minutes, plus 3 weeks refrigeration
COOKING TIME 6–8 hours
SERVES 12–15

FOR THE BRISKET

1½ cups (7¼ oz/210 g) salt

1½ cups (11½ oz/325 g) dark brown sugar

10 bay leaves

1 head garlic, cut in half across the middle

½ cup (3½ oz/100 g) black peppercorns

4 tablespoons coriander seeds

1 tablespoon cloves

1 (12–14 lb/5–6 kg) whole packer brisket, point and flat separated

Oak or cherry wood, for smoking

Rye bread and mustard, to serve

FOR THE RUB

1 cup (3½ oz/100 g) juniper berries

1½ cups (10¼ oz/290 g) coarsely ground black pepper

FOR THE BRISKET In a stockpot, combine the salt, sugar, and 6 quarts/5.6 L of water. Bring to a boil to dissolve the salt and sugar. Turn the heat off, then add the bay leaves, garlic, peppercorns, coriander seeds, and cloves. Set aside until the brine has cooled to room temperature.

In a large bowl, combine the brisket and the brine. Cover and refrigerate for 3 weeks, flipping the meat every 2–3 days.

FOR THE RUB Using the back of a knife or the bottom of a pan, crush the juniper berries. In a small bowl, combine the crushed juniper berries and black pepper.

Preheat a smoker to 250°F/120°C.

Transfer the brisket to a cutting board, then coat it with the juniper-pepper mixture. Place the brisket in the smoker and smoke for 6–8 hours, until the internal temperature reaches 200°F/93°C. Set aside to rest for 1 hour.

Thinly slice the pastrami across the grain and serve with rye bread and mustard.

Store pastrami in the refrigerator for up to 2 weeks.

The famous pit beef sandwich, from Baltimore, Maryland, piles thinly sliced grilled beef (top round or bottom round charred on charcoal with a medium-rare interior) on a Kaiser roll (or rye bread) with tiger sauce (mayo and horseradish) and sliced onions. Although individual pit beef shops use their own secret spices, the beef is usually marinated with salt, pepper, paprika, thyme, and onion powder.

PREPARATION TIME 10 minutes,
plus at least 1 day refrigeration
COOKING TIME 2 hours 20 minutes
SERVES 8

FOR THE PIT BEEF
2 tablespoons seasoning salt
1 tablespoon sweet paprika
1 teaspoon garlic powder
1 teaspoon dried oregano
½ teaspoon black pepper
1 (13-lb/6-kg) top round roast

FOR THE HORSERADISH SAUCE
1 cup (8 fl oz/240 ml) mayonnaise
½ cup (4 fl oz/120 ml) white horseradish
2 teaspoons lemon juice
Salt and black pepper, to taste

FOR THE SANDWICH
8 Kaiser rolls
1 sweet white onion, thinly sliced

FOR THE PIT BEEF In a small bowl, combine all the ingredients except the beef. Coat the beef in the rub, massaging it into the meat. Transfer the beef to a baking dish and cover with plastic wrap (clingfilm). Refrigerate for 1–3 days.

Preheat a grill to indirect high heat.

Sear the roast on all sides over high heat for 15–20 minutes, then move it to the cooler side of the grill and continue cooking, turning occasionally, for 1½–2 hours, or until it reaches a temperature of 120°F/49°C. Set aside to rest for 5 minutes, then slice across the grain.

FOR THE HORSERADISH SAUCE Whisk the ingredients in a small bowl. Season to taste.

FOR THE SANDWICH Cut each roll in half, then spread the horseradish sauce on the cut sides. Pile the sliced beef on the roll, then top with slices of onion and the top half of the bun.

The *chimichurri Dominicano*, or *chimi* burger, is classic street food in the Dominican Republic. These beef burgers are seasoned with Dominican flavors, topped with cabbage slaw, and then smothered in a creamy, sweet, and tangy pink sauce. Traditionally, these burgers are served with *pan de agua*, hard-crusted oblong rolls.

PREPARATION TIME 15 minutes, plus 30 minutes refrigeration
COOKING TIME 20 minutes
SERVES 6

FOR THE CHIMI SAUCE
½ cup (4 fl oz/120 ml) ketchup
½ cup (4 fl oz/120 ml) mayonnaise
4 tablespoons orange juice
1 tablespoon soy sauce
1 tablespoon Worcestershire sauce

FOR THE SLAW
1 tablespoon canola oil
2 tomatoes, sliced
1 red onion, thinly sliced
2 cups (5 oz/140 g) shredded cabbage

FOR THE BURGERS
2 cloves garlic
1 large red onion, coarsely chopped
1 red bell pepper, seeded, deveined, and coarsely chopped
1 tablespoon soy sauce
1 tablespoon Worcestershire sauce
2 lb/900 g ground (minced) beef chuck
6 hamburger buns or small baguettes
Salt and black pepper, to taste

FOR THE CHIMI SAUCE In a small bowl, combine all the ingredients. Divide the sauce between 2 bowls. Refrigerate both for 30 minutes.

FOR THE SLAW Heat the oil in a small skillet over medium-high heat. Add the tomatoes and onion and sear for 3–5 minutes, until softened. Transfer to a small bowl.

Add the cabbage to the skillet and sauté for 5 minutes, or until softened. Transfer the cabbage to the bowl of tomatoes. Add in a bowl of chimi sauce and mix well.

FOR THE BURGERS Preheat a grill to high heat.

In a food processor, combine the garlic, onion, bell pepper, soy sauce, and Worcestershire sauce. Season with salt and pepper, then process to form a paste.

In a medium bowl, combine the paste and beef and mix well. Divide the mixture into 6 portions and form each one into a patty. Place the patties on the grill and cook for 10 minutes, turning once, until cooked through.

Reduce the heat to medium-high. Add the buns or baguettes, cut side down, and briefly grill until toasted.

Transfer the buns or baguettes to serving dishes. On the bottom half of each, add a patty, a small scoop of slaw, and a tablespoon of the remaining chimi sauce. Finish with the top half of the bun or baguette.

Serve immediately.

BIRRIA TACOS

Birria originated in Jalisco, Mexico, as a goat or lamb stew prepared in the *barbacoa* style. The meat was marinated in a paste of dried chiles and spices and wrapped in maguey leaves for 12 hours. It was then simmered in a clay pot in a pit until the meat was juicy and tender. The broth from the meat juices was usually mixed with roasted tomatoes and spices. Centuries later and hundreds of miles north in Tijuana, the *birria* stew was transformed into tacos. The tortillas were dipped in the fat from the beef stew and stuffed with the stewed beef and sometimes cheese, then grilled until crunchy.

PREPARATION TIME 2 days, plus 15 minutes soaking and overnight refrigeration
COOKING TIME 4 hours 30 minutes
SERVES 6–8

FOR THE BIRRIA

2 large tomatoes, coarsely chopped
1 small white onion, coarsely chopped
6 guajillo chiles, stemmed and seeded
2 pasilla chiles, stemmed and seeded
1 chile de arbol, stemmed and seeded
2 cloves
1 teaspoon ground cumin
1 teaspoon ground cinnamon
3 cloves garlic
1 tablespoon dried Mexican oregano
2 tablespoons plus 1 teaspoon salt
½ teaspoon unsweetened cocoa powder
½ cup (4 fl oz/120 ml) white vinegar
1 (4-lb/1.8-kg) chuck roast, cut into 4 chunks
2 lb/900 g bone-in short ribs
2 bay leaves
6 cups (47 fl oz/1.4 L) beef stock or water

FOR THE TACOS

12–16 corn tortillas
2 cups (8 oz/225 g) shredded Oaxacan cheese
1 small red onion, chopped
4 tablespoons chopped cilantro (coriander)

FOR THE BIRRIA Preheat an oven to 400°F/200°C/Gas Mark 6.

Arrange the tomatoes and onion in a single layer on a baking sheet. Roast for 10–15 minutes, until softened and slightly charred.

Meanwhile, lightly toast the chiles in a cast-iron skillet for 5 minutes. Transfer the chiles to a bowl, then add enough hot water to cover them. Soak for 15 minutes. Drain the chiles, reserving the chile water.

In a blender, combine the soaked chiles, tomatoes, onion, cloves, cumin, cinnamon, garlic, oregano, 1 teaspoon of salt, cocoa, and vinegar. Pour the chile water into a measuring cup and add enough water to yield 1½ cups (12 fl oz/350 ml). Add this to the blender and blend for 2–3 minutes on high speed, until smooth. Strain the sauce.

In a large zip-top bag or bowl, combine the chuck roast, short ribs, and sauce. Seal or cover and refrigerate overnight.

Preheat an oven to 325°F/160°C/Gas Mark 3.

In a large Dutch oven (casserole) or baking dish, combine the meat and marinade, 2 tablespoons of salt, and the bay leaves. Add enough stock or water to mostly cover the meat. Cover and bake for 3–4 hours, until the meat is tender. Remove the bay leaves. Transfer the meat to a cutting board. Using two forks, shred all the meat.

Skim the fat from the surface of the sauce. Place it in a small skillet for frying the tortillas.

Warm the remaining sauce in a saucepan over low heat. Season to taste with salt. Add a ladle of sauce to the beef, then season again with salt. Cover the shredded meat with aluminum foil to keep warm.

FOR THE TACOS Gently heat the tortillas in a dry skillet or microwave. Warm the reserved grease in the skillet over medium heat. One by one, dip the warm tortillas into the grease. Stack them on a plate by the stove.

Heat a large skillet or grill (griddle) over high heat until very hot. Add a tortilla, then top with 2 spoonfuls of birria and a spoonful of cheese. Fold the taco in half, then press it down with a spatula. Cook for another 2–3 minutes, until the taco is crisp and golden on the bottom. Flip and cook on the other side for 2–3 minutes. Repeat with the remaining tortillas.

Place the tacos on a serving plate. Ladle the heated stock into a small bowl and top with onions and cilantro (coriander). Serve the tacos immediately with the stock.

CARNE ASADA

While *asada* technically means "grilled," the word often signifies the gathering of loved ones to help prep and cook the classic *carne asada*: a flap meat steak marinated in citrus and umami flavors, then grilled over high heat until charred on the outside while still pink inside. The meat is typically served with grilled scallions (spring onions), warm tortillas, and salsa.

PREPARATION TIME 20 minutes,
plus at least 2 hours marinating and 30 minutes standing
COOKING TIME 10–20 minutes
SERVES 6

FOR THE MARINADE

6 cloves garlic, finely chopped
1 tablespoon sea salt
1 teaspoon black pepper
½ teaspoon dried Mexican oregano
½ teaspoon smoked paprika
¼ teaspoon ground cumin
¾ cup (6 fl oz/175 ml) beer
½ cup (4 fl oz/120 ml) orange juice
4 tablespoons lime juice
4 tablespoons grapeseed oil
2½ teaspoons Worcestershire sauce
1 tablespoon apple cider vinegar

FOR THE STEAK

15 scallions (spring onions)
1 (2-lb/900-g) flap or skirt steak
2 serrano chiles, stemmed and halved lengthwise
1 small white onion, thinly sliced
1 cup (2¼ oz/60 g) chopped cilantro (coriander)

FOR SERVING

1 tablespoon grapeseed oil
Pinch of salt
12 corn tortillas, warmed
Pico de Gallo (page 339)

FOR THE MARINADE In a large bowl, combine all the ingredients and mix well.

FOR THE STEAK Cut 6 scallions (spring onions) in half lengthwise. In a large zip-top bag, combine the remaining ingredients with the halved scallions and marinade. Seal and shake to thoroughly mix. Refrigerate for 2–12 hours.

Preheat a grill to high heat.

Remove the steak from the marinade, then pat dry. Place the steak on a wire rack set over a rimmed baking sheet. Set aside for 30 minutes to bring to room temperature. Discard the marinade.

Place the steak on the grill and cook for 3–5 minutes on each side, until lightly charred and the internal temperature reaches 125°F/52°C for medium-rare. Transfer the steak to a cutting board, then set aside to rest for 5 minutes.

Meanwhile, in a small bowl, combine the remaining scallions, grapeseed oil, and salt. Toss until well coated. Place the scallions on the grill and cook for 4–6 minutes, turning occasionally, until softened and lightly charred.

Slice the steak against the grain, then arrange it in a serving dish. Serve it with the grilled scallions, warm tortillas, and pico de gallo.

Bò lá lốt, grilled rolls of ground (minced) beef wrapped in betel leaves, are found on almost every street corner in Saigon. This recipe adds pork to increase juiciness and replaces the betel leaves with grape leaves, but feel free to use betel leaves if you can find them. Serve these rolls with *nuoc cham* (Vietnamese Dipping Sauce, page 336) as an appetizer or side dish.

PREPARATION TIME 20 minutes, plus 1–2 hours marinating
COOKING TIME 10 minutes
SERVES 4

8 oz/225 g ground (minced) beef

8 oz/225 g ground (minced) pork

4 cloves garlic, minced

1 shallot, finely chopped

1 stalk lemongrass, finely chopped

2 tablespoons sugar

½ teaspoon black pepper

2 tablespoons fish sauce

20 brined grape (vine) leaves, drained, rinsed, and patted dry

Vegetable or peanut oil, for brushing

Vietnamese Dipping Sauce (page 336), to serve

In a large bowl, combine the beef, pork, garlic, shallot, lemongrass, sugar, black pepper, and fish sauce and mix well. Cover and refrigerate for 1–2 hours.

Preheat a grill to medium-high heat.

Remove the stems from the grape leaves. Spread the leaves out on a clean work surface. Place a table-spoon of the filling near the stem end of each leaf. Fold in the sides over the filling, then tightly roll the leaves to form cylinders. Lightly brush the beef rolls with oil, then place on the grill and cook for 8 minutes, turning often, until just cooked through.

Transfer the rolls to a serving dish and serve warm with a small bowl of Vietnamese dipping sauce.

This simple Japanese dish is called *negimaki*; *negi* is the Japanese word for "scallion (spring onion)" and *maki* means "roll." Pounded flank steak is wrapped around blanched scallions to form a roll, then grilled and served with a soy-based sauce.

PREPARATION TIME 20 minutes,
plus at least 15 minutes marinating
COOKING TIME 15 minutes
SERVES 4

FOR THE ROLLS

1 tablespoon salt
12 small scallions (spring onions), trimmed
1 (1-lb/450-g) flank steak, cut into 12 thin slices

FOR THE MARINADE

4 tablespoons sake
4 tablespoons mirin
3 tablespoons soy sauce
1 tablespoon sugar
1 tablespoon canola oil, for brushing

FOR THE ROLLS Fill a bowl with ice water. Bring a small saucepan of water to a boil. Add ½ tablespoon salt and the scallions (spring onions) and cook for 1 minute. Using tongs, transfer the scallions to the ice bath to cool. Remove and pat dry.

Pound the steak slices until very thin. Overlap 3 steak slices to make a square. Sprinkle with the remaining salt, then lay 3 scallions across the square in the direction of the grain. Roll the meat and tie it with kitchen string. Make 3 more.

Preheat a grill to high heat for indirect grilling.

FOR THE MARINADE In a medium bowl, combine the sake, mirin, soy sauce, and sugar. Add the rolls to the marinade and set aside to marinate for 15–30 minutes.

Remove the rolls from the marinade, then brush them with the oil. Reserve the marinade for later use. Cook the rolls on the hot side of the grill for 2–3 minutes on each side. Set aside for 5 minutes.

Bring the reserved marinade to a boil in a small saucepan. Reduce the heat to medium-low and simmer for 3–5 minutes, until reduced.

Remove the string from the rolls, then cut them into 1-inch/2.5-cm slices. Transfer the rolls to a serving plate and serve with a small bowl of the sauce.

CAMBODIAN PORK AND RICE

Bai sach chrouk is a popular breakfast dish, consisting of grilled pork, rice, and eggs. It is served on street carts all over Cambodia, typically with pickled carrots and daikon radish, a sweet-and-sour dipping sauce, a bowl of pork stock, and a glass of iced coffee.

PREPARATION TIME 20 minutes, plus at least 30 minutes marinating
COOKING TIME 15 minutes
SERVES 4

FOR THE PORK

5 cloves garlic, crushed and sliced
1 tablespoon sugar
1 tablespoon salt
1 teaspoon black pepper
1½ tablespoons oyster sauce
½ tablespoon vegetable oil
1 (2-lb/900-g) pork loin roast,
cut into ½-inch/1-cm-thick slices

FOR THE OMELET

4 eggs
1 teaspoon salt
1 teaspoon sugar
1 teaspoon fish sauce
1 tablespoon canola oil

FOR THE DIPPING SAUCE

6 cloves garlic
2 red bird's eye chiles
1 tablespoon sugar
1½ tablespoons fish sauce
½ teaspoon salt
Juice of 1 lime

FOR SERVING

Steamed rice
Vietnamese Pickles (page 300)

FOR THE PORK In a large bowl, combine all the ingredients except the pork and mix well. Add the pork and toss to coat. Cover and refrigerate for at least 30 minutes but, preferably, overnight.

Preheat a grill to medium heat.

Place the pork on the grill and cook for 5 minutes on each side. Transfer the pork to a cutting board, then slice it into thin strips. Set aside.

FOR THE OMELET In a medium bowl, combine the eggs, salt, sugar, and fish sauce. Using a whisk or fork, beat the mixture until frothy.

Heat the oil in a large skillet over medium heat. Pour in the egg mixture and fry for 2 minutes, or until the edges turn crispy. Flip, then fry for another 2 minutes. Transfer the omelet to a cutting board, then set aside for 3 minutes. Cut into thin strips.

FOR THE DIPPING SAUCE Combine all the ingredients in a food processor and pulse to combine.

Serve the omelet and pork over steamed rice alongside pickles and dipping sauce.

This maroon-tinged pork, often found in steamed pork buns, is a Cantonese dish called *char siu*, or "fork roasted," because the long strips of pork were traditionally held over a fire with large-pronged forks. Most red pork recipes call for boneless pork marinated in a sweet and spicy mixture, including hoisin sauce and five-spice powder. Although many restaurants use food coloring (or beet powder) to color the pork, the signature hue here comes from fermented red bean curd (available in Asian markets).

PREPARATION TIME 20 minutes, plus overnight marinating
COOKING TIME 40 minutes
SERVES 4–6

FOR THE MARINATED PORK

1 (2-lb/900-g) boneless pork shoulder with fat
3 cloves garlic, minced
1–2 cubes fermented red bean curd, mashed with 4 teaspoons of the sauce in the jar
2 tablespoons sugar
2 teaspoons salt
½ teaspoon five-spice powder
¼ teaspoon white pepper
1 tablespoon Shaoxing wine
1 tablespoon hoisin sauce
2 teaspoons molasses
½ teaspoon sesame oil

FOR THE BASTING SAUCE

1 tablespoon canola oil
1 tablespoon honey
1 tablespoon hoisin sauce
1 tablespoon warm water

FOR THE MARINATED PORK Cut the pork into long 1½–2-inch/3.5–5-cm-thick pieces.

Combine the remaining ingredients in a bowl, whisking to dissolve the bean curd. In a large zip-top bag, combine the pork and marinade. Seal and refrigerate overnight.

The next day, preheat a grill to high heat.

Transfer the pork to a baking sheet. Reserve the marinade.

FOR THE BASTING SAUCE In a small bowl, combine all the ingredients. Stir in the reserved marinade.

Place the pork on the grill and cook for 3 minutes on each side. Reduce the heat to medium-high and cook for another 20–30 minutes, turning frequently and brushing the pork with the basting sauce. Once the pork reaches an internal temperature of 145°F/63°C, transfer the meat to a cutting board. Set aside to rest for 5 minutes, then slice and serve.

In this popular party dish known as *costela de porco assada*, pork ribs are seasoned with garlic, ginger, citrus, and chiles and simmered until tender, then briefly blasted with heat so that they become sticky and golden.

PREPARATION TIME 15 minutes,
plus at least 4 hours marinating
COOKING TIME 1 hour 50 minutes
SERVES 4–6

4½ lb/2 kg pork ribs
3 cloves garlic, chopped
½ Thai red chile, finely chopped
4 tablespoons sugar
4 tablespoons finely chopped cilantro (coriander)
5 teaspoons finely chopped ginger
4 tablespoons white wine vinegar
2 tablespoons honey
Juice of 3 limes
Zest of 1 lime
Salt and black pepper, to taste

Place the ribs in a large saucepan and add enough water to cover them. Bring to a boil, then simmer for 1½ hours, or until tender. Drain, then let cool.

In a large bowl, combine the remaining ingredients and rub over the ribs. Cover and refrigerate for at least 4 hours but, preferably, overnight.

Preheat a grill to high heat.

Place the ribs on the grill and cook for 5–10 minutes on each side, basting them with any remaining marinade.

LEMONGRASS PORK CHOPS

These flavorful chops are beloved in both home and restaurant kitchens in Vietnam. The lemongrass adds a bright flavor to the quick-cooking pork. When served with rice and salad, this dish can be a substantial meal. Leftover meat is often thinly sliced as a filling for Bánh Mì Sandwiches (page 142).

PREPARATION TIME 20 minutes,
plus at least 3 hours marinating
COOKING TIME 20 minutes
SERVES 4–6

3 tablespoons sugar
4 tablespoons canola oil
3 tablespoons soy sauce
2 tablespoons fish sauce
6 tablespoons minced lemongrass
2 tablespoons minced garlic
2 tablespoons minced shallots
4–6 bone-in pork chops
Vietnamese Dipping Sauce (page 336), to serve

Combine the sugar, oil, soy sauce, and fish sauce in a bowl and stir until the sugar has dissolved. Stir in the lemongrass, garlic, and shallots. Add the pork chops and mix well. Refrigerate for at least 3 hours but, preferably, overnight.

Preheat a grill to high heat.

Using tongs, place the chops on the grill and sear for 2 minutes on each side. Discard the marinade. Reduce the heat to medium and cook for another 6–8 minutes, flipping every few minutes, until the pork reaches an internal temperature of 145°F/63°C.

Transfer to a serving dish and serve with Vietnamese dipping sauce.

BANH MI SANDWICH

Vietnam's famous *bánh mì* sandwich achieves a rare balancing act between richness and freshness. It starts with a crusty baguette spread with pâté and mayonnaise, then thin slices of pork, Vietnamese pickles, fresh herbs, and chiles layered on top. It's a refreshing and delicate yet satisfying sandwich that's easy to create (and recreate with twists) at home.

PREPARATION TIME 10 minutes
SERVES 4

4 small baguettes or long crusty rolls, sliced lengthwise

6 tablespoons pork or chicken pâté

6 tablespoons mayonnaise

6 thin slices head cheese

6 thin slices Vietnamese chicken loaf (*chả lụa*)

6 thin slices Lemongrass Pork Chops (page 140)

2 cucumbers, thinly sliced

4 scallions (spring onions), thinly sliced into strips

1 cup (5 oz/140 g) Vietnamese Pickles (page 300)

1½ cups (3¼ oz/90 g) chopped cilantro (coriander)

2 Thai red chiles, minced

On each roll, spread 1½ tablespoons of pâté on one side of the bread and 1½ tablespoons of mayonnaise on the other. Over the pâté, layer the meat, cucumber slices, and scallions (spring onions). Add the pickles and cilantro (coriander), then sprinkle with chiles.

Serve immediately.

COLOMBIAN PORK CHOPS

This version of an *asado* dish from Bogota uses an intensely spiced, fruity marinade that is easily sourced from the home pantry: Paprika is substituted for the traditional red achiote seeds, and cider vinegar replaces the apple wine. The marinade creates a rich coating for the pork chops, which turn a deep mahogany color when grilled.

PREPARATION TIME 20 minutes,
plus at least 2 hours marinating
COOKING TIME 15 minutes
SERVES 4

2 scallions (spring onions), chopped

2 bay leaves

2 cloves garlic

4 tablespoons sweet paprika

2 tablespoons packed brown sugar

2 teaspoons salt

1½ teaspoons ground cumin

1 teaspoon black pepper

1 teaspoon dried thyme

1 teaspoon ground allspice

3 tablespoons apple cider vinegar

2 tablespoons grapeseed or other neutral oil

4 bone-in pork loin chops,
about ¾-inch/2-cm thick, patted dry

Lime wedges, to serve

In a blender, combine all the ingredients except the pork. Add 4 tablespoons of water and blend until smooth. Measure ⅓ cup (2¾ fl oz/80 ml) of the paste into a small bowl, then stir in 2 tablespoons of water. Cover and refrigerate for later use.

In a large bowl, combine the pork chops and the remaining paste and rub the paste into the meat. Cover and refrigerate for at least 2 hours but, preferably, 24 hours.

Preheat a grill to high heat for direct grilling. Set aside the pork chops at room temperature for at least 15 minutes.

Place the chops on the grill. Cook, uncovered, for 5–7 minutes, until charred. Brush the pork with half of the reserved paste, then flip and brush with the rest. Cook for another 5–7 minutes, uncovered, until the other side is charred and the meat reaches an internal temperature of 135°F/57°C. Flip again and cook for another minute. Transfer to a serving dish and tent with aluminum foil. Set aside to rest for 10 minutes.

Serve with lime wedges.

GF DF NF 5

Pork ribs include baby back ribs and spareribs. Baby backs, which connect to the loin, are lean and cook quickly. Spareribs are connected to the pig's belly. They are fattier and require more time and skill, but they tend to have more flavor and a richer texture, especially if they are cooked properly.

PREPARATION TIME 15–20 minutes
COOKING TIME 4–5 hours
SERVES 4–6

2 racks spareribs, such as St. Louis-style

1 cup (7 oz/200 g) Pork and Poultry Rub (page 358), plus extra for serving

2 cups (16 fl oz/475 ml) apple cider or apple cider vinegar, in a spray bottle

1–2 cups (8–16 fl oz/240–475 ml) Texas Table Sauce (page 335), to serve (optional)

Oak or cherry wood, for smoking

Preheat a smoker to 250°F/120°C.

To remove the membrane from the underside of the ribs, slide a paring knife under the membrane of the largest rib at the end of the rack and slide it towards the end. This loosens the membrane, which you can grab with a towel and peel off.

Generously season the underside of the ribs with the rub, then set aside for 10 minutes. Flip the ribs and rub the top side.

Place the ribs in the smoker, meat side up, and smoke for 1 hour. Spray the ribs with the apple cider, then smoke for another 3–4 hours, spraying every 30 minutes, until the ribs are tender but not falling apart. Transfer the ribs to a serving dish, then set aside to rest for 15 minutes.

Sprinkle with more spice rub. Alternatively, serve with Texas table sauce over or alongside the ribs.

BERBERE RIBS

These baby back ribs are both rubbed and sauced with an Ethiopian spice blend called *berbere*, a spicy, tangy combination of toasted and ground spices. Some versions include lesser-known spices like *korarima*, which grows wild in Ethiopia.

PREPARATION TIME 30 minutes, plus 12 hours marinating
COOKING TIME 6 hours
SERVES 6–8

FOR THE RIBS

½ cup (3½ oz/100 g) brown sugar

3 tablespoons berbere

1½ tablespoons salt

1 tablespoon smoked paprika

1 tablespoon garlic powder

1 tablespoon onion powder

2 teaspoons dried thyme

4 racks baby back ribs or 2 racks St. Louis-style pork spareribs

FOR THE SAUCE

2 tablespoons olive oil

1 onion, chopped

5 tomatoes, seeded and chopped, or 2½ cups (1 lb 4 oz/560 g) canned chopped tomatoes

2 cloves garlic, minced

1 (2-inch/5-cm) piece of ginger, peeled and grated

1 serrano chile, seeded, deveined, and finely chopped

1 tablespoon tamarind paste

2 teaspoons berbere

¼ teaspoon ground cumin

¼ teaspoon coriander seeds, coarsely crushed

4 tablespoons strong coffee

4 tablespoons honey

FOR THE RIBS In a small bowl, combine all the ingredients except the ribs. Place the ribs on a baking sheet and sprinkle evenly with the rub, covering both sides of the ribs. Cover and refrigerate for 12 hours.

FOR THE SAUCE Heat the oil in a large saucepan over high heat. Add the onion and sauté for 5 minutes, or until softened. Add the tomatoes, garlic, and ginger. Bring to a boil, then reduce the heat to medium-low and simmer. Stir in the chile, tamarind paste, berbere, cumin, and coriander seeds. Pour in the coffee and 2 cups (16 fl oz/475 ml) of water and bring to a boil. Reduce the heat to medium-low and simmer for 40 minutes. Stir in the honey, then simmer for another 10 minutes, until the sauce has thickened. Set aside to cool.

Preheat an oven to 225°F/107°C/Gas Mark ¼.

Place a wire rack in a roasting pan, then lay the ribs on top. Brush half of the sauce over the ribs, then pour 1 cup (8 fl oz/240 ml) of water into the pan. Tightly cover with aluminum foil and roast for 5 hours, or until tender. Set aside to rest for 10 minutes.

Preheat a grill to medium-high heat.

Brush the ribs with the reserved sauce. Place the ribs on the grill and cook for 10–15 minutes, or until caramelized and slightly charred.

Transfer the ribs to a serving dish and serve immediately.

ADOBO BABY BACK RIBS

Although many pitmasters favor spareribs because of their fat content, baby backs, which sit on top of the loin and are therefore leaner, can be transcendent when done right. This means seasoned with either a dry rub or a marinade, then glazed with sauce and finished over high heat so that the sauce adheres to the ribs. These baby back ribs, covered in an Adobo Rub (page 357) and cooked in adobo sauce, were a beloved special at Mighty Quinn's in New York. They get sweetness from an apple cider spritz, but if you want to intensify the sweetness, add 2 tablespoons of dark brown sugar to every cup (7 oz/200 g) of Adobo rub.

PREPARATION TIME 10 minutes, plus 2 hours refrigeration
COOKING TIME 4½ hours
SERVES 4–6

2 racks baby back ribs
1 cup (7 oz/200 g) Adobo Rub (page 357)
4¼ cups (34 fl oz/1 L) apple cider, in a spray bottle
2 cups (16 fl oz/475 ml) Adobo Sauce (page 350)
Oak, cherry, or apple wood, for smoking

Remove the membrane from the ribs. Season both sides with the adobo rub. Cover and refrigerate for 2 hours but, preferably, overnight.

Preheat a smoker to 250°F/120°C.

Bring the ribs up to room temperature. Add the ribs to the smoker, meat side up, for 1 hour. Spray the ribs with the apple cider. Smoke for another 3 hours, spraying every 30 minutes, until the ribs are tender but not falling apart. Glaze them with the adobo sauce and smoke for another 15–20 minutes.

Remove them from the smoker and let them rest for 15 minutes. Slice the ribs between the bones, then transfer to a serving dish and serve with the remaining adobo sauce.

KOREAN PORK BELLY

Korean *samgyeopsal*, translating to "three-layer flesh," refers to the three layers of pork belly—the fat cap plus the two layers of leaner meat underneath it—that are grilled without fanfare. Serve it folded into fresh lettuce leaves with scallions (spring onions) and *ssamjang* (Korean Barbecue Sauce, page 347).

PREPARATION TIME 20 minutes, plus 30 minutes freezing
COOKING TIME 5 minutes
SERVES 4

FOR THE PORK
1 (3-lb/1.4-kg) pork belly
2 teaspoons salt
2 tablespoons canola oil

FOR THE SCALLIONS
16 scallions (spring onions), thinly sliced
2 tablespoons red pepper flakes
2 tablespoons sesame seeds
2 tablespoons soy sauce
1 tablespoon toasted sesame oil
2 teaspoons honey

FOR SERVING
1 head butter or bibb lettuce
Korean Barbecue Sauce (page 347)
2 carrots, cut into matchsticks
1 English cucumber, cut into matchsticks
10 cloves garlic, thinly sliced
3 jalapeños, chopped

FOR THE PORK Preheat a grill to medium-high heat.

Freeze the pork belly for 30 minutes. Slice into long ½-inch/1-cm-thick slices. Sprinkle with salt and brush with oil. Place the pork on the grill and cook for 5 minutes, flipping once, until golden brown. Transfer the pork to a serving dish and set aside.

FOR THE SCALLIONS Soak the scallions (spring onions) in cold water for 5 minutes. In a small bowl, combine the remaining ingredients and mix well. Drain the scallions, then add them to the sauce.

Serve the pork belly with lettuce leaves for wrapping, Korean barbecue sauce, and vegetables.

FILIPINO PORK BELLY

Inihaw na liempo, or "grilled pork belly," bathes the notoriously fatty belly meat in a distinctly Filipino marinade of citrus, fish sauce, garlic, and chiles and then sears it on a hot grill. The sweet, spicy, and sticky pork (no skewers needed) is traditionally served with a spiced vinegar dipping sauce known as *sawsawan.*

PREPARATION TIME 15 minutes, plus 8 hours marinating
COOKING TIME 15 minutes
SERVES 4

FOR THE MARINATED PORK
½ cup (4 fl oz/120 ml) lemon juice
4 tablespoons fish sauce
8 cloves garlic, minced
2 red bird's eye chiles, minced
2 tablespoons brown sugar
1 teaspoon salt
2 lb/900 g pork belly, cut into ½-inch/1-cm-thick slices

FOR THE DIPPING SAUCE
1 cup (8 fl oz/240 ml) rice vinegar
4 cloves garlic, minced
2 tablespoons finely chopped onions
2 bird's eye chiles, chopped
½ teaspoon salt
¼ teaspoon black pepper

FOR THE BASTING SAUCE
2 tablespoons oyster sauce
1 tablespoon canola or sesame oil

FOR THE MARINATED PORK In a large non-reactive bowl, combine all the ingredients except the pork and mix well. Add the pork and massage the marinade into the meat. Cover and refrigerate for 8 hours. Turn once.

Preheat a grill to high heat.

FOR THE DIPPING SAUCE In a medium bowl, whisk all the ingredients until combined.

Remove the pork from the marinade, then pour it into a small saucepan. Bring the marinade to a boil over high heat and boil for 5 minutes.

FOR THE BASTING SAUCE In a small bowl, combine the reduced marinade, oyster sauce, and oil.

Grill the pork for 2–3 minutes on each side. Brush one side with the basting sauce and grill for 2 minutes. Brush the other side with the basting sauce and grill for another 2 minutes.

Transfer the pork to a serving dish and serve with the dipping sauce.

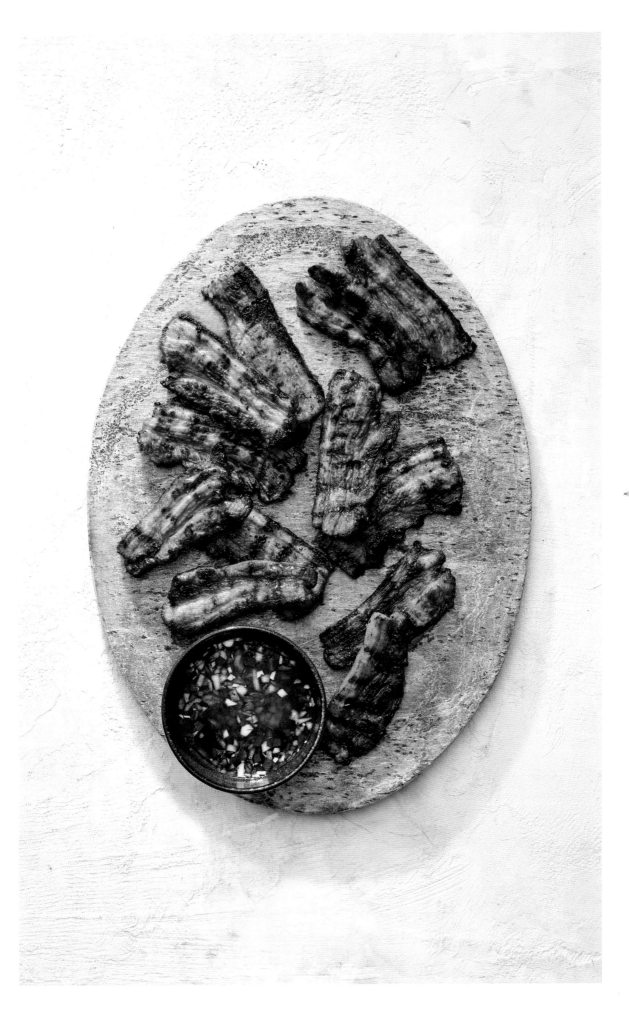

PULLED PORK

Pulled pork is to North Carolina what beef brisket is to Texas. Whether it comes from a whole hog, a shoulder, or a bone-in pork shoulder (or Boston butt), pulled pork is the language of love in North Carolina. The combination of smoke, meat, bark, and vinegar mop sauce is one of the pinnacles of American barbecue.

PREPARATION TIME 10 minutes, plus 24 hours refrigeration and at least 1 hour standing
COOKING TIME 10–12 hours
SERVES 8–20

1 (6–10-lb/2.7–4.5-kg) bone-in pork shoulder
2½ cups (1 lb 2 oz/500 g) Pork and Poultry Rub (page 358)
Texas Table Sauce (page 335), North Carolina Barbecue Sauce or South Carolina Mustard Sauce (page 334)
Oak, cherry, or apple wood, for smoking

In a large bowl, generously season the pork all over with the rub. Loosely cover and refrigerate for 24 hours.

Set the pork aside for 1–2 hours to come to room temperature.

Preheat a smoker to 250°F/120°C.

Place the pork in the smoker and smoke for 4 hours. Carefully transfer the pork to a roasting pan (to collect the juices) and place it back in the smoker. Smoke the pork for another 6–8 hours, until the internal temperature reaches 195°F/90°C. Transfer the pork to a cutting board, tent with aluminum foil, and set aside to rest for 20 minutes.

Using tongs or a fork, pull the pork apart. In a large bowl, combine the pork and your chosen sauce and toss to coat. Serve immediately.

PULLED PORK SANDWICHES

The pulled pork sandwich, typically served on a potato roll with vinegar mop sauce and coleslaw, is unparalleled: smoked pork and crispy bits of skin meet sweet, sour, and creamy. When done properly, the pulled pork sandwich fulfills the American barbecue promise.

PREPARATION TIME 5 minutes
SERVES 4

4 potato rolls, halved lengthwise
1 cup (9 oz/250 g) Pulled Pork (see left)
½ cup (4 fl oz/120 ml) North Carolina Barbecue Sauce (page 334)
½ cup (4¼ oz/120 g) American Coleslaw (page 296)

Layer the pulled pork, sauce, and coleslaw in the potato rolls. Serve.

Poc chuc, which is thought to have originated with the Mayans in Mexico, has become the signature dish of the Yucatan region. Thin slices of pork are marinated in fresh local citrus and tossed on the grill. The pork is usually served with charred red onions, pico de gallo, and homemade tortillas.

PREPARATION TIME 15 minutes, plus overnight marinating
COOKING TIME 15–20 minutes
SERVES 4–6

FOR THE MARINATED PORK

10 cloves garlic
1 cup (8 fl oz/240 ml) olive oil
1 teaspoon salt
½ teaspoon black pepper
½ teaspoon ground cumin
⅔ cup (5½ fl oz/160 ml) orange juice
⅓ cup (2¾ fl oz/80 ml) lime juice
Zest of 1 orange
Zest of 1 lime
1 (3-lb/1.4-kg) pork loin, cut into ¼-inch/5-mm-thick slices

FOR THE ONIONS

4 red onions, quartered
3 tablespoons orange juice
1 tablespoon lime juice
1 teaspoon salt
1 teaspoon black pepper
1 teaspoon dried Mexican oregano
½ teaspoon ground allspice
½ teaspoon ground clove

FOR SERVING

Pico de Gallo (page 339)
8–12 corn tortillas

FOR THE MARINATED PORK In a food processor or blender, combine all the marinade ingredients except the pork and blend until smooth. In a large zip-top bag or bowl, combine the pork and marinade. Seal or cover and refrigerate overnight.

FOR THE ONIONS Preheat a grill to high heat. Add the onions and grill for about 10 minutes, until charred. Transfer the onions to a bowl, then add the remaining ingredients and toss.

Add the pork to the grill and cook for 2–4 minutes on each side.

Transfer the pork to a serving dish, then serve warm with the onions, pico de gallo, and tortillas.

Lechón asado, which means "roast pork," typically features a suckling pig marinated in a mojo sauce of sour orange, garlic, oregano, and cumin, then slow-roasted. It's a celebratory dish in Cuba, popular on holidays and family gatherings. This recipe uses a grill to slow-cook a mojo-marinated pork shoulder.

PREPARATION TIME 20 minutes,
plus at least 12 hours marinating
COOKING TIME 2 hours 35 minutes
SERVES 6–8

2 heads garlic, cloves peeled and chopped
3 tablespoons salt
2 tablespoons dried oregano
1 tablespoon black pepper
1 tablespoon ground cumin
2½ cups (20 fl oz/600 ml) lime juice
1¼ cups (10 fl oz/300 ml) orange juice
1 (6-lb/2.5-kg) boneless pork shoulder
2 yellow onions, cut into rings

In a large bowl, combine all the ingredients except the pork and onions. Set aside for 10 minutes.

Using a sharp knife, make deep incisions all over the pork. Place it in a deep bowl or container, then add the marinade. Rub the mixture into the meat. Place the onion rings on the top. Cover and refrigerate for 12–24 hours.

Preheat a grill to high heat for indirect grilling.

Meanwhile, transfer the pork to a plate. Pour the marinade into a saucepan, add the onions, and boil for 2 minutes. Set aside to cool. Transfer the marinade and onions to a blender and purée until smooth.

Reduce the heat of the grill to 300°F/150°C. Place the pork, skin side down, on the cooler side of the grill. Cook for 2½ hours, basting frequently with the marinade and turning every 40 minutes, until the internal temperature reaches 150°F/66°C. Transfer the pork to a cutting board and set aside to rest for 10 minutes. Cut it into thick slices, then arrange on a serving dish.

Serve warm.

The Cubano, which originated in the late-night cafés of Havana, migrated in the early twentieth century to Tampa and then to Miami. where it became a lunch counter staple synonymous with the vibrant Cuban culture of south Florida. The sandwich usually contains Cuban Pork (page 157), ham, cheese, pickles, and yellow mustard and should be made with *pan cubano*, or firm Cuban-style bread.

PREPARATION TIME 5 minutes, plus overnight refrigeration
COOKING TIME 2 hours 40 minutes
SERVES 4

FOR THE ROAST PORK

8 cloves garlic, minced
1 onion, chopped
1 cup (2¼ oz/60 g) chopped cilantro (coriander)
4 tablespoons sugar
1 tablespoon salt
1 tablespoon smoked paprika
1 tablespoon ground cumin
1 teaspoon dried oregano
1 teaspoon black pepper
½ cup (4 fl oz/120 ml) olive oil
Juice of 3 oranges
Juice of 1 lime
1 (3–4 lb/1.3–1.8 kg) pork shoulder

FOR THE SANDWICH

4 Cuban-style rolls *(pan Cubano)*, halved lengthwise
2 large dill pickles, thinly sliced crosswise
½ lb/225 g ham, cut into wafer-thin slices
8 slices Swiss cheese
4 teaspoons yellow mustard
½ cup (4 oz/115 g) melted butter

FOR THE ROAST PORK In a large bowl, combine all the ingredients except the pork. Using a sharp paring knife, pierce the pork all over to allow the marinade to penetrate the meat. Submerge the pork in the marinade. Cover and refrigerate overnight.

Preheat an oven to 425°F/220°C/Gas Mark 7.

Place the pork in a roasting pan or large cast-iron skillet and discard the marinade. Roast for 30 minutes, basting it with the pan juices. Reduce the heat to 375°F/190°C/Gas Mark 5. Roast for 1½–2 hours, basting every 30 minutes, until the internal temperature reaches 160°F/71°C. Transfer the pork to a cutting board, then set aside to cool. Cut into ¼-inch/5-mm-thick slices.

FOR THE SANDWICHES Preheat the griddle side of a grill or a cast-iron skillet to medium-high heat.

For each roll, layer 2 slices of roast pork, 2 pickle slices, 1 slice of ham, and 2 slices of Swiss cheese on the bottom half. Brush the inside tops with 1 teaspoon of mustard. Close the sandwiches.

Generously butter the outside of the sandwiches. Place them on the grill and use a foil-lined grill weight or another heavy skillet to press down on them. Cook the sandwiches for 3–4 minutes on each side, until the cheese has melted and the bread is browned.

Cut them in half on a bias and serve.

Al pastor ("shepherd style" in Spanish) traditionally uses pork grilled on a spit. It resembles the shaved meat dish *shawarma*, which was brought by Lebanese immigrants to central Mexico. Al pastor tacos are popular street food throughout Mexico. The pork (usually shoulder) is marinated with chiles, garlic, pineapple, achiote, and oregano. For this recipe, it is cut into strips, grilled, and wrapped in warm corn tortillas.

PREPARATION TIME 15 minutes,
plus 20 minutes standing and 2 hours marinating
COOKING TIME 10 minutes
SERVES 6

FOR THE MARINATED PORK

2 ancho chiles
2 guajillo chiles
2 chiles de arbol
4 cloves garlic, chopped
1 small yellow onion, chopped
1 tablespoon brown sugar
1 tablespoon dried oregano
1 teaspoon ground cumin
1 teaspoon salt
⅓ cup (2¾ fl oz/80 ml) pineapple juice
4 tablespoons orange juice
4 tablespoons apple cider vinegar
2 tablespoons chipotle sauce
2 tablespoons achiote paste
1 (3-lb/1.4-kg) boneless pork shoulder, sliced into ½-inch/1-cm-thick strips

FOR THE TACOS

12 corn tortillas, warmed
Chopped jalapeño
Chopped tomato
Chopped cilantro (coriander)
Lime wedges
Hot sauce

FOR THE MARINATED PORK Toast the chiles in a large skillet over high heat for 3 minutes. Set aside until cool enough to handle, then remove the stems and seeds. Place the chiles in a medium bowl, add enough hot water to cover them, and set aside for 20 minutes.

In a food processor, combine the drained chiles and the remaining ingredients except the pork. Process until smooth.

In a large bowl, combine the pork and marinade. Cover and refrigerate for 2 hours.

FOR THE TACOS Preheat a grill to medium-high heat.

Remove the pork from the marinade and place it on the grill. Cook for 6–7 minutes, until cooked through. Transfer to a cutting board and cut into bite-sized pieces.

To serve, spoon the pork into warmed tortillas and top with jalapeño, tomato, cilantro (coriander), lime, and hot sauce.

GF DF NF

The name of this dish, *cochinita pibil*, comes from the Spanish word *cochinita* ("suckling pig") and the Mayan word *pibil* ("cooked underground")—a technique that dates to 400 AD. In this dish, the most celebrated Mexican barbecue dish in the Yucatan, pork is marinated in spices, achiote seeds, and sour orange juice, then wrapped in banana leaves and cooked in a pit overnight. The tender meat is shredded and served with tortillas and salsa. This recipe calls for a grill instead of a pit but still uses banana leaves to wrap the spiced pork.

PREPARATION TIME 20 minutes, plus 14 hours marinating
COOKING TIME 4 hours
SERVES 12–15

5 tablespoons achiote seeds

1½ tablespoons dried oregano

1½ tablespoons black peppercorns

1½ tablespoons ground cinnamon

1¼ teaspoons cumin seeds

½ teaspoon cloves

1 tablespoon salt, plus extra to taste

14 cloves garlic, chopped

1 cup (8 fl oz/240 ml) lime juice

½ cup (4 fl oz/120 ml) orange juice

2 (12-1b/5.4-kg) bone-in pork shoulder (pork butt), cut into 3-inch/7.5-cm-wide cross sections (ask your butcher)

1 (1-lb/450-g) package banana leaves, defrosted if frozen

FOR SERVING

Pickled Onions (page 297)

Pico de Gallo (page 339)

24–30 corn tortillas

In a spice grinder, combine the achiote seeds, oregano, black pepper, cinnamon, cumin, and cloves and grind to a powder.

In a blender, combine the ground spice mixture, salt, garlic, lime juice, and orange juice and blend until smooth.

Combine the meat and marinade in a large bowl. Cover and refrigerate overnight.

Preheat a grill to medium heat for indirect grilling.

Line the bottom and sides of a roasting pan with half the banana leaves, overlapping them and allowing them to hang over the sides. Place the pork in the center, cover with the marinade, and fold the leaves over the meat. Add the rest of the leaves to the top and tuck them around the sides. Roast for 4 hours, or until the pork is tender and the internal temperature reaches 145°F/63°C. Transfer the pork to a heat-resistant work surface. Remove the top banana leaves, spoon off the fat, and season to taste with more salt. When cool enough to handle, shred the meat and transfer to a serving bowl.

Serve with pickled onions, pico de gallo, and tortillas.

PUERTO RICAN ROAST PORK

Pernil, a beloved Puerto Rican dish often reserved for special occasions, is a garlicky slow-roasted pig. The meat becomes meltingly tender, although the crispy skin is most coveted. While the traditional recipe calls for a whole roasted pig, *pernil* is often made with a pork shoulder, which can be either roasted or smoked. Here are options for both methods.

PREPARATION TIME 30 minutes, plus overnight marinating
COOKING TIME 5–6 hours
SERVES 8–10

1 (8–9-lb/3.4–4-kg) bone-in, skin-on pork shoulder
8 cloves garlic, finely minced
4 tablespoons salt
4 teaspoons dried oregano
1 teaspoon black pepper
3 tablespoons olive oil
2 teaspoons fresh lime juice
2 teaspoons orange juice

Using a sharp paring knife, pierce the pork all over. (This allows the marinade to penetrate the meat.) Place the pork in a baking dish.

Combine the remaining ingredients in a bowl and mix well. Pour the marinade over the pork, massaging the marinade into the holes. Cover and refrigerate overnight.

Preheat an oven to 300°F/150°C/Gas Mark 2.

Remove the pork from the marinade, wiping off the extra marinade. Pat dry the pork with a paper towel, then season all over with 1 tablespoon of salt. Place in a roasting pan, then roast for about 6 hours, until the internal temperature reaches 160°F/71°C. For crispier skin, broil for another 10–15 minutes. Set aside to rest for 15 minutes. Cut or shred the meat and serve.

Alternatively, preheat a smoker to high heat for indirect smoking.

Place the pork over the cooler side. Cover and maintain the heat at 350°F/180°C. Smoke for 5 hours, or until the internal temperature of the pork is 160°F/71°C. Set aside to rest for 15 minutes.

Pork belly is one of the easiest and most rewarding cuts of meat to smoke because it offers so many great options—cubed and glazed or sliced into thick strips to be used like Bacon (page 175) on a BLT or bao bun. Pork belly loves sweet with heat, which this recipe achieves with maple sugar and a hearty rub. If you can't find maple sugar, substitute brown sugar.

PREPARATION TIME 15 minutes
COOKING TIME 8–10 hours
SERVES 20

1 (16–18-lb/7–8-kg) pork belly, rind removed
2 cups (14 oz/400 g) Pork and Poultry Rub (page 358)
1 cup (8 oz/225 g) maple sugar
4¼ cups (34 fl oz/1 L) apple cider, in a spray bottle
Texas Table Sauce (page 335) or North Carolina Barbecue Sauce (page 334), for glazing
Oak or cherry wood, for smoking

Preheat a smoker to 225°F/107°C.

Place the pork belly on a large cutting board and cut it into 4 equal pieces.

In a large bowl, combine the pork rub and maple sugar. Rub the seasoning all over the pork belly. Place the pork belly, fat side up, in the smoker and smoke for 1 hour. Smoke for another 7–9 hours, spritzing the pork belly with apple cider every 30 minutes, until the pork reaches an internal temperature of 200°F/93°C. Transfer the pork belly to a cutting board and set aside to rest for 15–20 minutes.

To serve, cut the belly into cubes and brush with the sauce. You can return the pork belly to the smoker or a grill for 10–15 minutes for some caramelization.

Alternatively, the pork belly can be cooled completely and then refrigerated. When ready to serve, cut it into ½-inch/1-cm slices and grill for 5–10 minutes to add to sandwiches.

Like *pernil* (page 164) in Puerto Rico, dove pork is often reserved for special occasions. The pork, flavored with garlic and a seasoning mix native to St. Croix in the Caribbean, is roasted or smoked, then covered in a light tomato sauce and broiled. "Cruzan," an alternate spelling of "Crucian," refers to a native of St. Croix. This spice mix is frequently used in St. Croix's cuisine.

PREPARATION TIME 20 minutes, plus overnight marinating
COOKING TIME 6¾ hours
SERVES 4–6

FOR THE CRUZAN SEASONING

16 cloves
10 cardamom pods
6 cloves garlic
½ Scotch bonnet chile
½ cup (2½ oz/70 g) salt
2 tablespoons finely chopped chives
2 teaspoons thyme leaves
1 teaspoon black pepper
¼ teaspoon mace
¼ teaspoon ground nutmeg
¼ teaspoon ground cinnamon

FOR THE PORK

1 (5-lb/2.3-kg) pork shoulder
4 tablespoons Cruzan seasoning (see above)
Oak wood, for smoking (optional)

FOR THE SAUCE

1 onion
4 sprigs parsley
4 sprigs thyme
4 cloves
1 (12-oz/340-g) can tomato sauce

FOR THE CRUZAN SEASONING Using a mortar and pestle, combine all the ingredients and grind the mixture to a fine powder. The seasoning can be stored in an airtight container for up to 1 week.

FOR THE PORK Using a sharp paring knife, pierce the pork all over. (This allows the marinade to penetrate the meat.) Place the pork in a baking dish and massage in the Cruzan seasoning. Cover and refrigerate overnight.

Preheat an oven to 300°F/150°C/Gas Mark 2. Roast the pork for 3–3½ hours, until the internal temperature reaches 160°F/71°C. Set aside to cool to room temperature.

Alternatively, preheat a smoker to high heat for indirect smoking. Place the pork on the cooler side and close the smoker. Reduce the temperature to 350°F/180°C and smoke for 3 hours. Set aside to rest for 15 minutes.

FOR THE SAUCE Preheat the broiler to high heat.

Transfer the pork to a large bowl.

In a food processor, blend all the ingredients until smooth. Pour the sauce into the bowl with the pork and toss to coat the pork. Transfer the pork to a baking sheet and broil for 15 minutes, or until browned. Cut or shred the meat, transfer to a serving dish, and serve.

This dish involves two cooking techniques. First, the pork cheeks are smoked with apple or cherry wood, then they're slowly cooked in fat until they practically melt (pork cheeks love smoke and are best cooked low and slow). The fatty pork is served with a tangy, herbaceous salsa verde.

PREPARATION TIME 20 minutes,
plus at least 4 hours marinating
COOKING TIME 5–6½ hours
SERVES 4–6

FOR THE SALSA VERDE

4 anchovy fillets
3 cloves garlic, coarsely chopped
1 teaspoon salt, plus extra to taste
½ cup (1 oz/30 g) arugula (rocket)
½ cup (1 oz/30 g) chopped basil
1 cup (8 fl oz/240 ml) extra-virgin olive oil
2 scallions (spring onions), thinly sliced
½ cup (1 oz/30 g) chopped cilantro (coriander)
½ cup (1 oz/30 g) chopped parsley
4 tablespoons capers, rinsed
4 tablespoons chopped tarragon
¼ teaspoon red pepper flakes
2 scallions (spring onions), thinly sliced
4 tablespoons capers, rinsed
Black pepper

FOR THE PORK CHEEKS

3 lb/1.3 kg pork cheeks
Salt and black pepper
2 cups (12 oz/350 g) rendered bacon fat, lard, or canola oil
Apple or cherry wood, for smoking

FOR THE SALSA VERDE In a food processor, combine the anchovies, garlic, and salt and blend to a paste. Add the arugula, basil, and 4 tablespoons oil and pulse for 15 seconds. Add the scallions (spring onions), cilantro (coriander), parsley, capers, tarragon, and red pepper flakes. Pulse to combine, adding the remaining ¾ cup (6 fl oz/175 ml) olive oil. Season to taste with salt and pepper. The salsa verde can be stored in an airtight container in the refrigerator for 3 days, ideally, but up to 1 week.

FOR THE PORK CHEEKS Generously season the pork cheeks with salt and pepper. Cover and refrigerate for at least 4 hours but, preferably, overnight.

Preheat a smoker with apple or cherry wood to 250°F/120°C for indirect smoking.

Set aside the pork cheeks for 1–2 hours to bring to room temperature. Arrange the pork cheeks in the smoker in a single layer, making sure they do not touch. Smoke for 2–2½ hours.

Transfer the smoked pork cheeks to a baking dish. Pour in the rendered bacon fat, lard, or canola oil. Cover with aluminum foil and return to the smoker for 3–4 hours, until fork tender. (Alternatively, roast in a 250°F/120°C/Gas Mark ½ oven.) Set aside for 10 minutes–1 hour.

Remove the pork from the fat and transfer to a serving dish. Serve with the salsa verde.

SMOKED PORK BUTT

Spiessbraten, a dish that is from the small town of Idar-Oberstein and popular throughout Germany, is essentially smoked pork butt, which gets its distinct flavor from onions and beechwood. A butterflied pork butt is smothered with seasoned onions and marinated overnight. The pork is then rolled onto a spit and smoked—while the onions travel a different route to become caramelized garnishes.

PREPARATION TIME 15 minutes, plus at least 6 hours marinating
COOKING TIME 5 hours
SERVES 8

5 onions, thinly sliced
4 tablespoons/40 g kosher salt, divided
½ cup (4 fl oz/120 ml) canola oil
2 tablespoons German mustard
2 teaspoons dried thyme
2 teaspoons dried oregano
2 teaspoons smoked paprika
1 teaspoon black pepper
1 teaspoon ground cumin
½ teaspoon cayenne pepper
1 (4-lb/1.8-kg) pork butt, butterflied
Soaked beechwood chips, for smoking

In a large bowl, combine the onions, 2 tablespoons of the salt, oil, mustard, thyme, oregano, paprika, black pepper, cumin, and cayenne. Using your hands, massage the onions to release their juices.

Spread half of the mixture onto a baking sheet, then place the pork on top. Coat the pork in the remaining mixture. Cover and refrigerate for at least 6 hours but, preferably, overnight.

Remove the pork from the refrigerator and separate the onions into a medium bowl. Roll the pork into a log shape, then secure it with kitchen string. Sprinkle with the remaining 2 tablespoons of salt. Thread the meat onto a rotisserie spit.

Prepare a smoker with coals and soaked beechwood chips to 250°F/120°C. Place the pork on the rotisserie 12 inches/30 cm above the coals and roast for 5 hours, or until the internal temperature reaches 195°F/90°C. If necessary, add more coals and wood chips.

Meanwhile, combine the onions and ½ cup (4 fl oz/ 120 ml) of water in a large skillet and cook over low heat for 30 minutes, until caramelized. Remove the pork from the spit and set aside to rest for 30 minutes.

Slice the pork against the grain, transfer to a serving dish, and serve with the caramelized onions.

Traditional Italian porchetta starts with a whole pork belly stuffed with aromatics, including fennel pollen and citrus zest, which is rolled up and tied (or wrapped around a pork loin). In this flavorful adaptation, the pork is seasoned with toasted fennel seeds as well as fennel pollen, garlic, and orange zest, then smoked before it roasts in the oven. In Italy, porchetta is often sliced and served on fresh Italian bread.

PREPARATION TIME 15 minutes,
plus at least 12 hours refrigeration
COOKING TIME 3½–4½ hours
SERVES 10–12

1 cup (3¼ oz/95 g) fennel seeds

2 heads garlic, cloves separated and peeled

Zest of 3–4 oranges

4 tablespoons fennel pollen

4 tablespoons salt

2 tablespoons black pepper

1 (10-lb/4.5-kg) skin-on pork belly

Apple or cherry wood, for smoking

Toast the fennel seeds in a small skillet over medium heat for 1–2 minutes, until fragrant. Set aside to cool.

In a food processor, combine the garlic and fennel seeds and pulse to form a paste. In a medium bowl, combine the paste, orange zest, fennel pollen, salt, and pepper. Mix to combine.

Place the pork belly, skin side up, on a cutting board. Using a sharp knife, cut ½-inch/1-cm-long slits into the thick skin. Slice both ways to create a crosshatch.

Flip the belly, skin side down, and spread over the garlic-fennel mixture. Tightly roll the pork belly into a log, then tie it with kitchen string in 1-inch/2.5-cm increments. Place the rolled belly on a rack set over a baking sheet, then refrigerate, uncovered, for 12–24 hours.

Preheat a smoker to 250°F/120°C and an oven to 450°F/230°C/Gas Mark 8.

Place the pork belly in the smoker and smoke for 1 hour. Transfer the pork belly to a rack set over a baking sheet, then roast it in the oven for 1 hour. Reduce the temperature to 325°F/160°C/Gas Mark 3 and roast for another 1½–2½ hours, until the internal temperature reaches 140°F/60°C. Set aside to rest for 30 minutes.

Slice, then serve.

BACON

Although few home cooks routinely make their own bacon, enthusiasts will be excited to learn that the process, while lengthy, is not difficult. This recipe provides a good basic strategy, but once you master the process, feel free to improvise using other flavorings like brown sugar, molasses, garlic, or even different smoking woods to develop your own signature bacon.

PREPARATION TIME 20 minutes, plus 8 days refrigeration
COOKING TIME 3 hours
SERVES 8–10

⅓ cup (2½ oz/70 g) sugar
3 tablespoons salt
2 tablespoons black pepper
2 teaspoons paprika
1 teaspoon pink curing salt
1 (3-lb/1.4-kg) skinless, boneless pork belly
Apple or cherry wood chips, for smoking

In a small bowl, combine all the ingredients except the pork belly.

Pat dry the pork belly with paper towels. Rub the mixture over both sides of the belly.

Place it in a zip-top bag, then refrigerate for 1 week. Gently massage any liquid in the bag over the pork belly.

Rinse the pork under cold running water. Pat dry, then place it on a rack set over a baking sheet. Refrigerate, uncovered, for 24 hours.

Preheat a smoker with apple or cherry wood chips to 200°F/93°C.

Place the pork belly in the smoker and smoke for 3 hours, or until the internal temperature reaches 150°F/65°C.

The bacon can be stored in an airtight container in the refrigerator for up to 1 week. Slice, then cook as desired.

Although Tasso ham isn't technically ham (it's not from the pig's hind legs), this cured meat from Louisiana is used like ham: added to beans, greens, or stews like gumbo to impart a rich smokiness. Pork shoulder chunks are cured in spices like chipotle and sage, then smoked to a low temperature so that they remain firm and flavorful.

PREPARATION TIME 30 minutes, plus 7 days marinating
COOKING TIME 2–3 hours
MAKES 5 lb/2.25 kg

4 tablespoons paprika

4 tablespoons salt

2 tablespoons cayenne pepper

2 tablespoons onion powder

2 tablespoons granulated garlic

1 tablespoon dark brown sugar

1 tablespoon sugar

1 tablespoon chipotle powder

1 tablespoon black pepper

1 tablespoon dried sage

1 teaspoon ground cloves

1 teaspoon pink curing salt

1 (5-lb/2.25-kg) bone-in pork shoulder blade roast, trimmed and cut into 3-inch/7.5-cm cubes

Oak, apple, or cherry wood, for smoking

In a large bowl, combine all the ingredients except the pork shoulder. Add the pork and toss to coat. Divide the pork among 3 large zip-top bags. Remove the air from the bags, then seal. Refrigerate for 7 days, turning every day to keep the liquid from settling.

Preheat a smoker to 225°F/107°C.

Place the pork in the smoker and smoke for 2–3 hours, until the internal temperature reaches 150°F/65°C.

The cured meat can be stored in the freezer, separated in batches, for up to 4 months.

Babi guling, or roast suckling pig, originated as a ceremonial offering to the Balinese Hindu gods. It is found all over Bali (a primarily Hindu island), although it's rarely seen on Indonesia's other (predominantly Islamic, non-pork-eating) islands. A whole pig is basted in a spice mixture, including turmeric, coriander, lemongrass, chiles, and galangal, then mounted on a spit and slow-roasted over an open fire. This recipe delivers the same spicy, succulent meat and crispy skin without the effort of cooking an entire pig.

PREPARATION TIME 20 minutes
COOKING TIME 1½–2 hours
SERVES 8

FOR THE SPICE PASTE

3 oz/85 g turmeric root, chopped
12 bird's eye chiles, chopped
8 golden shallots, chopped
5 large cloves garlic
2 large stalks lemongrass, outer leaves removed and white part only, chopped
2 tablespoons chopped ginger
2 tablespoons coriander seeds, crushed
2 tablespoons vegetable oil
1 tablespoon black peppercorns
1 tablespoon chopped galangal
2 teaspoons salt

FOR THE PORK

1 (3-lb/1.4-kg) boneless pork shoulder, skin-on
½ cup (4 fl oz/120 ml) vegetable oil

FOR SERVING

Steamed rice
Sambal Mata (page 346)

FOR THE SPICE PASTE In a food processor, combine all the ingredients and blend into a fine paste.

FOR THE PORK Starting 1-inch/2.5-cm from one end of the roast, cut a pocket almost to the other side. Place half of the spice paste into the pocket, then tie the roast at 1-inch/2.5-cm intervals with kitchen string. Spread the rest of the paste over the outside of the roast.

Preheat a grill to medium heat for indirect grilling.

Place the roast on the hot side of the grill, set over a drip pan. Cover and cook for 1½–2 hours, basting occasionally with the oil, until brown on all sides and the internal temperature reaches 190°F/88°C. Set aside to rest for 10 minutes. Remove the string, then thinly slice crosswise.

Serve with steamed rice and sambal mata.

LA CAJA CHINA PIG

La Caja China, a box barbecue technique, was invented in 1985 by Robert Guerra, who saw the method used in Chinatown in Havana, Cuba. The design was originally introduced by Chinese laborers in Cuba who were building railroads there. A whole pig (usually injected with mojo) is placed inside a box made of plywood and lined with aluminum. The metal lid is a tray for charcoal, which is added every hour until the skin is crispy. La Caja China is now sold around the world, and the pork dish, *cochinillo en caja China*, is a popular celebratory dish among Cuban families in south Florida. If you don't have a Caja China, see the recipe for Cuban Pork (page 157).

PREPARATION TIME 20 minutes, plus overnight marinating
COOKING TIME 4 hours
SERVES 12

FOR THE SPICE RUB

4 tablespoons coarse salt
4 tablespoons garlic powder
2 tablespoons onion powder
2 tablespoons ground oregano
2 teaspoons ground bay leaves
1½ teaspoons ground cumin
¼ teaspoon black pepper

FOR THE MOJO

6 heads garlic, separated and peeled
4 teaspoons coarse salt
4 teaspoons dried oregano
2 teaspoons black peppercorns
2 teaspoons ground cumin
2 teaspoons ground bay leaves
2 cups (16 fl oz/475 ml) orange juice
1 cup (8 fl oz/240 ml) lemon juice
1 cup (8 fl oz/240 ml) pineapple juice
1 (45–50-lb/20–22-kg) dressed pig, backbone split lengthwise (ask your butcher)

FOR THE SPICE RUB Combine all the ingredients in a medium bowl.

FOR THE MOJO Combine all the ingredients except the pig in a large bowl. Divide between 2 containers. Refrigerate half of the mixture. Strain the other half, reserving the solids.

Using a syringe, inject the pig with the liquid part of the mojo.

Sprinkle the interior and exterior of the pig with the spice rub and reserved mojo solids. Cover and marinate in the refrigerator overnight.

Bring the pork to room temperature. Using S-hooks, lock the pig into the rack of the Caja China, skin side down. Roast the pig for 3½ hours, starting with 16 lb/7 kg of charcoal and adding 8 lb/3.6 kg of charcoal every hour, until the pig reaches 185°F/85°C.

Turn the pig skin side up and, with a knife, make crosshatch cuts into the skin. Cook for another 30–45 minutes until the skin is crispy. Remove the pork from the Caja China and set aside to rest for 10 minutes. Carve it into pieces or slices.

Transfer the mojo to a serving bowl and serve with the pork.

The Philippines' unofficial national dish, called *lechón*, or *cebu lechón*, is ubiquitous at large gatherings and festivals. The name (*leche* means "milk" in Spanish) comes from the Spanish colonizers, but the dish was likely inspired by the Chinese who arrived on trade missions in the thirteenth century. The traditional recipe calls for a suckling pig, but these days, many Filipinos use a fully grown pig stuffed with lemongrass and garlic and slowly roasted on a bamboo spit over hot coals (or coconut husks). The evaporated milk glaze helps achieve that coveted crackling. Leftovers are often cooked in a vinegar-based gravy to create the next day's stew: *lechón paksiw*.

PREPARATION TIME 1 hour
COOKING TIME 5 hours
SERVES 20

FOR THE STUFFING
4 tablespoons ground star anise
4 tablespoons bay leaf powder
5 cups (1 lb 9 oz/700 g) crushed cloves garlic
4½ lb/2 kg scallions (spring onions), minced
2 tablespoons crushed black peppercorns
10 stalks lemongrass, cut in half and bundled together

FOR THE PIG
1 (44-lb/20-kg) whole pig, entrails removed and cleaned
3 (12-oz/354-ml) cans evaporated milk
Salt and black pepper

FOR SERVING
Liver Sauce (page 355)
Calamansi (Filipino lime) wedges

Set up a spit apparatus over a fire in a pit or container and heat to 225°F/107°C.

FOR THE STUFFING Combine all the ingredients except the lemongrass.

FOR THE PIG Wash the inside of the pig with boiling water, then set aside to drain. Rub salt and pepper on the interior and exterior of the pig. Skewer the pig on a long bamboo stick: Insert the spit rod into one end of the pig and slide the rod through the open body cavity and out the hole on the other side. Slide the pig into position along the spit, chest cavity facing up, until it is centered.

Stuff the pork belly with the stuffing. Put the bundle of lemongrass on top of the stuffing. Using a large embroidery needle and big looping stitches, stitch the belly from one end to the other. Roast the pig for 4–5 hours, turning the spit every hour and occasionally basting the skin with evaporated milk. If the ears and snout start to brown, wrap them in aluminum foil. The meat is cooked when it reaches an internal temperature of 185°F/85°C.

Serve with liver sauce and calamansi wedges.

The most popular food at Hawaiian celebrations or *luaus* is kalua pig (*kalua* means "from the pit"). A whole salted pig, wrapped in banana leaves, is cooked in a pit called an *imu*. The pit, usually about 4 feet (1.2 meters) deep with sloping sides, is filled with kindling and stones. Once the kindling is lit and the stones are hot, the pork is lowered onto the stones.

The wood and leaves infuse an earthy, smoky flavor into the pork, which is then usually shredded and accompanied by cooked cabbage and rice or *poi* (taro root pudding) and *lomi lomi* (raw salmon salad). Traditionally, the pig was served in braided baskets made of coconut fronds or on large banana leaves. This recipe uses a pork shoulder and an oven to simplify the traditional dish.

PREPARATION TIME 20 minutes
COOKING TIME 3 hours
SERVES 10

2½–3 lb/1–1.3 kg boneless pork shoulder, divided into 4 pieces

8–10 cloves garlic, cut in half

2 tablespoons olive oil

1½ tablespoons liquid smoke

1 large banana leaf, thawed if frozen and divided into 3 pieces

2 tablespoons sea salt

2 cups (16 fl oz/475 ml) water or chicken stock

FOR SERVING

Steamed white rice

Sautéed cabbage

Preheat an oven with a rack on the middle shelf to 325°F/160°C/Gas Mark 3.

Using a sharp paring knife, cut a few slits into each piece of pork shoulder. Insert the garlic into each pocket.

Heat the oil in a large Dutch oven (casserole) over medium-high heat. Add the pork and sear for 4–5 minutes on each side until browned. Transfer the pork to a plate, then set aside to cool.

Rub the salt and 1 tablespoon of liquid smoke all over the pork. Place the pork in the center of a banana leaf, then fold in the edges and wrap. Flip and set the wrapped pork, seam side down, on the next piece of banana leaf. Repeat the fold with the remaining pieces of banana. (It's okay if the leaf splits slightly.)

Place the banana leaf-wrapped pork, seam side down, into the Dutch oven. Pour in the water or stock around the sides. Cover, then transfer to the oven and roast for 3 hours, until the pork is very tender.

Using tongs or forks, shred the pork into bite-sized pieces and transfer to a large bowl. Season the pork with the remaining ½ tablespoon liquid smoke and 4 tablespoons of the cooking liquid.

Serve immediately with rice and cabbage.

The pork can be stored in an airtight container in the refrigerator for up to 5 days.

In North Carolina, whole hog barbecue—a slowly cooked pig, pulled or chopped, served with a vinegar-based barbecue sauce and coleslaw—is equal parts art and religion. Although it sounds simple, cooking a whole hog is a complex process requiring skill and patience to cook each part of the pig (shoulders, belly, loins, etc.) properly and achieve a perfectly crispy skin. (As a general rule of thumb, allow 2 hours of cooking time for every 10 lb/4.6 kg of hog.) Make this one for a crowd. The recipe yields a huge amount, and there is nothing quite like the spectacle of serving a whole hog.

PREPARATION TIME 15 minutes
COOKING TIME 10–15 hours
SERVES 20–50

1 (50–75-lb/22–34-kg) whole split hog
4 cups (1 lb 2 oz/800 g) Pork and Poultry Rub (page 358)
3 quarts/2.8 L North Carolina Barbecue Sauce (page 334)
Oak or cherry wood, for smoking

Preheat a smoker to 250°F/120°C.

Lay the split hog, belly side up, on a work surface. Generously season the belly side with the pork rub, making sure to get the rub into the cracks and crevices. (Don't season the skin because the rub won't stick.)

Place the hog, belly side down, in the smoker and smoke for 2–3 hours. Flip the hog, skin side down and belly side up. Roast for 8–12 hours, basting every 30 minutes with the sauce, until the hog reaches 190°F/88°C. Set aside to rest for 10–45 minutes.

Pull or chop the meat, then toss with more sauce.

CARIBBEAN GOAT LEG

This slow-grilled leg of goat (seasoned with a native blend of herbs and spices) is a popular dish in the U.S. Virgin Islands. It's rubbed with the earthy, smoky Cruzan Seasoning, which is less spicy than Jamaican jerk but just as flavorful. If you can't find a goat leg, try this with a leg of lamb.

PREPARATION TIME 2 hours, plus overnight marinating
COOKING TIME 3 hours
SERVES 6–8

1 (3–4-lb/1.3–1.8-kg) goat leg or lamb leg
½ cup (4 fl oz/120 ml) lime juice or white vinegar
4 tablespoons Cruzan Seasoning (page 167)
4 tablespoons melted butter

Rinse the goat or lamb with lime juice or vinegar, then rub the seasoning all over. Place on a tray with a rack. Refrigerate for at least 2 hours but, preferably, overnight. Remove the goat from the refrigerator at least 30 minutes prior to grilling.

Preheat a grill to medium heat for indirect grilling.

Place the meat on the cooler side of the grill and cook for 2–3 hours, turning and basting with butter every 30 minutes, until the outside is brown and crispy and the internal temperature reaches 160°F/70°C. Set aside to rest for 15 minutes.

Slice the goat meat, then arrange it in a serving dish and serve warm.

Grilled cabrito, or kid goat, is a dish that originated almost 450 years ago in the Mexican city of Monterrey. It remains a popular dish for large family gatherings in Mexico, Brazil, Argentina, and Spain. Recipes vary widely according to region and family, but the goat is typically brined and seasoned before being grilled or smoked. The tender meat is then shredded and served with tortillas, salsa, rice, and beans.

PREPARATION TIME 15 minutes, plus overnight brining
COOKING TIME 3 hours
SERVES 10

FOR THE BRINE
½ cup (4 fl oz/120 ml) white vinegar
1 tablespoon salt

FOR THE GOAT
1 (20-lb/9-kg) kid goat, skinned and gutted
Brine (see above)
1 cup (8 fl oz/240 ml) olive oil
1 tablespoon salt
1 tablespoon black pepper

FOR SERVING
20 flour tortillas
Pico de Gallo (page 339)

FOR THE BRINE In a container large enough to fit the goat, mix the vinegar, salt, and 8½ cups (68 fl oz/ 2 L) water.

FOR THE GOAT Submerge the goat in the liquid. Cover and refrigerate overnight.

Preheat a grill to medium heat.

Remove the goat from the brine, then brush with the oil and sprinkle with the salt and pepper. Place the goat on the grill and cook for 3 hours, turning every 30 minutes, until the outside is brown and crispy and the internal temperature reaches 160°F/71°C. Transfer the goat to a cutting board and set aside to rest for 10 minutes. Shred or cut the meat into small pieces, then transfer to a serving dish.

Serve warm with tortillas and pico de gallo.

Nyama choma, which means "roast meat" in Swahili, is a traditional Kenyan dish of goat meat grilled over charcoal. In this recipe, the goat leg meat is briefly grilled, then cooked with a deeply flavorful marinade in a foil packet on the grill.

PREPARATION TIME 15 minutes, plus overnight marinating
COOKING TIME 1½ hours
SERVES 6–8

FOR THE GOAT

1 (5-lb/2-kg) goat leg, cut into 4 pieces

FOR THE MARINADE

6 sprigs rosemary
2 heads garlic, halved
1 large yellow onion
1 (2-inch/5-cm) piece ginger
3 tablespoons salt
2 tablespoons ground paprika
1 tablespoon ground cumin
1 teaspoon black pepper
1–2 tablespoons honey
2 chicken bouillon cubes
Juice of 1 lemon

FOR THE GOAT Using a sharp paring knife, pierce the goat all over. (This allows the marinade to penetrate the meat.) Place the meat in a bowl.

FOR THE MARINADE Combine all the ingredients in a medium bowl. Pour the marinade over the goat and use your hands to massage the marinade into the holes. Cover and refrigerate overnight.

Preheat a grill to high heat.

Bring the goat to room temperature. Reserve the marinade. Place the goat on the grill and sear for 3 minutes on each side, then transfer the pieces to a large piece of aluminum foil. Top the meat with the reserved marinade, rosemary, and a halved bulb of garlic. Tent with the aluminum foil. Grill the packet, turning occasionally, for 1½ hours. Set aside to rest for 15 minutes.

Open up the packet, slice the meat, and transfer to a serving dish. Serve hot with the cooking juices.

Lamb *dibi*, or "barbecue" lamb, is a popular Senegalese street food sold at small vendors called *dibiteries*. The lamb is marinated in mustard and vinegar, then grilled until charred. The tangy lamb chunks are served with caramelized onions and mustard sauce (and often bread) in brown paper bags, which absorb the extra juices.

PREPARATION TIME 15 minutes, plus overnight marinating
COOKING TIME 10–15 minutes
SERVES 4

FOR THE LAMB AND ONIONS
1 (1-lb/450-g) boneless lamb shoulder, trimmed and cut into 3-inch/7.5-cm pieces
2 yellow onions, sliced into ½-inch/1-cm-thick pieces
3 tablespoons olive oil
2 tablespoons Dijon mustard
2 tablespoons minced garlic
2 tablespoons red wine vinegar
1 teaspoon red pepper flakes
Juice of 1 lemon
Salt and black pepper, to taste

FOR THE MUSTARD SAUCE
4 tablespoons Dijon mustard
3 tablespoons olive oil
2 tablespoons whole-grain mustard
1½ tablespoons red wine vinegar
¼ teaspoon red pepper flakes
Juice of 1 lemon

FOR SERVING
1 baguette, sliced

FOR THE LAMB AND ONIONS Place the lamb in a baking dish and the onions in a medium bowl. Generously season both with salt and pepper.

Combine the remaining ingredients in a small bowl. Pour half of the mixture over the lamb, then the other half over the onions. Toss to coat. Cover both and refrigerate overnight.

FOR THE MUSTARD SAUCE In a blender, combine all the ingredients and purée until smooth. Refrigerate until needed.

Preheat a grill to high heat.

Place the lamb on the grill and cook for 10–15 minutes, turning occasionally, until charred on the outside and the internal temperature reaches 145°F/63°C. Transfer to a cutting board and set aside to rest for 10 minutes.

Meanwhile, place the onions on the grill and cook for 8 minutes, turning, until lightly charred.

Thinly slice the lamb, place it in a serving dish, and serve warm with a small bowl of the mustard sauce and sliced baguette.

GREEK LAMB SHOULDER

In Crete, a traditional technique called *antikristo* ("across the fire") is used for cooking lamb. The animal is cut into four pieces, salted, and placed on posts in a circle around the fire, so the wind direction and distance from the flames control the heat. This recipe uses a deboned lamb shoulder and skewers to frame the meat over the heat.

PREPARATION TIME 10 minutes, plus overnight marinating
COOKING TIME 30 minutes
SERVES 6–8

1 clove garlic, minced
2 tablespoons salt
2 tablespoons dried oregano
1 tablespoon coriander seeds, crushed
½ teaspoon black pepper
Zest of 1 lemon
1 (4-lb/1.8-kg) lamb shoulder, butterflied

In a small bowl, combine all ingredients except the lamb. Rub the seasoning all over the lamb. Cover in plastic wrap (clingfilm) and refrigerate overnight.
  Preheat a grill to medium-high heat (425°F/220°C).
  Place the lamb on the grill and cook for 15 minutes on each side for medium-rare. Set aside to rest for 10 minutes.
  Slice, then serve.

SMOKED LAMB SHOULDER

Despite its size, lamb shoulder is easy to prepare, and the spectacle of an entire lamb shoulder coming off the smoker or grill is always a crowd-pleaser. Also, lamb meat is incredibly versatile and can be seasoned with just salt and pepper or, as in this recipe, a blend of simple spices and a rosemary-infused mop sauce. Serve with Lamb Sauce (page 353) or Chimichurri (page 340).

PREPARATION TIME 15 minutes, plus at least 2 hours refrigeration
COOKING TIME 8 hours
SERVES 8–10

FOR THE MOP SAUCE
2 cups (16 fl oz/475 ml) extra-virgin olive oil
2 cups (16 fl oz/475 ml) lemon juice
8 cloves garlic
4–5 sprigs rosemary, chopped
1 tablespoon red pepper flakes
1 tablespoon salt
1 tablespoon black pepper

FOR THE LAMB
2 cups (14 oz/400 g) Lamb Rub (page 360)
1 (7-lb/3-kg) bone-in lamb shoulder
Oak, apple, or cherry wood, for smoking

FOR THE MOP SAUCE In a blender or food processor, combine the oil, lemon juice, and garlic. Pulse until the garlic is blended. Transfer to a medium bowl, then whisk in the rosemary, red pepper flakes, salt, and pepper.

FOR THE LAMB Generously massage the lamb rub over the lamb. Cover and refrigerate for at least 2 hours or, preferably, overnight.
  Remove the lamb from the refrigerator and bring to room temperature. Meanwhile, heat a smoker to 250°F/120°C. Use a water pan to create humidity.
  Place the lamb in the smoker, skin side up, then close the lid and smoke for 1 hour. Brush the lamb with the mop sauce and cook for another 7 hours, brushing it with more mop sauce every 30 minutes. The lamb is cooked once it pulls easily into strands and reaches an internal temperature of 203°F/95°C.
  Remove the lamb from the smoker and set aside to rest for 20 minutes. Slice (or pull) the lamb meat and transfer it to a serving plate. Serve hot.

PATAGONIAN
SPIT-ROASTED LAMB

Lamb al asador is a classic Chilean dish in which a whole lamb is flayed and hung on a cross over a pit fire. It's often served and/or basted with Chimichurri (page 340). The recipe to the right is a simpler leg of lamb version that works well for home cooks.

PREPARATION TIME 1 hour
COOKING TIME 6–7 hours
SERVES 10

4 sprigs rosemary, finely chopped
Bunch of parsley, finely chopped
½ cup (2½ oz/70 g) salt
½ cup (3½ oz/100 g) sugar
2 tablespoons dried oregano
½ cup (4 fl oz/120 ml) red wine vinegar
Zest of 1 orange
1 (20–30-lb/9–13 kg) whole lamb, butterflied
Chimichurri (page 340), to serve

Build a fire pit.

In a medium bowl, combine all the ingredients except the lamb. Pour in 3 cups (25 fl oz/750 ml) of water, and set aside.

Tie the lamb's legs to cross bars with steel wire. Add support by tying wires through the mid-back and around the cross bars. The meat should be tilted on the stake, bone side down. Cook for 3 hours, then brush it with the sauce. Apply the sauce every 30 minutes for another 2–3 hours.

Turn the lamb, skin side down, and cook for 1 hour, until browned and crispy. Adjust the heat as needed. Remove the lamb from the cross, then slice the meat.

Transfer the lamb to a serving dish and serve with chimichurri.

PATAGONIAN ROASTED
LEG OF LAMB

CHILE

PREPARATION TIME 15 minutes, plus 4 hours marinating
COOKING TIME 30 minutes
SERVES 6

1 (5-lb/2.25-kg) leg of lamb, butterflied
Salt and black pepper
2 cups (16 fl oz/475 ml) Chimichurri (page 340)

Generously season the lamb with salt and pepper. Use about ½ cup (4 fl oz/120 ml) of chimichurri to coat all surfaces of the lamb. Cover and refrigerate for 4 hours.

Preheat an oven to 500°F/260°C/Gas Mark 10.

Place the lamb, skin side up, on a rimmed baking sheet. Cook for 30 minutes, or until the lamb is medium-rare. Transfer the lamb to a cutting board and cover with aluminum foil. Set aside to rest for 15 minutes.

Serve warm with the remaining chimichurri.

MOROCCAN SPIT-ROASTED LAMB

This is an adaptation of the traditional dish *méchoui,* which is made with a whole spit-roasted sheep or lamb and typically served at the beginning of a feast. This version, using a leg of lamb and a grill, captures the same Moroccan flavors—harissa, cumin, coriander— on a smaller scale. Both the original *méchoui* and this recipe finish the lamb with a sprinkling of cumin and flaky salt.

PREPARATION TIME 20 minutes,
plus at least 2 hours marinating
COOKING TIME 40–50 minutes
SERVES 8

FOR THE LAMB

1 (5-lb/2.25-kg) leg of lamb, butterflied
½ cup (2¼ oz/65 g) melted butter
2 tablespoons olive oil
4 cloves garlic, crushed
2 tablespoons thyme leaves
2 teaspoons paprika
2 teaspoons ground cumin, plus extra for sprinkling
2 teaspoons ground coriander
1 teaspoon salt, plus extra for sprinkling
1 teaspoon black pepper
1 teaspoon harissa paste
Zest and juice of 1 lemon

FOR THE SAUCE

1 cup (7 oz/200 g) Greek yogurt
½ cup (1 oz/30 g) cilantro (coriander) leaves, coarsely chopped
1 teaspoon harissa paste
Salt and black pepper

FOR THE LAMB Put the lamb in a large shallow dish and pat dry. In a medium bowl, combine the butter and oil, then stir in the remaining ingredients. Pour the marinade over the lamb, then use your hands to massage it into the meat. Cover and refrigerate for at least 2 hours but, preferably, overnight.

Preheat a grill to high heat.

Bring the lamb to room temperature. Place the lamb on the grill and cook, fat side down, for 5 minutes, until well browned. Flip and cook for another 5 minutes, until browned on the other side. Reduce the heat under the meat, leaving the rest of the grill at high heat. Cook the lamb for 30–40 minutes, turning occasionally. Transfer the lamb to a cutting board and cover tightly with aluminum foil. Set aside to rest for 10 minutes.

FOR THE SAUCE Combine all the ingredients in a medium bowl and mix well.

Cut the lamb into thick slices, then transfer it to a serving dish and sprinkle it with cumin and flaky salt. Serve warm with the sauce.

Traditional *barbacoa*, which likely originated in the Caribbean, was a method in which whole sheep were slow-cooked in pits covered with maguey leaves. (The indigenous word for this method, *barbaca*, became "*barbacoa*" and ultimately "barbecue.") The sheep (and later cow, goat, lamb, or pork) was usually cooked in a bland stock, then shredded and mixed with seasonings. These days, *barbacoa* (either beef or lamb) is particularly popular in Mexico, where it is slow-cooked in a seasoned stock, using chipotle and adobo peppers. This recipe smokes a lamb shoulder before slow-cooking it in a rich chile sauce to achieve the original dish's smoky flavor and tender meat.

PREPARATION TIME 20 minutes
COOKING TIME 5¼–6¼ hours
SERVES 8–10

FOR THE LAMB

2 tablespoons salt
2 tablespoons chili powder
1 tablespoon ground cumin
2 teaspoons dried oregano
2 teaspoons onion powder
2 teaspoons garlic powder
1 (5-lb/2.25-kg) boneless lamb shoulder roast, tied

FOR THE SAUCE

2 guajillo chiles, stemmed and seeded
1 ancho chile, stemmed and seeded
4¼ cups (34 fl oz/1 L) chicken stock
3 tablespoons vegetable oil
1 white onion, finely chopped
4 cloves garlic, crushed
1 teaspoon dried oregano
1 teaspoon ground cumin
¼ teaspoon ground cinnamon
⅓ cup (2¾ fl oz/80 ml) apple cider vinegar
3 tablespoons chopped chipotles in adobo plus 1 tablespoon adobo sauce
2 bay leaves
4 tablespoons lime juice
Salt, to taste
Oak or hickory wood, for smoking

FOR SERVING

16–20 corn tortillas
Chopped onion
Chopped cilantro (coriander)
Pico de Gallo (page 339)
Lime wedges

Preheat a smoker with oak or hickory wood to 250°F/120°C.

FOR THE LAMB In a small bowl, combine all the ingredients except the lamb. Massage the rub all over the lamb. Place the lamb in the smoker and smoke for 3 hours.

FOR THE SAUCE Toast the chiles in a Dutch oven (casserole) over medium heat for 5–10 minutes, turning frequently. Transfer the chiles to a small saucepan and cover with 2 cups (16 fl oz/475 ml) of chicken stock. Bring to a boil, then reduce the heat to medium-low and simmer for 15 minutes, or until the chiles are softened.

Meanwhile, heat the oil in a pan over medium-high heat. Add the onion and garlic and sauté for 7 minutes, or until softened. Add the oregano, cumin, and cinnamon and cook for 30 seconds, until fragrant. Stir in the remaining 2 cups (16 fl oz/475 ml) of stock, the vinegar, and chipotles and bring to a boil. Reduce the heat to medium and simmer for 20 minutes, or until the liquid is reduced by half. Transfer this mixture to a blender, then add the chiles and the soaking liquid. Purée until smooth and set aside.

Transfer the smoked lamb to the Dutch oven. Pour in the sauce, then add the bay leaves. Partially cover and place in the smoker or a 250°F/120°C/Gas Mark ½ oven. Cook for 2–3 hours, until the lamb is tender. Transfer the lamb to a plate and discard the bay leaves. Cook the sauce over medium-high heat for 5 minutes, until reduced by half. Stir in lime juice.

Untie the lamb, then shred or cut the meat into small pieces. Add the lamb to the pan, then season to taste with salt.

Serve immediately with tortillas, onion, cilantro (coriander), salsa, and lime.

Leftover barbacoa can be stored in an airtight container in the refrigerator for up to 5 days.

This celebratory Mongolian dish, or *khorkhog*, differs significantly from what many know as "Mongolian barbecue." Small pieces of seasoned lamb or goat meat and vegetables are layered in a metal pot or, traditionally, a milk jug, along with sizzling, coal-baked stones. The pot is covered so the hot stones steam the ingredients while imparting a smoky flavor. More of a nomadic technique than a specific recipe, *khorkhog* is typically eaten directly from the pot, while the stones, which are said to have healing powers, are cooled slightly and tossed among diners.

PREPARATION TIME 20 minutes
COOKING TIME 2–3 hours
SERVES 6–8

1 (2-lb/900-g) lamb, cut into 1-inch/2.5-cm cubes
2 onions, chopped
4–6 potatoes, chopped
4–6 carrots, chopped
Salt and black pepper, to taste
10–12 hot stones

Preheat a grill to medium-high heat. Heat the stones in the fire until they are red-hot.

In a Dutch oven (casserole dish), layer the lamb, onions, potatoes, and carrots. Season each layer with salt and black pepper. Using tongs, carefully place the hot stones over the ingredients, ensuring the stones do not touch the sides or bottom of the pan. Cover and cook for 2–3 hours, until the meat is tender. Remove the lid, then use the tongs to carefully remove the hot stones.

Serve hot.

The traditional Māori cooking method known as *hāngī* involves cooking food, such as lamb, pork, chicken, vegetables, and *kūmara* (sweet potatoes), in a hot-rock oven underground or a fire pit covered with volcanic stones. When the rocks are hot, the ashes are spread out and the area covered with seaweed or banana leaves. Then layers of food and leaves are added, ending with a cover or tarp of some kind. The food, steamed and smoked, acquires a distinctly earthy flavor. This hot-rock oven is called an *imu* in Hawaii and a *lovo* in Fiji. The method is called *pachamanca* in Peru. The following recipe mimics the technique and flavors of a New Zealand *hāngī*-style barbecue—without the pit. Cabbage leaves envelop and tenderize the meat and vegetables while the dish is slow-cooked in the oven.

PREPARATION TIME 45 minutes

COOKING TIME 4 hours

SERVES 8

FOR THE STUFFING

½ loaf white bread
1 onion, chopped
1 carrot, grated
2 tablespoons finely chopped parsley
2 teaspoons salt
7 tablespoons (3½ oz/100 g) melted butter

FOR THE MEAT

4 pork shoulder steaks
4 lamb shoulder steaks
6 chicken drumsticks
1 large cabbage, cored and leaves separated
4 potatoes, chopped into 1-inch/2.5-cm chunks
4 carrots, chopped into 1-inch/2.5-cm chunks
3 parsnips, chopped into 1-inch/2.5-cm chunks
2 sweet potatoes, chopped into 1-inch/2.5-cm chunks
1 butternut squash, chopped into 1-inch/2.5-cm chunks
Bunch of thyme, chopped
Salt

Preheat an oven to 400°F/200°C/Gas Mark 6.

FOR THE STUFFING In a food processor, briefly pulse the bread into small pieces. Transfer to large bowl, then add the remaining ingredients and mix well. Set aside.

FOR THE MEAT Generously salt the meat on both sides. Line a deep roasting pan with the cabbage leaves. Arrange the meat on top of the cabbage, then add the remaining vegetables over the meat. Top with the stuffing and thyme. Pour in 1 cup (8 fl oz/240 ml) of water evenly over the dish, then cover with more cabbage leaves. Cover with 2 layers of aluminum foil and roast for 2 hours. Reduce the temperature to 300°F/150°C/Gas Mark 2, then cook for another 2 hours.

Carefully remove the foil and top layer of cabbage leaves and discard. Serve hot.

In Uruguay, the backyard *asado*, or barbecue, often features a rack of lamb, or *costillar de cordero*. The fatty meat is simply seasoned with garlic, salt, and rosemary, then grilled and cut into individual ribs and served with Chimichurri (page 340).

PREPARATION TIME 5 minutes, plus 3 hours marinating
COOKING TIME 20 minutes
SERVES 4–6

1 teaspoon salt, plus extra to taste
3 cloves garlic, minced
2 sprigs rosemary, stemmed
Zest of ½ lemon
2 tablespoons olive oil
1 rack of lamb, French-trimmed with membrane removed
Black pepper, to taste
Chimichurri (page 340), to serve (optional)

In a large bowl, combine the salt, garlic, rosemary, lemon zest, and olive oil. Rub the marinade all over the rack of lamb, then refrigerate, uncovered, for 3 hours.

Preheat a grill to high heat.

Place the rack of lamb, rib side down, on the grill and cook for 10 minutes. Season with salt and pepper. Flip the rack and cook for another 10 minutes, or until the meat reaches an internal temperature of 140°F/60°C. Set aside to rest for 15 minutes.

Cut into individual ribs and serve with chimichurri (if desired).

Lamb belly (also called lamb breast or lamb ribs) is not only affordable but also one of the easiest and tastiest cuts to smoke or grill. It has more fat than lamb loin or lamb chops, so it gets divinely tender when slow-cooked. Also, the high skin-to-meat ratio allows more room for seasoning. Although any spice rub will work, this recipe uses za'atar, an earthy Middle Eastern spice blend that works exceptionally well with lamb.

PREPARATION TIME 15 minutes
COOKING TIME 4–5 hours
SERVES 8–10

½ cup (2½ oz/70 g) toasted sesame seeds
4 tablespoons ground cumin
4 tablespoons ground coriander
4 tablespoons sumac
4 tablespoons dried thyme
4 tablespoons dried oregano
2 tablespoons salt
1 tablespoon Aleppo pepper
1 (4-lb/1.8-kg) lamb belly
4¼ cups (34 fl oz/1 L) apple cider vinegar, in a spray bottle
2 cups (16 fl oz/475 ml) Lamb Sauce (page 353), to serve
Oak, apple or cherry wood, for smoking

Preheat a smoker to 250°F/120°C.

Toast the sesame seeds for 3–5 minutes over medium heat in a dry skillet. Place them in a heat-proof medium bowl, then add the remaining spices. Mix to combine. Rub the seasoning into the lamb.

Place the lamb in the smoker, bone side down, and smoke for 1 hour. Spritz with the vinegar. Smoke for another 3–4 hours, spritzing with the vinegar every 30 minutes, until tender. Set aside to rest for 15 minutes.

Slice the lamb, then arrange it in a serving dish. Serve warm with lamb sauce.

Kibbeh, from the Arabic word for "ball," is the national dish of Lebanon and has countless preparations. One of the most popular is this variation, *kibbeh mishwiyyeh*, a grilled dome-shaped lamb-bulgur dough ball stuffed with lamb fat. It's usually grilled on charcoal and served immediately so the rendered fats stay juicy.

PREPARATION TIME 30 minutes
COOKING TIME 20–30 minutes
SERVES 6

FOR THE KIBBEH DOUGH

1 lb/450 g lean ground (minced) lamb
1 red onion, chopped
¼ bunch mint
1 teaspoon dried marjoram
½ teaspoon salt
4 ice cubes
1½ cups (9 oz/250 g) bulgur wheat, rinsed

FOR THE KIBBEH STUFFING

5 oz/140 g frozen lamb tail fat or beef fat, cut into small cubes
1½ red onions
1½ oz/40 g parsley
1½ oz/40 g mint
½ teaspoon salt
½ teaspoon chili powder

Preheat a grill to medium-high heat.

FOR THE KIBBEH DOUGH In a food processor, combine all the ingredients except the bulgur wheat. Blend for 2–3 minutes, until the meat turns doughy and sticky. Add the bulgur wheat and blend for another minute. Transfer the dough to a bowl. Rinse the processor bowl.

FOR THE KIBBEH STUFFING In the same food processor, combine all the ingredients and blend at high speed for 3–5 minutes.

To make the domed kibbeh, line the inside of a small shallow bowl with a wet piece of plastic wrap (clingfilm), leaving about 1-inch/2.5-cm overhang. Take a ⅔-cup scoop of the dough and line the bowl with the mixture, pressing it down about ½ inch/1 cm thick.

Take another sheet of plastic wrap and place it on a clean work surface. Scoop ⅓ cup of the dough and place it on top of the plastic wrap. Flatten the mixture into a patty, about ½ inch/1 cm thick. Add a tablespoon of stuffing to the center.

Gently invert the dome in the small bowl onto the kibbeh patty, then press the bowl down firmly, so that the dome meets the patty. Slowly lift up the bowl and plastic, then press the kibbeh edges with your fingers to seal. Place on a lightly oiled plate, then repeat with the remaining mixture.

Grill the kibbeh for 20–30 minutes, until light brown. Serve warm.

Kati kati, originally from the Nkom people in the northwest province of Cameroon, calls for both grilling and sautéing chicken. Seasoned chicken pieces are seared over an open flame, then simmered with tomatoes and served with corn *fufu* (a cornmeal-dough ball) and vegetables.

PREPARATION TIME 15 minutes
COOKING TIME 40 minutes
SERVES 4

FOR THE CHICKEN

1½ tablespoons garlic powder
1 tablespoon salt, plus extra to taste
1 tablespoon onion powder
1 teaspoon white pepper, plus extra to taste
½ teaspoon cayenne pepper
1 (3–4-lb/1.3–1.8-kg) chicken, cut into 8 pieces and trimmed of fat
Canola oil, for brushing

FOR THE SAUCE

2 chicken bouillon cubes
2 tomatoes, chopped
1 tablespoon tomato paste (purée)
2 tablespoons palm or canola oil
Salt and black pepper, to taste

FOR SERVING

Fufu or polenta
Cooked vegetables

Preheat a grill to high heat.

FOR THE CHICKEN Combine the spices in a small bowl. Rub the seasoning over the chicken, then set aside at room temperature for 15 minutes.

Brush the chicken with the oil. Place the chicken on the grill and cook for 10 minutes, until browned on both sides. (The chicken does not have to be fully cooked at this point.)

FOR THE SAUCE In a blender, combine the bouillon, tomatoes, and tomato paste (purée). Pour in ½ cup (4 fl oz/120 ml) of water and blend until smooth.

Heat the oil in a large saucepan over medium heat. Add the tomato sauce and cook for 4–5 minutes, stirring occasionally.

Add the chicken and bring to a simmer over low heat. Pour in the sauce and ½ cup (4 fl oz/120 ml) of water and cook for 20 minutes, or until the chicken is cooked through and the sauce has reduced. Season to taste with salt and pepper.

Transfer the chicken and sauce to a serving dish. Serve warm with fufu or polenta and cooked vegetables.

COCONUT CHICKEN

Kuku paka (*kuku* means "chicken" in Swahili and *paka* means "delicious" in Punjabi) is a smoky stew made with chargrilled chicken in a rich coconut sauce. This dish, usually served with rice, has Arabic, Indian, and African influences and is especially popular among the Indian communities of Kenya, Tanzania, and Uganda.

PREPARATION TIME 15 minutes,
plus at least 1 hour marinating
COOKING TIME 45 minutes
SERVES 6

FOR THE CHICKEN
4 lb/1.8 kg bone-in chicken, trimmed
1 cup (2¼ oz/60 g) chopped cilantro (coriander) leaves, to garnish
Rice and/or Jordanian Flatbread (page 322), to serve

FOR THE SPICE PASTE
1 onion, quartered
1 (½-inch/1.2-cm) piece fresh ginger, peeled
4 cloves garlic
3 plum tomatoes
2–4 serrano chiles, stemmed and seeded
2 teaspoons salt
2 teaspoons ground cumin
1 teaspoon ground coriander

FOR THE SAUCE
2 tablespoons coconut oil
2 (13½-oz/400-ml) cans coconut milk
Juice of 1 lemon

Using a sharp knife, score each chicken piece in 2–3 places.

FOR THE SPICE PASTE Combine all the ingredients in a food processor and process into a paste. Rub 1 cup of the paste over the chicken and reserve the rest. Refrigerate the chicken for 1–5 hours.
Preheat a grill to high heat.

FOR THE SAUCE Heat the oil in a large skillet over medium heat. Add the remaining spice paste and cook, stirring occasionally, for 20 minutes, until thickened and the oil separates. Stir in the coconut milk and simmer for 20–25 minutes, until the sauce turns light orange.

Meanwhile, place the marinated chicken on the grill and cook for 10–15 minutes, turning frequently, until browned and the meat reaches an internal temperature of 165°F/74°C. Add the chicken to the sauce. Reduce the heat to low, cover, and simmer for 5 minutes. Season to taste with salt and lemon juice. Transfer to a serving bowl, then garnish with cilantro (coriander).

Serve with rice and/or flatbread.

TANDOORI CHICKEN

Tandoori chicken, originally from India but popular across Southeast Asia, is cooked in a *tandoor* (cylindrical clay oven) or grilled on charcoal. The skinless, bone-in chicken pieces are marinated in a mixture of yogurt and spices. It is typically served with Grilled Naan (page 329) and Indian Yogurt Sauce (page 352).

PREPARATION TIME 10 minutes,
plus at least 2 hours marinating
COOKING TIME 20–25 minutes
SERVES 4

FOR THE MARINATED CHICKEN

1 cup (7 fl oz/200 g) plain yogurt

2 tablespoons ginger paste

2 tablespoons garlic paste

1 tablespoon red chili powder

1 tablespoon ground cumin

1 tablespoon ground coriander

1 tablespoon garam masala

½ teaspoon ground turmeric

Juice of 1 lemon

Salt, to taste

1 (3–4-lb/1.3–1.8-kg) whole chicken, skinned and cut into pieces

Canola oil, for brushing

FOR SERVING

Grilled Naan (page 329)

Indian Yogurt Sauce (page 352)

In a large bowl, combine all the ingredients except the chicken and whisk.

Add the chicken and mix well to coat. Cover and refrigerate for 2–24 hours.

Preheat a grill to medium-high heat.

Brush the chicken with oil, then put it on the grill. Cook for 20–25 minutes, until it is slightly charred and the meat reaches an internal temperature of 165°F/74°C. (Alternatively, roast the chicken in a 500°F/260°C tandoori oven for 20 minutes.) Transfer the chicken to a serving platter.

Serve hot with naan and yogurt sauce.

Grilled chicken thighs *(dak)* are slathered in a rich, spicy sauce *(bul,* or "fire") made from *gochujang* and *gochugaru* chili powder to make the Korean street food dish, *buldak*. The saucy chicken is topped with a gooey layer of melted cheese.

PREPARATION TIME 45 minutes,
plus at least 45 minutes marinating
COOKING TIME 40 minutes
SERVES 4–6

½ cup (4 fl oz/120 ml) chicken stock
½ cup (4 fl oz/120 ml) soy sauce
4 tablespoons Korean rice syrup or honey
4 tablespoons Korean chili paste *(gochujang)*
4 tablespoons Korean chili powder *(gochugaru)*
2 tablespoons toasted sesame oil
2 tablespoons vegetable oil
8 large cloves garlic, minced
1 tablespoon grated fresh ginger
2 red bird's eye chiles, stemmed, seeded, and minced
1 tablespoon black pepper
1 cup (8 fl oz/240 ml) lemon-lime soda (drink)
6–7 boneless, skinless chicken thighs
1½ cups (5¾ oz/170 g) shredded low-moisture mozzarella
2 scallions (spring onions), thinly sliced
1 tablespoon toasted sesame seeds

In a large bowl, combine the chicken stock, soy sauce, Korean rice syrup or honey, chili paste, chili powder, and sesame oil. Mix well, then set aside.

Heat the oil in a medium saucepan over medium-high heat. Add the garlic and ginger and sauté for a minute. Add the chiles and black pepper and sauté for another 30 seconds.

Pour in the sauce and soda (drink) and bring to a boil. Reduce the heat to medium-low and simmer for 20 minutes, scraping down the sides of the saucepan with a rubber spatula, until reduced by half. Transfer the sauce to a bowl, then cool to room temperature.

In a large bowl or zip-top bag, combine the chicken and half of the sauce. Cover or seal and refrigerate for at least 45 minutes but, preferably, overnight.

Preheat a grill to high heat.

Place the chicken on the grill and cook for 5 minutes on each side. Brush both sides with the sauce and cook for another 2 minutes on each side.

Set an oven to broil (grill). Transfer the chicken to a baking dish and sprinkle the mozzarella evenly on top. Place the chicken in the oven and broil for 1–2 minutes, until the cheese is fully melted and bubbly. Sprinkle with scallions (spring onions) and sesame seeds.

Serve hot.

Many consider *maqluba*, chicken and caramelized onions served over *taboon* (Palestinian flatbread) to be Palestine's national dish. In this version, the chicken (often roasted in the oven) is grilled for added smokiness and to seal in the juices. Both the chicken and onions are seasoned with sumac and *baharat* (a Middle Eastern spice mixture that includes cumin, paprika, coriander, cloves, nutmeg, cinnamon, and cardamom) and placed on top of warm flatbread, then drizzled with pomegranate molasses.

PREPARATION TIME 20 minutes, plus overnight marinating
COOKING TIME 90 minutes
SERVES 4–6

FOR THE CHICKEN

¼ cup (2 fl oz/60 ml) olive oil
1½ teaspoons salt
1 tablespoon sumac
1 tablespoon minced garlic
1 teaspoon black pepper
1 tablespoon baharat spice mix
Juice of 1 lemon
6 chicken legs (or use a combination of legs and thighs)

FOR THE ONIONS

¾ cup (6 fl oz/175 ml) olive oil
4 yellow onions, diced
2 tablespoons sumac
1 teaspoon ground cumin
1 tablespoon salt
1 teaspoon baharat spice mix
1 tablespoon pomegranate molasses

FOR SERVING

6 pieces Grilled Naan (page 329) or store-bought flatbread
½ cup (½ oz/15 g) chopped parsley
3 tablespoons toasted pine nuts
2 tablespoons pomegranate molasses

FOR THE CHICKEN In a large bowl, combine the olive oil, salt, sumac, minced garlic, black pepper, baharat, and lemon juice. Add the chicken legs to the bowl and rub them with the marinade, including under the skin. Cover and refrigerate overnight.

FOR THE ONIONS Heat the olive oil in a large pot or Dutch oven (casserole) over medium heat. Add the onions and cook for about 10 minutes, stirring occasionally, until soft. Stir in the sumac, cumin, salt, and baharat. Cook for 40–45 minutes, stirring frequently, until the onions are caramelized. Stir in the pomegranate molasses and set aside.

Heat a grill to medium-high heat. Cook the chicken for 20–30 minutes, until the skin is golden brown and the internal temperature of the meat reaches 165°F/74°C. Remove the chicken from the grill to a plate.

Warm the naan on the hot grill and place it on a serving tray. Spread the onions over the bread and place the chicken (and any accumulated juices) on top of the onions. Serve with parsley, pine nuts, and pomegranate molasses.

This tangy and aromatic grilled chicken, or *djej mishweh*, is often considered a Sunday special in Lebanon because of its ubiquitous presence at weekend family gatherings. Bone-in chicken pieces are marinated in a warm spice rub and soaked in acid, garlic, and oil. The tenderized chicken is then grilled—preferably with apple wood because the fruity smoke is a perfect pairing with the marinade's cider vinegar—and served with Lebanese Garlic Sauce (page 352) and pita bread.

PREPARATION TIME 20 minutes,
plus at least 4 hours marinating
COOKING TIME 30–35 minutes
SERVES 4–6

FOR THE SPICE MIX

2 tablespoons ground cinnamon
1 tablespoon salt
1 tablespoon ground allspice
1 tablespoon ground coriander
2 teaspoons black pepper
1½ teaspoons ground cloves
1½ teaspoons ground cumin
1½ teaspoons ground nutmeg

FOR THE CHICKEN

1 (3–4-lb/1.3–1.8-kg) whole chicken, cut into 8 pieces
1 head garlic, cloves peeled and crushed
2 cups (16 fl oz/475 ml) apple cider vinegar
1½ cups (12 fl oz/350 ml) extra-virgin olive oil
1 cup (8 fl oz/240 ml) lemon juice

FOR SERVING

Lebanese Garlic Sauce (page 352)
4–6 pita breads

FOR THE SPICE MIX Combine all the ingredients in a small bowl.

FOR THE CHICKEN Make ½-inch/1-cm incisions all over the chicken. Massage the spice mix into the chicken, then place the chicken in large glass dish. Add the garlic, vinegar, oil, and lemon juice. Cover and refrigerate for at least 4 hours but, preferably, overnight.

Preheat a grill to high heat.

Place the chicken on the grill. Cook, skin side down, for 30–35 minutes, turning occasionally, until cooked through. Transfer to a serving dish.

Serve warm with garlic sauce and pita bread.

This juicy grilled chicken on the bone, marinated in a tomato-based sauce, has roots in Nepal. It is usually served with rice or flatbread, chutney, and salad.

PREPARATION TIME 15 minutes, plus at least 4 hours marinating
COOKING TIME 20 minutes
SERVES 6

1 cup (9 oz/250 g) canned tomatoes
5 cloves garlic, minced
1 tablespoon grated fresh ginger
2 teaspoons ground cumin
2 teaspoons ground coriander
2 teaspoons salt
1 tablespoon lime juice
4 tablespoons vegetable oil
1 (4-lb/1.8-kg) whole chicken, cut into pieces

In a food processor, combine all the ingredients except the oil and chicken. Transfer the paste to a small bowl, then stir in the oil. Rub the marinade into the chicken. Cover and refrigerate for 4–8 hours.

Preheat a grill to high heat.

Place the chicken on the grill and cook for 20 minutes, turning occasionally, until cooked through. Transfer to a serving dish.

Serve warm.

FILIPINO GRILLED CHICKEN

This grilled chicken dish called chicken *inasal*, from the city of Bacolod on Negros, the fourth largest island in the Philippines, uses vinegar, calamansi (Filipino lime), ginger, and lemongrass to season chicken pieces. The dish gets its orange hue from a basting sauce made with achiote oil, which is also poured over the accompanying rice.

PREPARATION TIME 20 minutes,
plus at least 1 hour marinating
COOKING TIME 45–50 minutes
SERVES 4–6

FOR THE CHICKEN
4 tablespoons brown sugar
2 tablespoons salt
1 cup (8 fl oz/240 ml) apple cider vinegar
3 cloves garlic
2 stalks lemongrass, outer leaves removed and chopped
1 (1-inch/2.5-cm) piece fresh ginger, peeled
½ tablespoon black pepper
Juice of 3 lemons
1 (2-lb/900-g) chicken, cut into 12–16 pieces
Steamed rice, to serve

FOR THE CHICKEN-ACHIOTE OIL
1 lb/450 g chicken skin with fat
1 cup (8 fl oz/240 ml) canola oil
4 tablespoons achiote seeds

FOR THE BASTING SAUCE
3 tablespoons chicken achiote oil (see above)
¼ teaspoon salt
5 tablespoons melted butter
1 teaspoon lemon juice

FOR THE CHICKEN In a small bowl, combine the sugar, salt, and vinegar and stir until the sugar and salt have dissolved. Pour the mixture into a food processor, then add the remaining ingredients except the chicken. Pulse for 2–3 minutes.

In a large glass bowl, combine the chicken and marinade. Cover and refrigerate for at least 1 hour but, preferably, overnight.

Preheat a grill to high heat for indirect grilling.

FOR THE CHICKEN-ACHIOTE OIL In a small saucepan, combine the chicken skin and just enough water to cover it. Boil for 15 minutes, or until the oil is rendered and the water has evaporated. Add the oil and cook for 10 minutes, until crispy. Using a slotted spoon, remove the chicken skin and discard.

Add the achiote seeds to the pan and cook for 1–2 minutes. Remove from the heat, then strain the oil.

FOR THE BASTING SAUCE Combine all the ingredients in a medium bowl.

Place the chicken on the grill and cook for 15–20 minutes, basting both sides with the sauce every few minutes, until cooked through. Transfer the grilled chicken to a serving dish, then set aside to rest for 5 minutes.

Serve with steamed rice and the extra chicken-achiote oil.

This dish, *gai yang*, from northeastern Thailand, is the most popular grilled chicken dish in the country (and beloved street food in Bangkok). A whole chicken is marinated in garlic, lemongrass, cilantro (coriander) roots, soy sauce, and fish sauce, then chargrilled. It's often served with sticky rice and the spicy dipping sauce, *nam jim jaew*.

PREPARATION TIME 20 minutes,
plus overnight marinating and at least 1 hour standing
COOKING TIME 50 minutes
SERVES 4–6

FOR THE MARINATED CHICKEN
8 cloves garlic, minced
2 shallots, chopped
1 stalk lemongrass, outer leaves removed and chopped
½ cup (1 oz/25 g) cilantro (coriander) with stems, chopped
4 tablespoons soy sauce
2 tablespoons vegetable oil
2 teaspoons sweet soy sauce or dark soy sauce
2 teaspoons fish sauce
2 tablespoons palm sugar or light brown sugar
1 teaspoon salt
½ teaspoon black pepper
½ teaspoon ground turmeric
1 (5–6-lb/2–3-kg) chicken, butterflied

FOR THE DIPPING SAUCE (NAM JIM JAEW)
1 tablespoon palm sugar or light brown sugar
2 tablespoons fish sauce
1 tablespoon tamarind paste
1 tablespoon toasted sticky rice (*kao khua*), ground (optional)
1 tablespoon chopped cilantro (coriander)
1 tablespoon chopped scallions (spring onions)
2 teaspoons red pepper flakes

FOR SERVING
Sticky rice
Lime wedges

FOR THE MARINATED CHICKEN In a food processor, combine the garlic, shallots, lemongrass, and cilantro (coriander) and blend until it forms a paste. Add the remaining ingredients except the chicken and blend well.

Rub the marinade over the chicken. Cover and refrigerate overnight or, preferably, 12 hours.

FOR THE DIPPING SAUCE Combine the sugar and 1 tablespoon hot water in a large bowl and stir until the sugar is dissolved. Add the remaining ingredients, then set aside.

Set aside the chicken for 1–2 hours to bring to room temperature.

Preheat a grill to high for indirect grilling.

Place the chicken, skin side up, on the cooler side of the grill and cook for 45 minutes, or until the internal temperature of the breast reaches 140°F/60°C. Flip the chicken and place it on the hot side of the grill. Cook for another 3 minutes, until the skin is crispy. Set aside to rest for 5–10 minutes.

Serve warm with sticky rice, the dipping sauce, and lime wedges.

Grilled chicken is a staple across Thailand, but this regional southern dish called *kai kawlae* is distinct by way of its rich curry marinade, made of coconut milk, Southeast Asian spices, lemongrass, tamarind, and ginger. It is continually brushed onto the chicken thighs as they cook, intensifying the flavor while also adding a smoky note.

PREPARATION TIME 30 minutes,
plus 30 minutes marinating
COOKING TIME 15 minutes
SERVES 4–6

FOR THE MARINADE

10 small dried guajillo chiles
5 mild dried chiles
2 teaspoons fennel seeds
1 teaspoon fenugreek seeds
12 cloves garlic, thinly sliced
4 shallots, thinly sliced
3 stalks lemongrass, outer leaves removed and thinly sliced
1 oz/30 g piece galangal, peeled and thinly sliced
1 oz/30 g piece ginger, peeled and thinly sliced
1 teaspoon salt
1 tablespoon Thai shrimp paste
1 tablespoon coconut oil or vegetable oil
3 cups (16 fl oz/475 ml) coconut milk
1 tablespoon tamarind paste

FOR THE CHICKEN

8–12 boneless, skin-on chicken thighs
1 teaspoon ground turmeric
1 teaspoon salt
1 cup (8 fl oz/240 ml) marinade (see above)
4 tablespoons coconut milk
Steamed rice, to serve

FOR THE MARINADE Place the dried chiles in a small saucepan, then add enough water to cover them. Bring to a boil over high heat, then cover and set aside for 15 minutes. Drain, then seed and thinly slice the chiles. Place them in a colander, then set aside to dry for 5 minutes.

Meanwhile, toast the fennel and fenugreek seeds in a small skillet over medium heat for 3 minutes, until fragrant. Transfer to a small bowl.

In the same skillet over medium-high heat, dry-roast the reserved chiles for 10 minutes.

In a food processor, combine the garlic, shallots, lemongrass, galangal, ginger, and salt and blend. Add the toasted spices, chiles, and shrimp paste and blend again until it forms a fine paste.

Combine the oil and paste in a medium saucepan and sauté over medium-high heat for 1 minute. Pour in ½ cup (4 fl oz/120 ml) of coconut milk and the tamarind paste and cook for 5 minutes. Stir in another ½ cup (4 fl oz/120 ml) of coconut milk. Add the remaining 2 cups (16 fl oz/475 ml) of coconut milk. Discard any tamarind seeds or stems, then set aside to cool. Reserve 4 tablespoons of marinade for serving.

FOR THE CHICKEN Preheat a grill to medium heat.

Combine all the ingredients in a large bowl. Set aside to marinate for 30 minutes.

Place the marinated chicken on the grill and cook for 5 minutes, until seared on one side. Flip over, then brush the chicken with some of the remaining marinade. Grill for another 15 minutes, flipping and basting occasionally, until the chicken is fully cooked yet tender.

Transfer the grilled chicken to a serving dish, then drizzle over the reserved marinade.

Serve warm or at room temperature with rice.

FIJI CHICKEN

FIJI

This dish, usually reserved for celebratory events, uses an indigenous method of cooking in an underground oven (or *lovo*). A hole in the ground is lined with coconut husks or banana leaves and heated stones. The food, usually fish or chicken and vegetables (including taro, cassava, and sweet potato) wrapped in banana leaves, along with *palusami* (taro leaves stuffed with onions and coconut cream), is cooked on the hot stones. A simpler, oven-baked version of the dish can be found on the right.

PREPARATION TIME 30 minutes
COOKING TIME 1 hour
SERVES 8

2 (3½-1b/1.6-kg) whole chickens
4 tablespoons sweet soy sauce
Coconut palm fronds
16 taro leaves, stemmed
1 large onion, chopped
1 cup (3½ oz/100 g) unsweetened dried shredded (desiccated) coconut
1 cup (8 fl oz/240 ml) coconut milk
3 taro tubers, chopped
4 sweet potatoes, chopped
2 breadfruits, chopped
Banana leaves

Dig a square hole in the ground, about 2 feet/0.5 meters deep. Fill it with a layer of rounded stones and build a wood fire on top. Once the wood turns to ember, remove the wood but leave the hot stones.

Place the chickens in a large bowl and coat them with the sweet soy sauce.

Lay out two coconut palms on a clean work counter, then place the chickens on the cut end. Braid the individual leaves over the chicken, continuing the braid to the very end of the leaves, past the chicken. Carefully place the wrapped chicken on the hot coals.

Cut out a square of aluminum foil, then layer 4 taro leaves in the center. In a bowl, combine the onion and dried shredded (desiccated) coconut. Add a scoop of the coconut mixture. Add 4 tablespoons of coconut milk, and then carefully fold the taro leaf and wrap it tightly in foil. Repeat with the remaining leaves, onion mixture, and coconut milk.

Place the vegetables, breadfruit, and taro packets on top of the chicken. Cover the food with banana leaves and coconut palm fronds. Cover the banana leaves and palm fronds with dirt. Cook for 1 hour, then slowly uncover to check the internal temperature of the chicken (it should reach 165°F/74°C). When the banana leaves turn yellow-brown, remove from the "oven."

Serve all together on a platter.

OVEN-BAKED FIJI CHICKEN

PREPARATION TIME 30 minutes, plus at least 2 hours marinating
COOKING TIME 3 hours
SERVES 8

1 cup (8 fl oz/240 ml) sweet soy sauce
1 cup (3½ oz/100 g) unsweetened dried shredded (desiccated) coconut
2 cups (16 fl oz/480 ml) coconut milk
2 (3½-1b/1.6-kg) whole chickens, cut into quarters
1 breadfruit, peeled and cut into 1-inch/2.5-cm chunks
4 sweet potatoes, peeled and cut into 1-inch/2.5-cm chunks
4 taro tubers, peeled and cut into 1-inch/2.5-cm chunks
Salt and pepper, to taste
Banana leaves or aluminum foil, for wrapping (optional)

In a large bowl, mix the sweet soy sauce, dried shredded (desiccated) coconut, and coconut milk. Add the chicken pieces to the bowl and coat with the marinade. Cover and refrigerate for at least 2 hours, preferably overnight.

When ready to cook, heat an oven to 325°F/165°C/Gas Mark 3.

In a large bowl, toss the breadfruit, sweet potatoes, and taro tubers with salt and pepper.

Line a large baking dish with banana leaves (or aluminum foil). Place the marinated chicken pieces in the baking dish. Arrange the breadfruit, sweet potatoes, and taro tubers around the chicken. Pour the remaining marinade over the chicken and vegetables.

If using banana leaves, wrap them over the chicken and vegetables to enclose them. If using foil, cover the dish tightly with aluminum foil.

Bake for about 3 hours, or until the chicken is fully cooked and tender and the vegetables are soft.

Carefully remove the banana leaves or foil. Transfer the chicken and vegetables to a serving platter. Serve hot, with some of the coconut sauce spooned over the chicken and vegetables.

BAHAMIAN GRILLED CHICKEN

A Bahamian outdoor celebration is not complete without spicy grilled chicken. Unlike Jerk Chicken (page 222) from Jamaica, this dish has a citrus-forward heat which is cooled with a tangy, creamy sauce. The lime juice both tenderizes the meat and brightens the flavors.

PREPARATION TIME 20 minutes, plus 2¼ hours marinating
COOKING TIME 20–25 minutes
SERVES 4

FOR THE SAUCE

1 cup (9 oz/250 g) sour cream
2 tablespoons lime juice
1 teaspoon smoked paprika
1 teaspoon sugar
½ teaspoon cayenne pepper
¼ teaspoon ground cinnamon
¼ teaspoon ground nutmeg
¼ teaspoon ground allspice

FOR THE CHICKEN

4 bone-in, skin-on chicken breast halves
1 cup (8 fl oz/240 ml) lime juice
4 cloves garlic, minced
2 scallions (spring onions), thinly sliced on the bias
½–2 habaneros, seeded and finely chopped
½ sweet onion, finely chopped
2 tablespoons thyme
1 tablespoon smoked paprika
1 teaspoon salt
1 teaspoon white pepper
1½ tablespoons vegetable oil

FOR THE SAUCE Combine all the ingredients in a large bowl. Cover and refrigerate.

FOR THE CHICKEN Pat the chicken dry. In a medium bowl, combine the chicken and lime juice. Set aside for 15 minutes to marinate. Pour off the lime juice from the chicken and discard.

In a small bowl, combine the remaining ingredients. Add to the chicken, then toss to coat. Cover and refrigerate for 2 hours.

Preheat a grill to high heat.

Place the chicken on the grill and cook for 8–12 minutes. Turn and grill for another 8–12 minutes, until it reaches an internal temperature of 165°F/74°C. Transfer the chicken to a serving dish, then set aside to rest for 5 minutes.

Serve warm with the sauce.

PERUVIAN GRILLED CHICKEN

More than 155 million Peruvian grilled chicken dishes, or *pollos a la brasa*, are consumed annually in Peru. Most are cooked on a rotisserie over wood fires (*brasa* means "ember") and served with a creamy green sauce made with *ají amarillo* (a fruity, mild chile) paste. This recipe uses a grill to cook a butterflied chicken but preserves the traditional flavors and sauce.

PREPARATION TIME 10 minutes
COOKING TIME 50 minutes
SERVES 4–6

1 (3½–4-1b/1.6–1.8-kg) whole chicken, spatchcocked
3 cloves garlic, minced
2 tablespoons ground cumin
2 tablespoons paprika
4 teaspoons salt
1 teaspoon black pepper
2 tablespoons white vinegar
2 tablespoons canola oil
1 cup Ají Amarillo Sauce (page 336), to serve

Preheat a grill to high heat for indirect grilling.

Combine all the ingredients except the chicken in a small bowl and mix well. Rub the paste all over the chicken.

Place the chicken, skin side up, on the cooler side of the grill. Cook for 40 minutes, or until the internal temperature reaches 110°F/43°C. Flip the chicken and cook for another 10 minutes, or until the internal temperature reaches 155°F/68°C.

Serve with a small bowl of ají amarillo sauce.

JERK CHICKEN

Jamaica's most celebrated dish features bone-in chicken or pork marinated in a complex blend of spices and hot peppers and slow-cooked over pimento wood. The dish likely originated with African slaves who escaped Spanish-owned plantations and had to smoke wild hogs underground to stay out of sight. Jerk refers less to a specific seasoning (the spice mix has many variations) and more to a cooking technique. The distinct flavor comes from the smoked leaves and branches of the pimento tree (also known as the "allspice tree").

PREPARATION TIME 15 minutes,
plus at least 1 day marinating and 20 minutes soaking
COOKING TIME 1½ hours
SERVES 4

FOR THE MARINATED CHICKEN

6 Scotch bonnet chiles, stemmed and seeded
3 scallions (spring onions), trimmed and coarsely chopped
2 cloves garlic
4 tablespoons thyme leaves
2 tablespoons strong coffee
1½ tablespoons allspice berries
1½ tablespoons grated fresh ginger
2 teaspoons salt
1 teaspoon coriander seeds
¼ teaspoon ground cinnamon
Pinch of freshly grated nutmeg
¾ cup (6 fl oz/175 ml) vegetable oil
2 tablespoons distilled white vinegar
1 tablespoon dark Jamaican rum
1½ teaspoons molasses
1 (3–4-lb/1.4–1.8-kg) whole chicken, quartered
Pimento wood chips, and leaves, for smoking

FOR SERVING

Lime wedges
Hot sauce

FOR THE MARINATED CHICKEN In a food processor, combine all the ingredients except the chicken and pulse until blended. Reserve a quarter of the marinade for serving and refrigerate until needed.

In a large bowl or zip-top bag, combine the chicken and the remaining marinade. Cover or seal and refrigerate for 1–2 days.

Soak the pimento wood chips and leaves in separate bowls of water for 20 minutes.

Preheat a grill to medium-high heat for indirect grilling.

Spread out the soaked pimento leaves in a single layer, then add the soaked chips in another layer on top. Place the chicken, skin side up, on the leaves. Cover and cook for 1¼ hours, or until the chicken skin is charred and the internal temperature reaches 155°F/68°C. Transfer the chicken to a serving dish.

Serve warm with lime wedges, hot sauce, and the reserved marinade on the side.

This popular Hawaiian dish originated in 1955 when a Honolulu businessman grilled chicken that he had marinated in his mother's teriyaki sauce. He named the dish *huli-huli* (or "turned turned") because he grilled the chicken between two racks, which he continuously turned. These days, most cooks use a rotisserie to flip the whole (or cut up) chicken. A combination of flavors—sweet (often ketchup), salty (soy sauce), and tangy (in this case, pineapple juice and rice wine vinegar)—creates that distinctive sweet-smoky aroma that wafts up from roadside stands, food carts, and restaurants across the Hawaiian Islands.

PREPARATION TIME 20 minutes,
plus at least 1 hour marinating
COOKING TIME 1 hour
SERVES 4

FOR THE BRINE

2 cups (16 fl oz/475 ml) soy sauce

1 tablespoon canola oil

5 cloves garlic, minced

1 tablespoon grated fresh ginger

4 chicken halves, split

FOR THE GLAZE

2 cloves garlic, minced

2 tablespoons brown sugar

1 tablespoon grated fresh ginger

¾ cup (6 fl oz/175 ml) pineapple juice

2 tablespoons soy sauce

2 tablespoons ketchup

2 tablespoons rice vinegar

2 teaspoons Sriracha

FOR THE BRINE In a large bowl, combine the soy sauce and 8½ cups (68 fl oz/2 liters) cold water.

Heat the oil in a small saucepan over medium-high heat. Add the garlic and ginger and sauté for 30 seconds until fragrant. Add the garlic and ginger to the diluted soy sauce and stir. Add the chicken, cover, and refrigerate for 1–8 hours.

FOR THE GLAZE Combine all the ingredients in a medium saucepan and bring to a boil. Reduce the heat to medium-low and simmer for 30 minutes.

Preheat a grill to high heat for indirect grilling.

Pat dry the marinated chicken. Cook for 15 minutes, skin side up, on the cooler side of the grill. Flip the chicken and cook for another 15 minutes, or until the skin turns crispy. Flip again and brush the chicken with the glaze. Transfer the chicken to a serving dish, then set aside to rest for 10 minutes.

Serve warm.

More Tex-Mex than authentic Mexican, fajitas are usually served on a sizzling platter with grilled meats and peppers, plus sour cream, guacamole, and tortillas. The word "fajita" comes from the Spanish word *faja*, or "belt," because the original fajita, which likely came from the cattle ranches of west Texas and northern Mexico, used skirt steak, which is long and thin like a belt. This simple recipe uses grilled chicken breasts and vegetables sautéed on the grill.

PREPARATION TIME 15 minutes, plus 30 minutes marinating
COOKING TIME 15–20 minutes
SERVES 4

FOR THE MARINATED CHICKEN

⅓ cup (¾ oz/20 g) coarsely chopped cilantro (coriander)

3 cloves garlic, minced

1 teaspoon ground cumin

1 teaspoon brown sugar

½ teaspoon salt

5 tablespoons olive oil

4 tablespoons lime juice

3 boneless, skinless chicken breasts

FOR THE PEPPERS

1 red bell pepper, seeded, deveined, and cut into ¼-inch/5-mm strips

1 green bell pepper, seeded, deveined, and cut into ¼-inch/5-mm strips

1 white onion, cut into ¼-inch/5-mm strips

1 tablespoon salt

½ cup (4 fl oz/120 ml) olive oil

FOR SERVING

1 cup (9 oz/250 g) sour cream

8 tortillas

FOR THE MARINATED CHICKEN In a small bowl, combine all the ingredients except the chicken. Place the chicken in a large zip-top bag and pound each piece to a ½ inch/1 cm thickness. Add the marinade and mix well to coat the chicken. Refrigerate for 30 minutes.

Preheat a grill to high heat.

Place the chicken on the grill and cook for 3–5 minutes on each side, until brown and cooked through. Set the chicken aside to rest for 10 minutes. (Keep the grill on high heat.)

FOR THE PEPPERS Preheat a cast-iron skillet on the grill over medium-high heat.

In a bowl, combine the peppers, onion, salt, and oil and toss to coat. Place the peppers and onions on the grill and sauté for 5–10 minutes, until the peppers are softened.

Slice the chicken into strips, then transfer the chicken and vegetables to a serving dish and serve with warm tortillas and sour cream.

YUCATECAN GRILLED CHICKEN

This popular and vibrant dish from the Yucatan, *pollo asado*, uses citrus, spices, and smoke to make grilled chicken soar, while the sweet and peppery achiote gives a beautiful red hue. Feel free to use bone-in thighs, but boneless thighs are easier to cut and/or shred, allowing the meat to be enveloped by warm tortillas and pickled onions.

PREPARATION TIME 20 minutes, plus at least 4 hours marinating
COOKING TIME 25 minutes
SERVES 6

FOR THE MARINATED CHICKEN

4 cloves garlic, minced
2½ tablespoons achiote powder
1 teaspoon dried oregano
1 teaspoon ground cumin
1 teaspoon paprika
1 teaspoon salt
½ teaspoon black pepper
2 tablespoons vegetable oil
Juice of 3 oranges
Juice of 2 limes
12 boneless, skinless chicken thighs

FOR SERVING

Pickled Onions (page 297)
12 corn tortillas

In a large bowl, combine all the ingredients except the chicken and mix well.

In a large bowl or zip-top bag, combine the chicken and marinade. Cover or seal and refrigerate for at least 4 hours but, preferably, overnight.

Preheat a grill to medium-high heat for indirect grilling.

Place the chicken directly over the hot side of the grill and cook for 3–5 minutes on each side. Move the chicken to the cooler side of the grill and cook for another 10–15 minutes, until it reaches an internal temperature of 165°F/74°C. Transfer the chicken to a serving dish, then set aside to rest for 3–5 minutes.

Serve warm with pickled red onions and tortillas.

HALF CHICKEN

This recipe starts with whole chickens (cut in half), which are fairly inexpensive and smoke quickly. Plus, keeping the meat on the bone helps retain moisture. The rub acts as a penetrating, dry brine, and, because the chicken skin can get rubbery after it's smoked, the grill helps the skin crisp up while sealing in the flavor.

PREPARATION TIME 20 minutes,
plus at least 2 hours refrigeration
COOKING TIME 2¼ hours
SERVES 4–6

2 (3-lb/1.4-kg) whole chickens (roasters),
split in half through the backbone
1 cup (7 oz/200 g) Pork and Poultry Rub (page 358)
1 cup (8 fl oz/240 ml) Texas Table Sauce (page 335) or Alabama White Sauce (page 353)
Oak, pecan, cherry, or apple wood, for smoking

Lay the split chickens, skin side down, on a baking sheet. Season the underside with the rub, then set aside for 5 minutes. Flip the chicken and season the skin side with the rub. Leave uncovered and refrigerate for at least 2 hours but, preferably, overnight.

Preheat a smoker to 250°F/120°C.

Bring the chicken to room temperature. Place it in the smoker and close the lid. Smoke for 1½–2 hours, until the chicken reaches an internal temperature of 155°F/68°C.

After the chicken has been on the smoker for 1 hour, preheat a grill to medium-high heat. Once the chicken reaches the correct temperature, transfer it to the grill, skin side up. Brush it all over with Texas table sauce. (If using Alabama white sauce, brush only after it's finished grilling.) Flip the chicken and grill for 5–10 minutes, until it reaches an internal temperature of 160°F/71°C. Set it aside to rest for 10 minutes. If using Alabama sauce, brush it all over the chicken.

Serve the chicken in halves or cut them between the breast/wing and the thigh/drumstick.

You'll find these juicy, sticky, charred wings at Singapore's hawker centers (or food courts), where there's usually at least one vendor flipping them over a charcoal grill. The chicken wings are marinated in dark soy sauce, oyster sauce, and garlic, then served with a spicy dipping sauce made of chiles and lime.

PREPARATION TIME 10 minutes, plus overnight marinating
COOKING TIME 20–25 minutes
SERVES 4

FOR THE MARINATED CHICKEN

½ cup (4 fl oz/120 ml) soy sauce

4 tablespoons dark soy sauce

4 tablespoons oyster sauce

2 tablespoons sesame oil

2 tablespoons dried basil

1 tablespoon garlic powder

1 teaspoon onion powder

1 teaspoon black pepper

24 whole chicken wings

FOR THE HOT SAUCE

6 red bird's eye chiles

2 cloves garlic

2 tablespoons grated fresh ginger

1 teaspoon sugar

¼ teaspoon salt

½ cup (4 fl oz/120 ml) hot chicken stock

1 teaspoon calamansi (Filipino lime) juice or lime juice

FOR THE MARINATED CHICKEN In a large bowl, combine all the ingredients except the chicken. Add the chicken and mix well to coat. Cover and refrigerate overnight.

FOR THE HOT SAUCE In a food processor, combine the chiles, garlic, ginger, sugar, and salt. Blend until it forms a paste, then transfer the paste to a medium bowl. Stir in the hot stock, then add the juice.

Preheat a grill to medium-high heat.

Place the wings on the grill and cook for 8–12 minutes on each side, until cooked through and slightly charred.

Transfer the wings to a serving dish and serve with the hot sauce.

The benefits of this smoke-then-fry method are twofold. Not only do the crispy wings gain a delicious smokiness, the smoking of the wings prior to frying them takes the guesswork out of cooking chicken to the correct temperature. If you don't want to fry, finish the wings in a 400°F/200°C/Gas Mark 6 oven.

PREPARATION TIME 10 minutes
COOKING TIME 35 minutes
SERVES 4–6

2 cups (14 oz/400 g) Pork and Poultry Rub (page 358)

4 lb/1.8 kg whole chicken wings

Vegetable or canola oil, for deep-frying

1 cup (8 fl oz/240 ml) Chili-Lime Wing Sauce (page 335) or Alabama White Sauce (page 353)

Oak or cherry wood, for smoking

Preheat a smoker for indirect low heat.

Place the rub in a large bowl. Dredge the chicken wings in the rub, then place them on a baking sheet or, preferably, a perforated pan. Grill or smoke for 30 minutes, or until the internal temperature of the wings reaches 155°F/68°C.

Heat the oil in a deep-fryer or deep saucepan to 350°F/180°C. Carefully lower the wings into the hot oil and deep-fry for 3–4 minutes, until crispy. Using a spider or slotted spoon, transfer the wings to a paper towel–lined plate to drain for 30 seconds.

In a large bowl, combine the wings and sauce and toss to coat. Serve immediately.

In this traditional North African dish, a whole chicken, flavored with the Moroccan spice blend ras el hanout, cumin, chili, and garlic, is smoked and then combined with sautéed vegetables and potatoes. The combined chicken, vegetable, and potato mixture is then smoked again to produce a deeply flavored stew with fall-off-the-bone chicken. It's typically served with a bowl of steaming couscous.

PREPARATION TIME 45 minutes
COOKING TIME 3 hours
SERVES 6

FOR THE CHICKEN

4 tablespoons ras el hanout
2 tablespoons salt
1 teaspoon lemon zest
½ teaspoon chili powder
½ teaspoon ground ginger
½ teaspoon ground cumin
½ teaspoon garlic granules
½ teaspoon onion powder
½ teaspoon brown sugar
1 (4-lb/1.8-kg) whole chicken
Apple wood, for smoking

FOR THE VEGETABLES

1 tablespoon butter
6 pearl onions
6 cloves garlic
½ cup (4¼ oz/120 g) baby carrots
2–3 potatoes, cut into ½-inch/1-cm cubes
3 tablespoons chicken stock

FOR SERVING

2 tablespoons finely chopped parsley
1 tablespoon finely chopped cilantro (coriander)
1 teaspoon finely chopped mint
4 tablespoons Greek yogurt
Couscous

Preheat a smoker with apple wood to 250°F/120°C.

FOR THE CHICKEN In a bowl or large zip-top bag, combine all the ingredients except the chicken. Add the chicken and toss to coat. Place the chicken in the smoker and smoke for 2 hours, until a crust forms.

FOR THE VEGETABLES Melt the butter in a cast-iron skillet over medium-high heat. Add the onions, garlic, and baby carrots and sauté for 7–10 minutes, until brown. Transfer to a small plate. Add the potatoes and sauté for 10–15 minutes, until brown.

In a Dutch oven (casserole), arrange the sautéed vegetables and chicken stock in an even layer. Top with the chicken, then cover and place in the smoker. Smoke for 1 hour, or until the chicken reaches an internal temperature of 165°F/74°C.

Transfer the chicken and vegetables to a serving dish. Garnish with herbs and yogurt. Serve hot with couscous.

SMOKED CHICKEN WITH ROOT VEGETABLES

Jordanian *zarb* (or Bedouin barbecue) is an ancient nomadic technique in which the food is cooked for hours—usually in a metal rack or bin buried in the ground. The ingredients (often sheep or chicken plus root vegetables) are seasoned and piled into a container buried in a hole on top of embers. The hole is filled with sand and, hours later, the unearthed dish has meat so tender it practically falls off the bone. The following recipe provides an option for making this dish in the oven.

PREPARATION TIME 20 minutes,
plus at least 2 hours refrigeration
COOKING TIME 1½ hours
SERVES 6

1 (4-lb/1.8-kg) whole chicken, cut into parts,
or 8 large thighs
4 carrots, cut into 2½-inch/6-cm pieces
4 potatoes, cut into wedges
2 onions, quartered
3 tablespoons vegetable oil
2 tablespoons salt
1 teaspoon black pepper
2 teaspoons ground cumin
1 teaspoon ground allspice

Combine all the ingredients in a large bowl and mix well. Cover and refrigerate for at least 2 hours but, preferably, overnight.

Use a charcoal grill or smoker to heat 2 cups of coals. Dig a hole in sandy soil and insert a large stockpot. Replace the soil around the pot, leaving only the top edge sticking out.

Place the hot coals into the pot and set a rack over the coals. Layer the chicken and vegetables over the rack and cover the pot. Lay a tarp or large blanket over the pot to retain the heat. Cook for 1½ hours, or until the internal temperature of the chicken reaches 165°F/74°C.

Alternatively, preheat an oven to 300°F/150°C/ Gas Mark 2. Transfer the vegetables and chicken to a large roasting pan. Cover the pan tightly with aluminum foil and cook for 3–4 hours, until the chicken is tender and the vegetables are soft. Remove the foil, then increase the oven heat to 400°F/200°C/ Gas Mark 6. Roast for 15 minutes to brown the top.

Transfer the chicken and vegetables to a serving dish and serve warm.

In Quechua (a language of Indigenous Peruvians), *pachamanca* (which means "earth-pot") is an ancient spiritual ritual intended to show respect for the earth. A brick-lined hole in the ground is filled with hot volcanic rocks. Potatoes and meat, marinated in a mixture of garlic, salt, and herbs (including the Peruvian herb *huacatay*), are piled in. A layer of damp banana leaves covers the food to help build steam. Then fava (broad) beans, corn on the cob, and sweet tamales are added. Hours later, an entire meal is unearthed and enjoyed. This recipe, which uses corn husks to create layers and steam, simplifies the dish for home cooks.

PREPARATION TIME 30 minutes, plus 2 hours marinating
COOKING TIME 1 hour
SERVES 8

FOR THE MARINATED MEAT
½ cup (1 oz/30 g) chopped mint
½ cup (1 oz/30 g) chopped cilantro (coriander)
½ cup (1 oz/30 g) chopped parsley
½ teaspoon salt
½ teaspoon black pepper
½ teaspoon ground cumin
½ teaspoon dried oregano
½ cup (4 fl oz/120 ml) vegetable oil
1 tablespoon red wine vinegar
4 teaspoons garlic paste
2 teaspoons ají panca paste or
1 teaspoon Ají Amarillo Paste (page 336)
1 (12-oz/350-g) pork shoulder, cut into thirds
3 skin-on, bone-in chicken thighs

FOR THE VEGETABLES
24 corn husks, plus extra if needed
3 potatoes, halved
2 sweet potatoes, cut into thirds
1½ cups (9 oz/250 g) cooked hominy
1½ cups (12 fl oz/350 ml) vegetable stock
4–6 tablespoons vegetable oil

FOR THE MARINATED MEAT In a food processor or blender, combine all the ingredients except the pork and chicken and blend until smooth. Place the pork and chicken in a bowl, then pour over half of the marinade. Cover and refrigerate for 2 hours.

Heat a large saucepan over medium-high heat. Add the pork and sear on all sides for 5–10 minutes. Transfer the pork to a plate, then set aside.

FOR THE VEGETABLES Arrange a layer of corn husks along the bottom of the same pan. Add the pork and cover with another layer of corn husks. Repeat this with the chicken, then add a final layer of potatoes, sweet potatoes, and hominy. Pour the remaining marinade over the vegetables, then cover them with more corn husks.

Pour in the stock, then cover pan with a round piece of parchment paper. Cover with the lid and cook over low heat for 1 hour, or until the meat is cooked through and the vegetables are tender.

Serve hot.

Brined and smoked whole turkey breast packs a delicious punch and delivers moist, delicate meat that, when sliced, can make a hearty sandwich. Don't forgo the brining or air-drying—the (mostly passive) time is well worth it. Allowing the turkey to dry for at least 12 hours improves the skin or coating of the proteins on the meat's surface and, thus, creates a stronger outer layer for smoking. (This is known as the pellicle.)

PREPARATION TIME 40 minutes,
plus at least 12 hours brining and 12 hours drying
COOKING TIME 2–2½ hours
SERVES 8–12

3–4 bay leaves

1 head garlic, unpeeled and split in half

Bunch of rosemary

Bunch of thyme

2 cups (15½ oz/440 g) brown sugar

1 cup (5 oz/140 g) salt

½ cup (3½ oz/100 g) black peppercorns

1 tablespoon red pepper flakes

8½ cups (68 fl oz/2 L) apple cider

2–3 skin-on, boneless turkey breasts

1 cup (7 oz/200 g) Pork and Poultry Rub (page 358)

Oak, cherry, or apple wood, for smoking

In a large stockpot, combine all the ingredients except the turkey and poultry rub. Pour in 1 gallon/3.8 L water and bring to a boil. Turn off the heat, then add 8½ cups (68 fl oz/2 L) of ice water to the pot to cool the brine temperature. Once the brine is cold, add the turkey to the pot and submerge. Cover and refrigerate for 12–24 hours.

Set a wire cooling rack over a baking sheet. Using tongs, transfer the turkey breasts onto the rack. Refrigerate for 12–24 hours to dry the skin.

Preheat a smoker to 250°F/120°C.

Bring the turkey to room temperature. Pat the turkey dry with paper towels and season it with the rub. Place the turkey in the smoker, skin side up, and smoke for 1 hour. Check the temperature of the turkey to gauge where it is in the cooking process. Smoke for another 1–1½ hours, until it reaches an internal temperature of 155°F/68°C. Set the turkey aside to rest for 20 minutes, or until the internal temperature reaches 165°F/74°C.

To serve, slice the turkey or make a sandwich.

SMOKED TURKEY LEGS

Although meaty drumsticks with their built-in handles conjure medieval royalty, smoked turkey legs have exploded in popularity during the last couple of decades. In this recipe, the legs are brined to add flavor and texture, smoked, and then caramelized with barbecue sauce on a grill. If feeding a large group, be sure to prepare two days in advance of the occasion.

PREPARATION TIME 20 minutes,
plus at least 12 hours brining
COOKING TIME 2½–3 hours
SERVES 4–6

3–4 bay leaves

1 head garlic, unpeeled and split in half

Bunch of rosemary

Bunch of thyme

2 cups (15½ oz/440 g) brown sugar

1 cup (5 oz/140 g) salt

½ cup (3½ oz/100 g) black peppercorns

1 tablespoon red pepper flakes

8½ cups (68 fl oz/2 L) apple cider

4–6 whole turkey legs

2 cups (14 oz/400 g) Pork and Poultry Rub (page 358)

2 cups (16 fl oz/475 ml) Texas Table Sauce (page 335), to serve

Oak or cherry wood, for smoking

In a large stockpot, combine all the ingredients except the turkey and poultry rub and bring to a boil. Turn off the heat, then add 8½ cups (68 fl oz/2 L) of ice water to the pot to cool the brine temperature. Once the brine is cold, add the turkey to the pot and submerge. Cover and refrigerate for 12–24 hours.

Preheat a smoker to 250°F/120°C.

Pat the turkey dry with paper towels and season it with the rub. Place the turkey in the smoker and smoke for 1 hour. Gauge the temperature of the turkey. Smoke for another 1–1½ hours, until it reaches an internal temperature of 155–160°F/68–71°C.

Meanwhile, preheat a grill over high heat. Place the cooked turkey legs on the grill and cook for 10 minutes, brushing them with the sauce, until caramelized and the internal temperature reaches 165°F/74°C.

MAINS

TURKEY PASTRAMI

Turkey pastrami is a leaner take on the Jewish deli favorite that's typically made from brisket (page 122). Turkey breasts are brined for one day or more, then rubbed with a blend of classic pastrami spices and smoked to bring out the flavor. Slice and serve on rye with spicy brown mustard and pickles.

PREPARATION TIME 30 minutes, plus overnight brining
COOKING TIME 3 hours
SERVES 6–8

FOR THE TURKEY

6 sprigs thyme

4 bay leaves

1 head garlic, cloves separated and crushed

½ cup (3¾ oz/110 g) brown sugar

½ cup (2½ oz/70 g) salt

½ cup (2¼ oz/60 g) black peppercorns

½ cup (1¾ oz/50 g) cracked juniper berries

1 teaspoon red pepper flakes

1 (4–6-lb/1.8–3-kg) whole turkey breast

Oak or cherry wood, for smoking

FOR THE RUB

4 tablespoons juniper berries

4 tablespoons garlic powder

4 tablespoons black peppercorns

4 tablespoons brown sugar

2 tablespoons mustard seeds

1 teaspoon red pepper flakes

FOR THE TURKEY Combine all the ingredients except the turkey in a stockpot. Pour in 3 cups (25 fl oz/750 ml) of water, then warm over medium-high heat until the sugar and salt have dissolved. Set aside, then add 3 cups (25 fl oz/750 ml) of ice water to the pot to cool the brine temperature. Once the brine is cold, add the turkey to the pot and submerge. Cover and refrigerate overnight.

FOR THE RUB Combine all the ingredients in a spice grinder and grind to a fine powder. Apply the rub liberally to the turkey. Place on a tray with a rack and refrigerate overnight.

Preheat a smoker with oak or cherry wood to 250°F/120°C.

Pat the turkey dry with paper towels. Place the turkey in the smoker and smoke for 2–3 hours, until it reaches an internal temperature of 160°F/71°C.

Remove the turkey from the smoker and tent with aluminum foil, until ready to serve.

Thinly slice against the grain, arrange on a serving dish, and serve immediately.

Zhangcha duck, a quintessential Sichuan dish, is made by smoking a marinated duck with tea leaves and twigs from the camphor plant. It's not an easy dish—the duck is smoked plus marinated, boiled, roasted, and fried—which is why Zhangcha duck is more often found at banquets than at dinner tables. If you can't find camphor wood, use ground edible camphor crystals, which release the same traditional flavors.

PREPARATION TIME 30 minutes,
plus overnight marinating and 2 hours drying
COOKING TIME 1 hour 50 minutes
SERVES 6

FOR THE MARINATED DUCK

1 tablespoon ginger paste
1 tablespoon salt
1 teaspoon Sichuan pepper powder
½ teaspoon ground star anise
1 (5-lb/2.25-kg) duckling
2 tablespoons sesame oil
1 tablespoon Shaoxing wine

FOR THE DIPPING SAUCE

4 teaspoons peanut oil
2 teaspoons sweet bean paste
2 teaspoons sugar

FOR COOKING AND SERVING

4 tablespoons camphor wood
2 tablespoons lapsang souchong tea leaves
2 tablespoons jasmine tea leaves
8½ cups (68 fl oz/2 L) peanut oil
20–30 scallions (spring onions),
cut into 2-inch/5-cm pieces, to serve

FOR THE MARINATED DUCK In a small skillet, combine the ginger paste, salt, Sichuan powder, and ground star anise. Cook for 3–5 minutes, until fragrant. Set aside to cool. Divide the mixture in half.

Rub half of the mixture inside and outside of the duckling. In a small bowl, combine the other half of the mixture, the sesame oil, and wine together. Massage the marinade into the duckling. Leave the duckling, uncovered, and refrigerate overnight.

Bring a large saucepan of water to a boil. Briefly plunge the duckling into the water, then remove and towel dry. Set aside the duckling to dry at room temperature for 2 hours, until the skin is tight.

FOR THE DIPPING SAUCE Heat the peanut oil in a small skillet over medium-high heat. Add the sweet bean paste, sugar, and 2 teaspoons of water, and cook for 5 minutes. Transfer to a small bowl.

Preheat an oven to 400°F/200°C/Gas Mark 6.

Set a wire rack over a baking sheet. Place the duckling on the prepared rack and roast for 1 hour.

Meanwhile, preheat a smoker with the wood and tea leaves to 225°F/107°C. Place the duckling in the smoker and smoke the duckling for 30 minutes to infuse the flavors.

Heat the peanut oil in a large wok or deep saucepan to 380°F/193°C. Carefully lower the duckling into the hot oil and fry for 8 minutes, turning frequently, until the skin is crispy. Transfer the duckling to a paper towel–lined plate to drain. Cut into bite-size pieces and arrange In a serving dish.

Serve warm with the dipping sauce and scallions (spring onions).

Mufete de peixe is a popular Angolan dish often served at family gatherings and celebrations. A whole fish, like tilapia, is seasoned with acid, onions, and spices and then grilled. It's served on a large platter with palm oil beans (*feijão de óleo de palma*), boiled plantains, sweet potatoes, and cassava.

PREPARATION TIME 15 minutes, plus 30 minutes marinating
COOKING TIME 50 minutes
SERVES 4

FOR THE VEGETABLES

3 sweet potatoes, chopped
1 cassava, chopped
Salt

FOR THE BEANS

3 tablespoons olive oil
1 onion, finely chopped
1 clove garlic, minced
2 (14-oz/400-g) cans lima (butter) beans

FOR THE ONION SALAD

1 green bell pepper, seeded, deveined, and finely chopped
½ onion, finely chopped
4 tablespoons extra-virgin olive oil
2 tablespoons white wine vinegar

FOR THE FISH

5 cloves garlic
1 malagueta chile, seeded and minced
1 teaspoon salt
2 lb/900 g tilapia fillets
2 tablespoons white vinegar
1 tablespoon olive oil, for brushing

FOR THE VEGETABLES Bring a large saucepan of salted water to a boil. Add the sweet potatoes and cassava and simmer for 10–15 minutes, until softened. Drain, then set aside.

FOR THE BEANS Heat the oil in a large skillet over medium heat. Add the onion and garlic and sauté for 5 minutes. Add the beans and pan-fry for 10 minutes. Pour in ½ cup (4 fl oz/120 ml) of water and cook for another 10 minutes, or until softened. Season to taste with salt.

FOR THE ONION SALAD Combine all the ingredients in a medium bowl and toss well.

FOR THE FISH In a food processor, or with a mortar and pestle, combine the garlic, chile, and salt and blend until it forms a paste. Rub the paste over the fish, sprinkle the vinegar on top, and set aside to marinate at room temperature for 30 minutes.

Preheat a grill to high heat.

Brush the fish with the oil. Add the fish to the grill and cook for 5–7 minutes on each side until cooked through. (If desired, use a fish grill basket to prevent the fish from sticking to the grill.) Transfer the fish to a large serving dish.

Arrange the onion salad, beans, and vegetables around the fish. Serve.

Samak mashwi, a traditional party dish often served during Ramadan, is a whole fish (head on, eyes removed) seasoned with Middle Eastern spices, rolled in farina (semolina), and grilled. It's served with pickles, mayonnaise, olives, parsley, and peppers.

PREPARATION TIME 15 minutes, plus 30 minutes marinating
COOKING TIME 30 minutes
SERVES 6

FOR THE FISH

2 teaspoons ground cumin	
2 teaspoons ground coriander	
1 teaspoon chili powder	
1 teaspoon paprika	
½ teaspoon ground turmeric	
1 teaspoon white vinegar	
Juice of 1½ lemons	
2 (2.5-lb/1-kg) striped bass, sea bass, or red snapper, cleaned	
1 cup (6 oz/180 g) farina (semolina)	
1 tablespoon salt	

FOR GARNISHING

Sliced pickles	
Sliced green and black olives	
Sliced roasted red peppers	
Chopped parsley	
Mayonnaise	

FOR THE FISH Preheat a grill to medium-high heat.

In a food processor, combine the cumin, coriander, chili powder, paprika, turmeric, vinegar, and lemon juice to make the marinade.

Make 3 slits on each side of the fish, then rub the marinade over the fish, stuffing some of it into the incisions and the belly. Refrigerate for at least 30 minutes.

Put the farina and salt into a shallow bowl, then dredge the fish until coated. Place the fish on the grill and cook for 10–15 minutes on each side, until cooked through and golden. (If desired, use a fish grill basket to prevent the fish from sticking to the grill.)

Transfer the fish to a serving dish and garnish with pickles, olives, peppers and parsley. Serve immediately with mayonnaise on the side.

The popular Thai dish *pla pao* transforms a simple fish into a symphonic meal. Stuffed with the aromatics lemongrass and makrut lime leaves and coated in salt, a whole fish is grilled over charcoal until the skin slides off to reveal moist and smoky fillets—which are best served with a spicy dipping sauce and Thai sticky rice.

PREPARATION TIME 15 minutes
COOKING TIME 25 minutes
SERVES 2–4

2 (1½–2-lb/680–900-g) white fish, such as snapper or trout, cleaned
10 makrut lime leaves
4–6 stalks lemongrass, bruised
2 cups (1 lb 1 oz/480 g) salt
2 tablespoons all-purpose (plain) flour

FOR SERVING
Thai Dipping Sauce (page 338)
Steamed rice

Preheat a grill to low heat.

Stuff each fish with the makrut lime leaves and lemongrass, folding the stalks in half if necessary.

In a large bowl, combine the salt, flour, and 3 tablespoons of water. Stir until fully mixed and moist. Pat and rub the fish with the salt mixture, making sure to cover the entire fish.

Add the fish to the grill and cook for 25 minutes, or until firm and the white salted skin has turned crusty and golden. (If desired, use a fish grill basket to prevent the fish from sticking to the grill.) Transfer to a serving dish.

Using a knife or scissors, cut through the skin from the head to the tail. Serve with Thai dipping sauce and rice.

Pepes ikan, a traditional Indonesian dish (also popular in Malaysia) that varies slightly among regions, usually features a whole fish rubbed with a rich spice paste, wrapped in a banana leaf, and grilled over charcoal. The banana leaf seals in the moisture and keeps the fish from sticking to the grill.

PREPARATION TIME 25 minutes
COOKING TIME 30 minutes
SERVES 4–6

FOR THE SPICE PASTE

6 red bird's eye chiles, seeded and chopped
5 shallots, chopped
5 macadamia nuts, coarsely chopped
3 cloves garlic, minced
1 large tomato, chopped
1 (¼-inch/5-mm) slice fresh ginger, peeled
2 teaspoons salt, plus extra to taste
1 teaspoon ground turmeric
1 teaspoon tamarind pulp
1 teaspoon sugar, plus extra to taste
4 makrut lime leaves, thinly sliced
1 stalk lemongrass, outer leaves removed and thinly sliced
1 (¼-inch/5-mm) slice galangal, peeled

FOR THE FISH

3 banana leaves
2 (2-lb/900-g) whole snapper or tilapia, cleaned, or 4–6 white fish fillets

FOR THE SPICE PASTE In a food processor, combine all the ingredients except the makrut lime leaves, lemongrass, and galangal. Blend until smooth. Transfer the mixture to a large bowl. Stir in the lemongrass, makrut lime, and galangal. Season to taste with salt and sugar.

FOR THE FISH Soak the banana leaves in hot water for 10 minutes.

Preheat a grill to high heat.

Remove the banana leaves from the water, then wipe with paper towels to remove any dirt. Add 2 tablespoons of paste to the center of each leaf. Top with a whole fish (or 2 fillets), then spread another 2 tablespoons of paste over the fish and inside their cavities. Fold the leaf around the fish to make a packet and secure the ends with toothpicks. In a large steamer, steam the fish packets for 20 minutes.

Transfer the steamed fish packets to the grill and cook for 5 minutes on each side, or until cooked through. Transfer the packets to a large platter, then carefully open the leaves to reveal the cooked fish. Serve immediately.

Ikan bakar is a popular street food in both Malaysia and Indonesia. Although the sambal-seasoned fish is often fried at food stalls in outdoor markets, this version uses white fish marinated in a spicy and aromatic sambal, then grilled over banana leaves.

PREPARATION TIME 20 minutes,
plus at least 2 hours marinating
COOKING TIME 10 minutes
SERVES 4

FOR THE SAMBAL MARINADE

1 teaspoon *belacan* (Malaysian shrimp paste), finely chopped

2 red bird's eye chiles

4 shallots, coarsely chopped

1 large onion, coarsely chopped

2 stalks lemongrass, outer leaves removed and finely chopped

4 cloves garlic, coarsely chopped

1 (1-inch/2.5-cm) piece fresh ginger, minced

1 (1-inch/2.5-cm) piece galangal, peeled and finely chopped

2 teaspoons ground turmeric

2 tablespoons coconut oil

2 tablespoons lime juice

⅓ cup (2¾ fl oz/80 ml) sweet soy sauce

FOR THE FISH

4 fillets firm white fish, such as snapper, skate, grouper, or tilapla

1 tablespoon salt

4–6 large banana leaves

½ cup (4 fl oz/120 ml) canola oil

FOR SERVING

½ cup (4 fl oz/120 ml) sambal oelek

1 lime, cut into wedges

FOR THE SAMBAL MARINADE Preheat an oven to 450°F/230°C/Gas Mark 8. Line a baking sheet with parchment paper.

Spread out the belacan on the prepared baking sheet and roast for 2 minutes, or until the edges start to brown. Set aside to cool.

Combine all the ingredients in a blender or food processor and blend until it forms a smooth paste. If the mixture seems dry, add a teaspoon of water at a time. Transfer the paste to a large bowl.

FOR THE FISH Pat the fish dry with paper towels, then sprinkle with the salt. Place the fillets in the bowl of marinade and toss to coat. Cover and refrigerate for at least 2 hours or, preferably, overnight.

Preheat a grill to medium heat. Line the grill with 2 layers of banana leaves, trimming leaves that are too large to fit.

Arrange the fish fillets in rows over the banana leaves. Drizzle 1 tablespoon of oil over each fillet and grill for 5 minutes. Flip, then drizzle another 1 tablespoon of oil over each fillet and grill for 5 minutes, until charred and slightly crispy. Transfer to a serving dish.

Serve immediately with sambal oelek and lime wedges.

This popular Greek dish proves that lemon juice, good olive oil, and a smattering of fresh herbs can transform a fresh fish into a spectacular dish. The most commonly grilled fish in Greece is branzino, which is native to western and southern Europe, as well as northern Africa, and has a delicate, slightly sweet taste. It's fine, however, to substitute another small white fish (like sea bass or sea bream), or to use fillets.

PREPARATION TIME 5 minutes
COOKING TIME 15 minutes
SERVES 4–6

4 (1½–2-lb/680–900-g) whole sea bass
or sea bream, cleaned
¾ cup (6 fl oz/175 ml) olive oil
4 tablespoons lemon juice
2 teaspoons chopped parsley
1 tablespoon chopped oregano
Salt and black pepper

Preheat a grill to medium-high heat.

Season the fish outside and inside with salt and pepper. Brush each with ½ tablespoon of oil. Place the fish on the grill and cook for 6 minutes on each side, turning occasionally, until cooked through. (If desired, use a fish grill basket to prevent the fish from sticking to the grill.)

Meanwhile, in a small bowl, combine the remaining olive oil, the lemon juice, parsley, and oregano. Season with salt and pepper.

Transfer the fish to a serving platter, then drizzle over the dressing. Serve immediately.

EMIRATI GRILLED FISH

Seafood is a significant part of the cuisine of the United Arab Emirates. This simple grilled fish is flavored with citrus, ginger, and lemongrass. Although the recipe calls for a butterflied sea bream, feel free to use fillets from any small white fish.

COOKING TIME 15 minutes, plus 30 minutes marinating
PREPARATION TIME 20 minutes
SERVES 2–4

½ small onion, chopped

3 tablespoons grated fresh ginger

1½ tablespoons saffron threads

1 tablespoon chopped mild green chiles

1 tablespoon chopped lemongrass

½ teaspoon salt, plus extra to taste

¼ cup ice

½ cup (4 fl oz/120 ml) vegetable oil

⅓ cup (2¾ fl oz/80 ml) orange juice

3 tablespoons lemon juice

2 (1½–2-lb/680–900-g) whole sea bream,
butterflied (ask your fishmonger)

In a blender or food processor, combine all the ingredients except the sea bream and blend to form a smooth paste.

With a sharp knife, cut small slits in the fish skin. Season with salt. Brush the marinade over both sides of the fish, reserving the rest for later use. Set aside to marinate for 30 minutes.

Meanwhile, preheat a grill to 400°F/200°C.

Place the fish, skin side down, on the grill and cook for 8–10 minutes. (If desired, use a fish grill basket to prevent the fish from sticking to the grill.) Brush with the marinade. Flip, then cook for another 8–10 minutes.

Transfer to a serving dish and serve immediately.

Iraq's national dish, *masgouf* (meaning "covered" in Arabic), features a butterflied carp covered in a spicy tomato-based sauce, which is grilled over hot coals. This recipe substitutes fillets of any white fish (such as flounder, tilapia, or snapper) and uses a grill basket or perforated pan to prevent the coated fish from sticking to the grates while it absorbs the smoky flavor.

PREPARATION TIME 15 minutes, plus 30 minutes marinating
COOKING TIME 30 minutes
SERVES 2

FOR THE FISH

1 lb/450 g white fish fillets
1 teaspoon salt
1 teaspoon curry powder
1 tomato, thinly sliced
½ onion, thinly sliced
Steamed rice, to serve

FOR THE SAUCE

3 tablespoons vegetable oil
½ onion, chopped
2 cloves garlic, minced
1 tomato, chopped
1½ cups (3¼ oz/90 g) chopped parsley
⅓ cup (2¾ oz/80 g) tomato paste (purée)
1 teaspoon salt
1 teaspoon curry powder
½ teaspoon cayenne pepper
2 tablespoons red wine vinegar
2 tablespoons lemon juice

FOR THE FISH Rub the fish fillets with a teaspoon each of salt and curry powder. Place the fish on a plate, cover, and refrigerate for 30 minutes.

Preheat a grill to high heat.

FOR THE SAUCE Heat the oil in a large skillet over medium-high heat. Add the onion and garlic and sauté for 7 minutes, or until the onion is translucent. Add the remaining ingredients and simmer for 10 minutes. Set aside to cool.

Remove the fish from the refrigerator and cover it with the cooled tomato sauce. Arrange the tomato and onion on top. Slide the fish into a fish grill basket and grill for 5 minutes on each side, until cooked through.

Transfer to a serving dish and serve immediately with rice.

SPANISH
GRILLED SARDINES

GF DF NF 5 ◖ ◎

Espetos de sardinas—whole, fresh sardines skewered on sharpened sugar cane and roasted over an open (traditionally olive wood) fire—is a dish so popular in the Spanish coastal city of Málaga (especially at summer beach bars) that the city erected a statue in its honor. The salty snack, made on metal or bamboo skewers over a grill, is ideally eaten straight from the fire—no forks necessary.

PREPARATION TIME 5 minutes, plus 30 minutes soaking
COOKING TIME 10 minutes
SERVES 4–6

24 small sardines, cleaned but not gutted or filleted
2 tablespoons salt

Preheat a grill to medium heat.
  Soak the sardines in ice water for 30 minutes.
  Insert a skewer through the belly and under the spine of a sardine. Repeat with 5 more on the same skewer, ensuring the sardines all face the same direction. Salt the sardines well on both sides.
  Place the sardine skewers, spine side down, on the grill and cook for 3–4 minutes on each side, until golden brown. Transfer to a serving dish and serve immediately.

PORTUGUESE
GRILLED SARDINES

GF DF NF ◖ ◎

Portugal's grilled sardine dish is zestier than the Spanish version (see left). The sardines are flavored with herbs and spices and usually some heat, then served with thick slices of crusty bread to absorb the savory juices.

PREPARATION TIME 10 minutes,
plus at least 3 hours marinating
COOKING TIME 10 minutes
SERVES 4

4 sprigs rosemary, leaves only and bruised
3 cloves garlic, sliced
2 tablespoons olive oil, plus extra for drizzling
1 red bird's eye chile, seeded and finely chopped
1 tablespoon smoked paprika, plus extra for sprinkling
Zest of ½ lemon
8 sardines, cleaned
Lemon wedges, to serve

In a small bowl, combine all the ingredients except the sardines. Pour the marinade into a baking dish, then add the sardines and toss. Cover and chill for 3 hours.
  Preheat a grill to high heat.
  Place the sardines on the grill and cook for 4–5 minutes on each side until charred. Transfer to a serving dish, drizzle with oil, and sprinkle with paprika.
  Serve immediately with the lemon wedges.

This dish from the Yucatan called *tikin xic* (meaning "dry fish") is a whole fish marinated in achiote paste and guajillo chiles, wrapped in banana leaves, and grilled. It is traditionally cooked in an underground oven lined with volcanic rocks, but this simpler version uses fish fillets cooked on a charcoal or gas grill.

PREPARATION TIME 20 minutes,
plus at least 1 hour marinating
COOKING TIME 10 minutes
SERVES 6

6 (6-oz/170-g) boneless white fish fillets, such as red snapper, grouper, or branzino

1 teaspoon coarse sea salt

¼ teaspoon black pepper

2 guajillo chiles, stemmed and seeded

½ cup (4 fl oz/120 ml) orange juice

½ cup (4 fl oz/120 ml) lime juice

2 tablespoons white vinegar

¾ cup (5 oz/140 g) achiote paste

4 tablespoons coarsely chopped onion

6 cloves garlic

4 cloves, stems removed

¼ teaspoon ground allspice

1 tablespoon vegetable oil

2 large banana leaves

FOR SERVING

6 warm flour or corn tortillas

Grilled Pineapple Salsa (page 338) or Pico de Gallo (page 339)

Pickled Onions (page 297)

Place the fish fillets in a glass dish and season with the salt and pepper.

Toast the guajillo chiles in a skillet for 3–5 minutes over medium-high heat. Cover with water and simmer over medium heat for 15 minutes.

In a blender, combine the rehydrated chiles with 2 tablespoons of their cooking liquid, the orange juice, lime juice, vinegar, achiote paste, onion, garlic, cloves, allspice, and oil. Blend until smooth. Pour the marinade over the dish, then cover and refrigerate for 1–12 hours.

Preheat a grill to medium heat for indirect grilling.

Cut the banana leaves into 12-inch/30-cm squares. Make 6 in total. Place the fish in the center of each square. Fold over the sides to cover the fish, then tie kitchen string around the packages to keep them closed.

Grill the fish packages for 3–4 minutes on each side, until the leaves are charred. Transfer the fish to the cooler side and cook until the internal temperature of the fish reaches 140°F/60°C.

Serve immediately with warm tortillas, salsa, and pickled onions.

PORTUGUESE GRILLED OCTOPUS

In *polvo grelhado*, a Portuguese seafood dish, fresh octopus is tenderized with a braise (traditionally, it was wrapped in sackcloth and beaten with a stick) and then grilled to form a smoky crust. The final product gets a kick from a parsley and garlic sauce—ideally made with the freshest garlic you can find.

PREPARATION TIME 15 minutes, plus 30 minutes standing
COOKING TIME 2¼ hours
SERVES 4

FOR THE PARSLEY-GARLIC SAUCE

½ cup (4 fl oz/120 ml) olive oil
2 sprigs parsley, finely chopped
4 cloves garlic, finely chopped
Salt and black pepper

FOR THE OCTOPUS

1 (6 lb 8-oz/3-kg) octopus, cleaned
2 tablespoons olive oil, for brushing
Salt and black pepper
1 lemon, cut into wedges, to serve

FOR THE PARSLEY-GARLIC SAUCE Combine all the ingredients in a medium bowl and mix well. Set aside at room temperature for 30 minutes.

FOR THE OCTOPUS Preheat an oven to 250°F/120°C/Gas Mark ½.

Bring 7½ cups (60 fl oz/1.75 L) of water to a boil in a stockpot. Carefully lower the octopus into the pot and blanch for 2 minutes. Using tongs, transfer the octopus to a Dutch oven (casserole). Cover and roast in the oven for 2 hours, or until the octopus is tender. Remove the octopus from the pan, then set aside to cool.

Preheat a grill to high heat.

Brush the octopus with oil, then place it on the grill and char all over for 10 minutes. Transfer the octopus to a serving dish, drizzle with the sauce, and season with salt and pepper. Mix well, then cut the octopus into pieces and serve with lemon wedges.

SPANISH GRILLED OCTOPUS

This dish starts with octopus that is softened and then grilled with olive oil. Unlike the Galician-style octopus tapas, which are only boiled or braised, this recipe adds brief, high heat to crisp the cooked octopus's exterior. The result is a succulent and smoky main course, often served with roasted potatoes and salad.

PREPARATION TIME 15 minutes
COOKING TIME 1 hour 40 minutes
SERVES 4

1 bay leaf
4 tablespoons salt
1 tablespoon black peppercorns
1 (5½-lb/2.5-kg) octopus (fresh or frozen), cleaned
3–4 Yukon Gold potatoes
3 tablespoons olive oil
1 tablespoon lemon juice
1 teaspoon flaky sea salt, for sprinkling
¼ teaspoon paprika, for sprinkling
Parsley leaves, for sprinkling

Bring 7½ cups (60 fl oz/1.75 L) of water to a boil in a stockpot. Add the bay leaf, salt, and peppercorns. Carefully lower the octopus into the pot, then reduce the heat to low and simmer for about 1 hour, until almost tender.

Preheat a grill to high heat.

Add the whole potatoes and cook for another 25 minutes, until both the potatoes and octopus are tender. Drain. Separate the tentacles and cut the head in half.

When cool enough to handle, slice the potatoes about ¼ inch/5 mm thick.

Brush the octopus with oil. Place the octopus on the grill and cook, turning often, for about 4 minutes, until lightly charred. Transfer the octopus and potatoes to a large serving dish.

Drizzle with lemon juice, then sprinkle with flaky sea salt, paprika, and parsley. Serve immediately.

GRILLED SQUID WITH FISH SAUCE

A favorite roadside treat in Thailand, *pla muek yang* consists of grilled squid covered in a spicy, tangy sauce—made with lime juice, fish sauce, garlic, chiles, and sugar—and then topped with peanuts and cilantro (coriander).

PREPARATION TIME 15 minutes
COOKING TIME 10 minutes
SERVES 4

FOR THE SAUCE
10 cloves garlic, coarsely chopped
6 green bird's eye chiles, stemmed, seeded, and coarsely chopped
½ cup (3½ oz/100 g) brown sugar
4 tablespoons fish sauce
4 tablespoons lime juice

FOR THE SQUID
2 lb/900 g squid tubes and tentacles, cleaned
1 teaspoon salt
½ teaspoon black pepper
2 tablespoons canola oil

FOR GARNISHING
4 tablespoons chopped peanuts
½ cup (1 oz/30 g) chopped cilantro (coriander)

FOR THE SAUCE Combine the garlic and chiles in a food processor and blend to form a paste. Add the brown sugar and process until the sugar has dissolved. Stir in the fish sauce and lime juice and process again for 10 seconds.

FOR THE SQUID Preheat a grill to medium-high heat.
Make several shallow 1-inch/2.5-cm-long cuts along the squid tubes, taking care not to cut through them. Season with the salt and pepper, then brush the squid with oil. Place the squid tube and tentacles on the grill and cook for 6–8 minutes, until charred. Transfer the squid tubes to a cutting board, then cut into rings.
Place the squid in a serving dish. Drizzle with the sauce and garnish with peanuts and cilantro (coriander). Serve immediately.

CEDAR PLANK SALMON

CANADA

This dish, popular in Canada and the Pacific Northwest, comes from the Indigenous peoples, who tied a whole salmon to a plank of sacred Western red cedar and stood it vertically next to a fire pit. The more modern interpretation is a salmon fillet marinated in spices or a mixture of mustard and maple syrup, then cooked on a hot cedar plank to absorb the smokiness and moisture of the wood.

PREPARATION TIME 15 minutes
COOKING TIME 15 minutes
SERVES 6

1 large untreated cedar plank,
soaked in water for at least 12 hours before using
1 cup (5¾ oz/170 g) coarse salt
6 (4-oz/115-g) salmon fillets
½ cup (4 fl oz/120 ml) olive oil
1 large red onion, chopped
1 lemon, thinly sliced
½ tablespoon black peppercorns, crushed

Preheat a grill to high heat.

Place the cedar plank on the hot grill. Sprinkle the plank with some of the coarse salt, then close the grill lid and heat for 3 minutes. Reduce the grill temperature to medium.

Coat the salmon in oil and generously sprinkle with the remaining salt. Place the fillets on the plank, then top with the onion, lemon, and peppercorns. Cook for 10–12 minutes, until the salmon is flaky and cooked through.

MAPLE-SMOKED SALMON

Smoked salmon is popular in many cuisines, from Alaska to Norway, but this version, which uses the aromatic sweetness of maple syrup to complement the richness of salmon, is distinctly Canadian. Plan ahead because the fish needs to marinate for 24 hours.

PREPARATION TIME 10 minutes, plus 24 hours marinating
COOKING TIME 1 hour 35 minutes
SERVES 4

4 (5-oz/140-g) skinless salmon fillets
1 cup (8 fl oz/240 ml) maple syrup
2 teaspoons sea salt
1 teaspoon black pepper
2 tablespoons butter
Oak or apple wood, for smoking

Combine the fillets and maple syrup in a shallow baking dish and mix well to evenly coat the fillets. Sprinkle the salt and pepper over both sides of the fish. Cover and refrigerate for 24 hours.

Preheat a smoker to 200°F/93°C.

Place the fillets in the smoker and smoke for 1½ hours.

Melt the butter in a small skillet over medium heat. Add the fillets and cook for 2 minutes on each side to create a rich glaze. Transfer to a serving dish.

Serve warm or cold. The smoked salmon will keep in the refrigerator for 1 week.

SMOKED WHITEFISH

Eastern European Jews brought smoked whitefish to the United States in the late 1800s. The smoking was originally used as a preservation method. Now that whitefish is smoked and salted for flavor rather than preservation, it tends to be less salty and more delicate than the original version.

PREPARATION TIME 10 minutes,
plus at least 4 hours marinating and 2 hours refrigeration
COOKING TIME 2 hours
SERVES 4

½ cup (2½ oz/70 g) salt
½ cup (3¾ oz/110 g) brown sugar
1 tablespoon black peppercorns
1 teaspoon onion salt
1 teaspoon granulated garlic
½ cup (4 fl oz/120 ml) soy sauce
4 skinless whitefish fillets
Cherry or apple wood, for smoking

In a large bowl, combine all the ingredients except the fish. Pour in 8½ cups (68 fl oz/2 L) cool water, then add the fish. Cover and refrigerate for 4–12 hours.

Rinse the fish fillets under cold running water. Place them on a plate and refrigerate for 2 hours.

Preheat a smoker to 200°F/93°C.

Place the fish in the smoker and smoke for 2 hours. Transfer to a serving dish, then set aside to cool.

Serve cold.

CLAMBAKE

The traditional clambake uses a shallow hole in the sand, where a fire is built using wood and hot stones. The food is cooked on a hot grate between layers of seaweed and covered with a seawater-soaked tarp. The seaweed and seawater produce salty steam to cook the seafood, sausage, potatoes, and corn. If you don't have access to a fire pit, use the grilled adaptation of this recipe on the right.

PREPARATION TIME 20 minutes
COOKING TIME 1 hour
SERVES 8

FOR THE BAKE

10–15 lb/4.5–7 kg rockweed seaweed
4 lb/1.8 kg new potatoes
8 ears of corn, with husks
4 lb/1.8 kg kielbasa, cut into 1-inch/2.5-cm pieces
8 dozen cherrystone or littleneck clams, cleaned

FOR THE HERB BUTTER

1 cup (8 oz/225 g) butter, softened
½ cup (½ oz/15 g) grated Parmesan
½ cup (1 oz/30 g) finely chopped parsley
Salt and black pepper

FOR THE BAKE Dig a hole into the ground, about 2–3 feet/60–90 cm deep. Use stones and wood to create a fire in the pit. Secure a grate on top of the pit. Place a layer of seaweed across the grate, then layer with the potatoes. Repeat this process for the corn, kielbasa, and clams, separating each layer with a layer of seaweed. Cover with burlap or a tarp soaked in water. (Pour room-temperature water over the tarp to keep it wet.) Cook for 1 hour, until the potatoes are tender.

FOR THE HERB BUTTER Combine all the herb butter ingredients in a medium bowl and mix well.

Transfer all the food except the corn onto a large serving dish. Remove the husks from the corn, then brush with the herb butter. Add them to the dish and serve hot.

GRILLED CLAMBAKE

PREPARATION TIME 25 minutes
COOKING TIME 30 minutes
SERVES 8

1½ cups (12 oz/350 g) butter
2 tablespoons Old Bay seasoning, plus extra for sprinkling
2 baguettes, each cut into 8 slices
4 ears of corn, shucked
28 oz/800 g kielbasa
2 lb/900 g large shrimp (prawns), peeled and deveined
24 oz/700 g new potatoes, thinly sliced
2 small red onions, cut into ½-inch/1-cm-thick pieces
48 littleneck clams (about 4 lb/1.8 kg), cleaned
1½ cups (12 fl oz/350 ml) white wine
4 tablespoons lemon juice
2 cloves garlic, minced
Salt and black pepper, to taste
Lemon wedges, to serve

Preheat a grill to medium-high heat.

Melt the butter in a small saucepan over medium heat. Stir in the Old Bay seasoning. Brush 6 tablespoons of the butter mixture across all the baguette slices, then place them on a baking sheet.

Brush the corn and kielbasa with 6 tablespoons of the melted butter, then add them to the baking sheet. Toss the shrimp (prawns) with 6 tablespoons of the butter mixture, then add them to the same sheet. Reserve the remaining melted butter mixture.

Cut 6 (25-inch/63-cm) lengths of aluminum foil. Place one sheet on top of another, perpendicularly, to form a cross. Place the potatoes, onions, and clams in the center, then season with salt and pepper. Fold the sides of the aluminum foil inwards to create a bowl. Add the wine, lemon juice, garlic, and the remaining 6 tablespoons of the melted butter. Tightly seal the foil packet, then wrap the remaining piece of foil around it.

Place the foil packet, corn, and kielbasa on the grill. Cook for 15–20 minutes, flipping the corn and kielbasa, until they are charred. Add the shrimp and sauté for 5 minutes. Add the baguette and grill for 1 minute, until toasted.

Cut each ear of corn into 4 pieces and slice the kielbasa diagonally. Divide the shrimp, corn, kielbasa, potatoes, and clams among 8 bowls. Add the sauce and sprinkle with Old Bay. Serve with lemon wedges and the grilled baguette.

"Paella," the Catalan word for "skillet," is a traditional Valencian rice dish made in a shallow pan over a fire fueled by orange and pine branches. The short-grain rice, which turns yellow from the saffron, develops a crispy layer (called *socarrat*) at the bottom of the pan. Paella was originally made with rabbit, green beans, and tomatoes but evolved in regions closer to the coast to include seafood and other fresh vegetables.

PREPARATION TIME 20 minutes
COOKING TIME 40–45 minutes
SERVES 6

2 tomatoes, cored and halved
16 large shrimp (prawns), peeled and deveined
1 teaspoon smoked paprika
8 boneless, skinless chicken thighs, cut into 1-inch/2.5-cm pieces
8 oz/225 g Spanish chorizo, thinly sliced
2 tablespoons olive oil
1 onion, chopped
2 cloves garlic, chopped
1 teaspoon saffron threads
2 cups (15 oz/425 g) bomba or Valencia rice
4 cups (32 fl oz/960 ml) chicken stock
18 mussels, cleaned
2 tablespoons chopped parsley
Salt and black pepper, to taste
2 lemons, cut into 8 wedges each, to serve

Preheat a grill to high heat (450°F/230°C).

Using a box grater, grate the flesh side of the tomatoes over a medium bowl.

In a separate bowl, combine the shrimp (prawns) and ¼ teaspoon of the smoked paprika. Season with salt and pepper. Toss.

Place the chicken in another bowl and season with salt and pepper.

Place a large paella pan or a large cast-iron skillet on the grill. Close the grill lid and heat for 2 minutes. Add the chorizo and sauté for 3 minutes, or until the fat has rendered. Transfer the chorizo to a large bowl.

Add the chicken. Close the grill lid and cook, opening the lid and stirring occasionally, for 6 minutes. Add the chicken to the bowl with the chorizo.

Add the olive oil and onion to the pan, then season with salt and pepper. Cook, stirring occasionally, about 5 minutes. Add the garlic, the remaining ¾ teaspoon paprika, and the saffron and sauté for 30 seconds.

Stir in the tomato pulp and juice and cook for 3 minutes, or until the mixture has darkened. Add the rice and 2 teaspoons of salt and stir. Pour in the stock, stirring so that the rice mixture is in an even layer.

Add the chorizo and chicken to the pan and spread them out over the rice. Close the grill lid and simmer for 10 minutes, checking occasionally, until the rice has absorbed most of the liquid. Rotate the pan every few minutes to distribute the heat.

Add the shrimp and mussels. Close the grill lid and cook for another 10–12 minutes, until the mussels have opened and the shrimp are just cooked through. Discard any unopened mussels.

Remove the pan from the grill, cover with aluminum foil, and set aside for 5 minutes.

Sprinkle parsley over the paella and serve warm with lemon wedges.

Grilled cabbage is a favorite dish in Australia, where it is often made with a savory, sticky yeast-based spread called Vegemite. (The British version is known as Marmite.) This rich dish, studded with bacon and dressed with a tangy vinaigrette, is a delicious and unique addition to any barbecue spread.

PREPARATION TIME 10 minutes
COOKING TIME 20–30 minutes
SERVES 4

FOR THE DRESSING

2½ tablespoons Vegemite or Marmite
2 tablespoons red wine vinegar
3 egg yolks
1 cup (8 fl oz/240 ml) canola oil

FOR THE CABBAGE

1 green cabbage, quartered
1 tablespoon canola oil
7 slices (rashers) smoked bacon or pancetta, cut into ¼-inch/5-mm cubes
7 oz/200 g goat cheese
1 tablespoon plain yogurt

Preheat a grill to medium heat.

FOR THE DRESSING In a medium bowl, whisk together the Vegemite, vinegar, and egg yolks. Continue to whisk the mixture, slowly drizzling in the oil until the dressing is emulsified. Whisk in 3–4 tablespoons of cold water.

FOR THE CABBAGE Bring a large saucepan of salted water to a boil. Add the cabbage and cook for 30 seconds. Remove and pat dry.

Place the cabbage on the grill and cook for 10 minutes, turning occasionally, until the surface is charred on all sides. Wrap the cabbage in aluminum foil and cook for another 5–10 minutes.

Heat the oil in a skillet over high heat. Add the bacon and sauté for 5–10 minutes, until crisp. Transfer to a paper towel–lined plate.

In a small bowl, combine the goat cheese and yogurt and mix until smooth.

Unwrap the foil around the cabbage and discard any black outer leaves. Place the cabbage in a serving dish, spoon the goat cheese mixture between the layers, and then sprinkle with the bacon. Drizzle the dressing over the cabbage.

Serve at room temperature.

GRILLED LEEKS WITH ROMESCO SAUCE

V · VG · DF

Catalonia hosts an annual outdoor barbecue festival called Calçotada, where recently harvested scallions (spring onions) called *calçots* are served with Spanish romesco sauce. This iconic Spanish dish is replicated here with steamed and grilled leeks.

PREPARATION TIME 20 minutes, plus 15 minutes soaking
COOKING TIME 25 minutes
SERVES 4–6

FOR THE ROMESCO SAUCE

1 small ancho chile, seeded
3 tablespoons hazelnuts
1 slice white toast, cut into 1-inch/2.5-cm pieces
1 clove garlic, chopped
3 tablespoons roasted almonds, coarsely chopped
2 plum tomatoes, peeled, seeded, and coarsely chopped
1 roasted red pepper, cut into 1-inch/2.5-cm pieces
2 teaspoons sherry vinegar
4 tablespoons extra-virgin olive oil
1 tablespoon chopped parsley
Salt and black pepper

FOR THE LEEKS

6 fat leeks or 12 baby leeks, white and light green parts only
2 tablespoons extra-virgin olive oil
Salt and black pepper

Preheat an oven to 350°F/180°C/Gas Mark 4. Preheat a grill to medium heat.

FOR THE ROMESCO SAUCE In a small bowl, combine the chile and enough hot water to cover it. Soak for 15 minutes, then drain.

Place the hazelnuts on a baking sheet and roast for 10 minutes, or until lightly browned. Set aside to cool, then use a dish towel to rub them and remove the skins. Coarsely chop.

In a food processor, combine the drained chile, hazelnuts, toast, garlic, and almonds. Blend until it forms a smooth paste. Add the tomatoes, red pepper, and vinegar and purée again. With the machine still running, slowly pour in the oil.

Pour the sauce into a small bowl, then stir in the parsley. Season with salt and pepper.

FOR THE LEEKS Add 1 inch/2.5 cm of water to the bottom of a double boiler and bring to a boil. Cut the leeks lengthwise into quarters, then rinse well under cold running water. Place the leeks in the top pan and steam for 10 minutes.

In a bowl, combine the leeks, olive oil, salt, and pepper. Place the leeks on the grill and lightly char for 5 minutes. Transfer to a serving dish.

Serve warm with romesco sauce.

Any eggplant (aubergine)—globe, Italian, Japanese—can be used to make this unique Vietnamese dish called *ca nuong*. Vietnamese cooks use small clay charcoal-fired braziers, but a standard grill works well to char and soften the meaty eggplant, which is then shredded and topped with scallion (spring onion) oil and a fiery fish sauce.

PREPARATION TIME 10 minutes
COOKING TIME 20 minutes
SERVES 4–6

2 large eggplants (aubergines)
3 tablespoons fish sauce
2 cloves garlic, minced
2 chiles, minced
3 tablespoons canola oil
1 scallion (spring onion), thinly sliced

Preheat a grill to medium-high heat.

Pierce the eggplants (aubergines) all over with a fork. Place them on the grill and cook for 15 minutes, turning occasionally, until charred all over. Set aside to cool, then remove the skin and cut the flesh into thin strips.

Meanwhile, in a small bowl, combine the fish sauce, garlic, and chiles. Whisk well.

Heat the oil in a small skillet over high heat until it smokes. Set the skillet aside, then add the scallion (spring onion) and stir.

Arrange the eggplant strips on a serving dish, drizzle with the scallion oil, and top with the fish sauce mixture.

GRILLED EGGPLANT WITH TAHINI

Grilling transforms a whole eggplant (aubergine) into a smoky, creamy dip with its own crispy-skin bowl. A staple in Levantine cuisine, this dish takes very little effort and creates a colorful and elegant side dish or first course. Nutty tahini and a splattering of herbs (and hot sauce, if you like spiciness) add depth and complexity to this simple concept.

PREPARATION TIME 10 minutes
COOKING TIME 10–15 minutes
SERVES 2–4

FOR THE TAHINI SAUCE

¾ cup (6 fl oz/175 ml) tahini
2 cloves garlic, minced
1 teaspoon salt
¼ teaspoon ground cumin
Juice of 1 lemon

FOR THE EGGPLANT

1 large eggplant (aubergine)
½ teaspoon salt
4 tablespoons chopped parsley
1 tablespoon harissa paste (optional)

FOR SERVING

Pita bread

Preheat a grill to medium-high heat.

FOR THE TAHINI SAUCE Combine all the ingredients in a medium bowl. Add ½ cup (4 fl oz/120 ml) ice water and mix well. Season to taste with salt.

FOR THE EGGPLANT Place the eggplant (aubergine) on the grill and cook for 10–15 minutes, turning occasionally, until the eggplant is blackened and soft. Transfer it to a platter, then cut it open lengthwise. Flatten it against the plate with a spoon. Season the flesh with the salt. Drizzle over the tahini sauce, then sprinkle with parsley. Add the harissa paste, if desired.

Serve with pita for dipping.

RATATOUILLE

V VG GF DF NF

Ratatouille is a rustic vegetable stew from southern France, typically made with eggplant (aubergine), zucchini (courgettes), summer squash, onions, and tomatoes. The vegetables are often slow-cooked together until they practically melt. In this bright, acidic version, which pairs beautifully with smoked or grilled meat, the vegetables are charred over high heat.

PREPARATION TIME 30 minutes
COOKING TIME 30 minutes
SERVES 4–6

3 red onions, sliced into ½-inch/1-cm rings

3 zucchini (courgettes), sliced in half lengthwise

2 yellow summer squash, sliced in half lengthwise

1 head garlic, cloves separated, peeled, and chopped

2 teaspoons salt

6 tablespoons extra-virgin olive oil

2 Japanese eggplants (aubergines), sliced in half lengthwise

1 lb/450 g cherry tomatoes

Bunch of oregano, leaves picked and coarsely chopped

Red pepper flakes, to taste

Balsamic or sherry vinegar (optional)

Black pepper, to taste

Preheat a grill to high heat.

Place the red onions on the grill and cook for 10 minutes, or until they are softened and charred on both sides. Set aside to cool.

Meanwhile, in a large bowl, combine the zucchini (courgettes), summer squash, one-third of the garlic, 1 teaspoon salt, pepper, and 2 tablespoons of oil. Place the zucchini and summer squash on the grill and cook for 10–15 minutes, until softened and charred. Set aside to cool.

In a large bowl, combine the eggplant (aubergine), one-third of the garlic, 1 teaspoon salt, and pepper. Grill the eggplant in the same way as the zucchini and summer squash. Remove the eggplant from the grill and reserve. Set aside to cool.

In a medium bowl, combine the cherry tomatoes, the remaining one-third of garlic, salt, and pepper. Grill the tomatoes (on a perforated pan, if possible) for 5–10 minutes, until they burst. Transfer them into a large bowl. Once all the grilled vegetables except the tomatoes are cool enough to handle, cut them into ½-inch/1-cm cubes.

In a bowl, combine the cut vegetables and grilled tomatoes. Season with salt, pepper, oregano, red pepper flakes, and a splash of vinegar (if using).

Serve warm or at room temperature.

GRILLED YUCA WITH MOJO SAUCE

V VG GF DF NF

Yuca *con mojo* is a popular Cuban dish that starts with boiled or softened yuca (a potato-like root vegetable also called cassava or manioc). The yuca is cut into strips, seasoned with a garlic-herb marinade, and grilled until crispy. It's a tasty appetizer or side dish for any barbecue meal.

PREPARATION TIME 15 minutes
COOKING TIME 40 minutes
SERVES 6

3 tablespoons minced onion

3 cloves garlic, crushed

3 tablespoons minced parsley

3 tablespoons minced cilantro (coriander)

2 tablespoons hot sauce

6 tablespoons red wine vinegar

Scant ½ cup (4½ fl oz/130 ml) canola oil

5 lb/2.25 kg yuca, peeled

Salt and black pepper, to taste

Preheat a grill to high heat for indirect grilling.

In a large bowl, combine all the ingredients except the yuca and mix well.

Bring a large saucepan of salted water to a boil over high heat. Add the yuca and boil for 15–20 minutes, until fork tender. Cut the yuca into strips.

Generously brush the yuca with the mojo sauce, covering all sides. Place the yuca on the cooler side of the grill and cook for 20 minutes, or until crispy. Add salt and pepper to taste. Transfer the yuca to a serving dish.

Serve the crispy yuca with a small bowl of mojo sauce for dipping.

COAL-ROASTED VEGETABLES

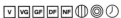

This ratatouille-like vegetable dish, *escalivada*, originated with Catalan shepherds who made fires in the morning to stay warm. As the fires died out, they would add vegetables to the embers. (The Catalan word *escalivar* means "coal roasting.") The vegetables would slowly tenderize in time for dinner, at which point they would be tossed with local olive oil. While modern cooks often use an oven to re-create this dish, coal-roasting on a charcoal grill is a tastier method.

PREPARATION TIME 5 minutes
COOKING TIME At least 2 hours
SERVES 4–6

1 eggplant (aubergine)
1 large red bell pepper
1 small onion, unpeeled
½ cup (4 fl oz/120 ml) extra-virgin olive oil
2 tablespoons chopped parsley leaves
Salt and black pepper, to taste

Preheat a charcoal grill to high heat until the coals are white.

In a large bowl, combine the eggplant (aubergine), bell pepper, onion, and 4 tablespoons of oil. Season with salt and pepper. Wrap each vegetable individually in aluminum foil.

Place the foil-wrapped vegetables directly onto the coals. Cook for 2 hours (and up to 12 hours).

Remove the vegetables from the coals, unwrap them, and discard the skins and seeds. Roughly chop the vegetables.

In a large bowl, combine the vegetables with the remaining 4 tablespoons of olive oil and the parsley. Season to taste with salt and pepper.

A popular component of the South African *braai* (or barbecue) is grilled cheese sandwiches. The *braaibroodjie*, however, is very different from what's served at American diners. Garlicky sautéed veggies and sweet chutney elevate the sandwich and make it a perfect companion to the *braai*'s other guests: grilled meats, South African Relish (page 350), and Piri-Piri Sauce (page 348). You can use any sweet chutney, although mango is the traditional choice.

PREPARATION TIME 10 minutes
COOKING TIME 10 minutes
SERVES 2

FOR THE VEGETABLES

1 tablespoon canola oil
1 yellow onion, thinly sliced
1 large tomato, thinly sliced
1 clove garlic, minced
Salt and black pepper, to taste

FOR THE SANDWICHES

4 tablespoons butter
4 slices country white or sourdough bread
2 tablespoons chutney
4½ cups (8 oz/225 g) shredded Gruyère

FOR THE VEGETABLES Heat the oil in a large skillet over medium heat. Add the onion, tomato, and garlic and sauté for 5 minutes, or until the vegetables have softened. Season to taste with salt and pepper. Transfer the vegetables to a small bowl.

FOR THE SANDWICHES Butter both sides of the bread. On two of the slices, spread 1 tablespoon of chutney, then top each with a small scoop of the sautéed vegetables and 4 tablespoons of cheese. Cover each one with a piece of bread.

Preheat a grill to medium heat.

Place the sandwiches on the grill and grill for 5 minutes on each side, flattening them with a heat-proof spatula as you cook them.

Cut each sandwich in half and serve.

SIDES

This refreshing salad is often served with *khorovats*—grilled meats—such as the Armenian Beef Skewers (page 34) or Lamb Skewers (page 38). It begins with grilled chopped eggplants (aubergines) and bell peppers, which are added to raw tomatoes, onions, and fresh herbs. The multifaceted salad is enlivened with olive oil and lemon juice and can be served cold or at room temperature.

PREPARATION TIME 15 minutes, plus 15 minutes standing
COOKING TIME 30 minutes
SERVES 8

2 eggplants (aubergines)
3 red bell peppers, seeded and deveined
1–2 tablespoons olive oil
Juice of 1 lemon, plus extra to taste
3 tomatoes, chopped
1 small onion, minced
Bunch of parsley or cilantro (coriander), finely chopped
Salt and black pepper, to taste

Preheat a grill to high heat.

Using a fork, prick the eggplants (aubergines) all over. Grill the eggplants and bell peppers for 15 minutes, turning continuously, until the skins are charred. Transfer the peppers into a large bowl and cover with plastic wrap (clingfilm). Set aside for 15 minutes.

When cool enough to handle, peel the eggplants. Peel the peppers, then remove the seeds and stems. Chop both of them into chunks and mix together in a large bowl. Set aside to cool to room temperature.

Dress with olive oil and lemon juice, then season with salt and pepper. Add the tomatoes, onion, and parsley or cilantro (coriander) and toss well. Season to taste with salt, pepper, or lemon juice.

MEXICAN
CORN SALAD

Esquites is the spoonable version of *elote* (page 314) and delivers all the smoky, cheesy, spicy flavors of Mexican street corn. While it's also possible to char raw kernels in a cast-iron pan, grilling the cobs adds depth to the dish.

PREPARATION TIME 5 minutes
COOKING TIME 10–15 minutes
SERVES 4

2 oz/55 g cotija cheese or feta
½ cup (1¾ oz/50 g) thinly sliced scallions (spring onions)
½ cup (1 oz/30 g) finely chopped cilantro (coriander)
1 teaspoon red pepper flakes, plus extra to taste
2 cloves garlic, minced
3 tablespoons mayonnaise
1 tablespoon lime juice
Salt, to taste
4 ears of corn, shucked

Preheat a grill to medium-high heat for indirect grilling.
In a large bowl, combine all the ingredients except the corn. Place the corn on the hot side of the grill and cook for 10–15 minutes, until charred in spots. Set aside to cool, then remove the kernels. Add the corn to the cheese mixture and stir to combine.
Serve immediately.

SWISS
SAUSAGE SALAD

`GF` `NF`

Switzerland's beloved sausage, *cervelat* (page 75), is often transformed into *wurstsalat*, a common salad in Switzerland, Germany, Austria, and eastern France. Sliced sausage, cheese, pickles, and onions are dressed in a simple vinaigrette. Feel free to substitute mortadella or ham for the *cervelat*.

PREPARATION TIME 10 minutes
SERVES 4

FOR THE DRESSING
6 tablespoons olive oil
3 tablespoons apple cider vinegar
½ teaspoon Dijon mustard
½ teaspoon sugar
Salt and black pepper

FOR THE SALAD
3–4 baby dill pickles, thinly sliced
2 (3-oz/85-g) Swiss Sausages (page 75), thinly sliced
Bunch of radishes, thinly sliced
½ red onion, thinly sliced
5¾ oz/170 g Gruyère or Emmental cheese, cut into ½-inch/1-cm squares
4 tablespoons chopped parsley

FOR THE DRESSING Combine all the ingredients in a small bowl and whisk together.

FOR THE SALAD In a large bowl, combine all the ingredients and mix well. Add the dressing and toss again.
Serve immediately.

AMERICAN POTATO SALAD

GF DF NF

This classic potato salad uses buttery Yukon Golds, which have just enough starch to hold their shape while remaining creamy. The salad gets crunch from freshly diced celery and onions and richness from smoky bacon and hard-boiled eggs.

PREPARATION TIME 10 minutes, plus 10 minutes cooling, 10 minutes drying, and 1 hour refrigeration
COOKING TIME 25 minutes
SERVES 10–12

12 eggs

5 lb/2.25 kg Yukon Gold potatoes, cut into 1-inch/2.5-cm cubes

1 lb/450 g bacon, chopped

10–12 ribs celery, chopped

2 red onions, chopped

2 cups (16 fl oz/475 ml) mayonnaise

1 cup (8 fl oz/240 ml) pickle relish

½ cup (4 fl oz/120 ml) Dijon mustard

Salt and black pepper

Place the eggs in a medium saucepan and cover with cold water. Bring the water to a boil, then turn off the heat and cover for 12 minutes. Fill a large bowl with ice water. Using a slotted spoon, carefully transfer the eggs into the ice bath. Set aside to cool for 10 minutes, then peel and chop the eggs.

Place the potatoes in a saucepan, then add enough cold water to cover them by 1 inch/2.5 cm. Bring to a boil and cook for 10 minutes, or until the potatoes still hold their shape but can be easily pierced with a fork. Drain, then set aside to air-dry for 10 minutes.

Cook the bacon in a skillet over medium heat for 10 minutes, or until just crispy. Using a slotted spoon, transfer the bacon to a paper towel–lined plate to drain. Reserve the bacon fat.

In a large bowl, combine the potatoes, celery, red onions, eggs, and bacon. Add the mayonnaise, relish, and mustard and toss to mix. Season to taste with salt and pepper. Add 1 tablespoon of the bacon fat and toss again. Cover and refrigerate for at least 1 hour.

The potato salad can be stored in the refrigerator for up to 5 days.

GERMAN POTATO SALAD

GF DF NF

Usually served warm or at room temperature, Germany's traditional potato salad is flavored with bacon and tossed with vinegar. This dish lasts for 5 days in the refrigerator and can be reheated (covered with foil) before serving.

PREPARATION TIME 15 minutes
COOKING TIME 35 minutes
SERVES 4

4 russet potatoes, chopped

4 slices (rashers) bacon

1 small onion, chopped

4 tablespoons white vinegar

1½ tablespoons sugar, plus extra to taste

1 teaspoon salt

⅛ teaspoon black pepper

1 tablespoon chopped parsley, to garnish

Place the potatoes in a saucepan, then add enough cold water to cover them by 1 inch/2.5 cm. Bring to a boil and cook for 10 minutes, or until the potatoes still hold their shape but can be easily pierced with a fork. Drain, then set aside.

Cook the bacon in a skillet over medium heat for 10 minutes, or until just crispy. Using a slotted spoon, transfer the bacon to a paper towel–lined plate to drain. Crumble the bacon into small pieces.

Heat the bacon fat in the skillet over medium heat. Add the onion and sauté for 6–8 minutes, until brown. Add the vinegar, 2 tablespoons of water, the sugar, salt, and pepper and bring to a boil. Boil for 3 minutes, then add the drained potatoes and half of the crumbled bacon. Cook for 3–4 minutes, until heated through.

Transfer the potato salad to a serving dish. Sprinkle with the remaining bacon and garnish with parsley.

DUTCH PEPPER SLAW

V | VG | GF | DF | NF

Coleslaw originated in the Netherlands (*kool* means "cabbage" and *sla* is "salad") in the eighteenth century, before the invention of mayonnaise. Cabbage was usually the base, although other vegetables were often added. The mayo-less slaw is more of a pickled cabbage salad—and a refreshingly sweet and sour side for any barbecue.

PREPARATION TIME 10 minutes, plus 2 hours refrigeration
COOKING TIME 5 minutes
SERVES 8–10

¾ cup (6 fl oz/175 ml) apple cider vinegar
1 cup (7 oz/200 g) sugar
1 teaspoon celery seeds
1 teaspoon mustard powder
2 teaspoons salt, to taste
1 green cabbage, cored and finely chopped
1 carrot, grated
1 red bell pepper, seeded, deveined, and finely chopped
1 green bell pepper, seeded, deveined, and finely chopped

In a small saucepan, combine the vinegar, 4 tablespoons of water, the sugar, celery seeds, mustard, and salt. Bring to a boil, stirring, until the sugar has dissolved. Set aside to cool.

In a large bowl, combine the vegetables and cooled dressing and toss. Refrigerate for at least 2 hours.

Serve cold.

SALVADOREAN SLAW

V | VG | GF | DF | NF

Curdito is a slightly fermented slaw made with cabbage, red onions, carrots, and oregano. Served with everything from *pupusas* to grilled meats, this slaw is often spiced with chiles, which are optional in the following recipe.

PREPARATION TIME 10 minutes, plus at least 1 hour marinating
SERVES 4

½ head green cabbage, shredded
2 carrots, shredded
1 jalapeño, thinly sliced (optional)
½ red onion, thinly sliced
1 tablespoon salt
½ teaspoon dried oregano
½ cup (4 fl oz/120 ml) white vinegar

Bring 4 cups (32 fl oz/960 ml) of water to a boil in a small saucepan.

Place the cabbage in a colander, then pour the boiling water on top. Rinse under cold running water. Drain well.

In a large bowl, combine all the ingredients and toss to combine. Set aside to marinate at room temperature for 1–3 hours.

Store in an airtight container in the refrigerator for up to 1 week.

BACON BROCCOLI SLAW

This slaw, a staple at Mighty Quinn's in New York, pairs fresh vegetables with smoky bacon and sweet cranberries. This combination produces stark contrasts in texture but also a harmony of ingredients, as the rich fattiness meets the crunchy raw broccoli, tangy dried fruit, and acidic vinaigrette.

PREPARATION TIME 15 minutes,
plus 30 minutes refrigeration
COOKING TIME 15 minutes
SERVES 8

16 slices (rashers) smoked bacon,
cut into ½-inch/1-cm-thick strips

1 cup (3½ oz/100 g) sliced almonds

2 cups (16 fl oz/475 ml) mayonnaise

½ cup (4 fl oz/120 ml) apple cider vinegar

2 cloves garlic, minced

2 heads broccoli, cut into 1-inch/2.5-cm florets

1 large red onion, chopped

1 cup (5¾ oz/170 g) dried cranberries

Salt and black pepper, to taste

Cook the bacon in a skillet over medium heat for 10 minutes, or until just crispy. Using a slotted spoon, transfer the bacon to a paper towel–lined plate to drain. Reserve the bacon fat for the dressing.

In a small skillet, toast the almonds for 3 minutes, or until lightly golden and fragrant. Let cool.

In a medium bowl, whisk the mayonnaise and vinegar together. Add the garlic and season to taste with salt and pepper. Whisk in 1 tablespoon of the rendered bacon fat. Season to taste with more bacon fat.

In a large bowl, combine the broccoli, red onion, cranberries, bacon, and almonds. Add the dressing and toss to mix. Cover and refrigerate for 30 minutes.

Serve cold.

V VG GF DF NF 5

Coleslaw is a staple of American barbecue, whether served alongside a protein or in a sandwich. Use the vinegar-based dressing to make a bright, crunchy slaw that complements unctuous slow-smoked pork. The mayonnaise-based dressing creates a phenomenal slaw that is especially at home alongside smoked chicken (page 237) and beef.

PREPARATION TIME 5 minutes, plus 15–20 minutes standing
SERVES 8–10

½ head purple cabbage, cored and cut into ribbons
1 head green cabbage, cored and cut into ribbons
3–4 carrots, grated
2 cups (16 fl oz/475 ml) Vinegar Coleslaw Dressing or Creamy Coleslaw Dressing
Salt and black pepper, to taste

Place the purple cabbage in a large bowl and cover with cold water. Set aside for 10 minutes to prevent the color from bleeding throughout the slaw.

In a large bowl, combine the green cabbage and carrots. Drain the purple cabbage, then add it to the slaw. Add 1 cup (8 fl oz/240 ml) of dressing and toss. Set aside for 5–10 minutes so the cabbage softens, then toss again. Add more dressing if desired. Season to taste with salt and pepper.

VINEGAR COLESLAW DRESSING

V VG GF DF NF

PREPARATION TIME 10 minutes
MAKES 1 quart /1 L

2 cups (16 fl oz/475 ml) apple cider vinegar
2 cups (14 oz/400 g) sugar
2 tablespoons extra-virgin olive oil
2 tablespoons celery seeds
1 tablespoon garlic granules
1 tablespoon onion powder
1 tablespoon salt
2 teaspoons black pepper

Combine all the ingredients in a bowl and whisk.
The dressing can be stored in an airtight container in the refrigerator for up to 2 weeks.

CREAMY COLESLAW DRESSING

VG GF DF NF

PREPARATION TIME 10 minutes
MAKES 2 quarts/1.8 L

2 cups (16 fl oz/475 ml) mayonnaise
2 cups (16 fl oz/475 ml) apple cider vinegar
2 cups (14 oz/400 g) sugar
2 tablespoons extra-virgin olive oil
2 tablespoons celery seeds
1 tablespoon garlic granules
1 tablespoon onion powder
1 tablespoon salt
2 teaspoons black pepper

Combine all the ingredients in a bowl and whisk.
The dressing can be stored in an airtight container in the refrigerator for up to 2 weeks.

KIMCHI

DF NF

Like many pickled condiments, Korean kimchi, made with cabbage and red pepper flakes, has been used for thousands of years to preserve vegetables during the winter. Many Koreans still eat kimchi every day.

PREPARATION TIME 30 minutes, plus 6 hours marinating, 1 hour draining, and 24 hours pickling
COOKING TIME 10 minutes
MAKES 4 quarts

FOR THE CABBAGE
1¼ cups (8 oz/225 g) salt
4 lb/1.8 kg napa cabbage, quartered with core intact

FOR THE KIMCHI PASTE
1 tablespoon glutinous rice flour
¾ cup (7 oz/200 g) Korean chili powder (gochugaru)
12 oz/350 g daikon radish, cut into matchsticks
1 tablespoon salted fermented shrimp (saeu-jeot), minced
½ tablespoon fine sea salt
2 tablespoons fish sauce
2 carrots, cut into matchsticks
½ large onion, grated
1½ oz/45 g chives, cut in 2-inch/5-cm lengths
5 cloves garlic, minced
1 teaspoon grated fresh ginger
1 tablespoon sugar

FOR THE CABBAGE In a large bowl, combine 1 cup (6 oz/175 g) of the salt and 7½ cups (60 fl oz/1.75 L) of water and stir until the salt has dissolved. Dip the cabbage into the water, then place it onto a baking sheet. Reserve the salt water. Sprinkle the cabbage with the remaining salt, making sure to get the salt into all the crevices of the cabbage.

Put the cabbage into a large bag or bowl, then pour in the reserved salt water. Cover, then set aside to marinate for 6 hours, rotating every 2 hours. Rinse the cabbage under cold running water, then set aside in a colander to drain for 1 hour.

FOR THE KIMCHI PASTE In a saucepan, combine the rice flour and ¾ cup (6 fl oz/175 ml) of water. Bring to a boil, then simmer for 5–8 minutes, until thickened. Transfer to a bowl, then set aside to cool. Stir in the Korean chili powder (gochugaru).

In a large bowl, combine the radish, salted shrimp, sea salt, and fish sauce. Set aside for 10 minutes. Add the carrots, onion, chives, garlic, ginger, sugar, and chili mixture.

Arrange the cabbage on a baking sheet and spread the paste on top, coating each leaf. Transfer to an airtight container, cover, then set aside at room temperature for 24 hours. Chill until ready to serve.

Kimchi can be stored in an airtight container in the refrigerator for up to 6 months.

PICKLED ONIONS

V VG GF DF NF 5

This easy condiment brightens barbecue dishes, from Carne Asada (page 130) to Birria Tacos (page 128) to Yucatecan Grilled Chicken (page 228). These tangy, delicate onions can also enhance a sandwich, a bowl of chili, or even a salad.

PREPARATION TIME 5 minutes, plus at least 1 hour refrigeration
COOKING TIME 5 minutes
SERVES 12

2 small red onions, thinly sliced
2 cups (16 fl oz/475 ml) white vinegar
⅓ cup (2¼ oz/65 g) sugar
2 tablespoons sea salt

Divide the onions among 2–3 sterilized glass jars.

In a medium saucepan, combine the vinegar, sugar, and salt. Pour in 2 cups (16 fl oz/475 ml) of water and stir over medium heat until the sugar has dissolved. Set aside to cool for 5 minutes, then pour the mixture over the onions. Set aside to cool to room temperature. Refrigerate for at least 1 hour.

The pickled onions can be stored in the refrigerator for up to 2 weeks.

NEW YORK PICKLES

V | VG | GF | DF | NF

Pickled vegetables are a great foil for the richness and assertiveness of barbecue. The crisp and colorful condiment adds brightness and cleanses the palate. The following brine recipe, which is similar to the kosher dill pickle recipe that Jewish immigrants from Eastern Europe brought to New York, can pickle almost any vegetable.

PREPARATION TIME 15 minutes,
plus at least 2 hours marinating
COOKING TIME 10 minutes
SERVES 4–6

3 cups (1 lb/450 g) chopped vegetables, such as onions, cauliflower, radishes, green beans, sweet corn, carrots, Fresno chiles, and/or celery
2 tablespoons coriander seeds
2 tablespoons black peppercorns
2 teaspoons yellow mustard seeds
3 cups (25 fl oz/750 ml) apple cider vinegar
5 cloves garlic
2–3 bay leaves
4 tablespoons sugar
4 tablespoons salt
1 teaspoon red pepper flakes

Place the vegetables and chiles in sterilized glass jars.

In a medium saucepan, combine the coriander, peppercorns, and mustard seeds. Toast over medium-high heat for 1–2 minutes, until fragrant. Pour in the vinegar and 3 cups (25 fl oz/750 ml) of water. Add the remaining ingredients and bring to a boil. Remove the pan from the heat, then pour the brine into the jars.

Refrigerate for at least 2 hours and up to 2 weeks.

INDIAN PICKLES

V | VG | GF | DF | NF

This tangy, sweet pickled condiment, called *achar* or *achaar*, has many variations—from a salted mango with fenugreek (below) to a version made with sugar, chili powder, and cumin. In northern India, *achar* is typically made with mustard oil, while the South Indian style uses sesame oil.

PREPARATION TIME 15 minutes, plus 5 days marinating
COOKING TIME 5 minutes
SERVES 15–20

7 cups (4½ lb/2 kg) raw mango, peeled and cut into 1-inch/2.5-cm cubes
½ cup (4¼ oz/125 g) salt, plus extra to taste
3 tablespoons ground turmeric
4 tablespoons coriander seeds
4 tablespoons mustard seeds
4 tablespoons fenugreek seeds
½ cup (1½ oz/40 g) chili powder
4 tablespoons fennel seeds
4 tablespoons nigella seeds
3 cups (25 fl oz/750 ml) + 3–5 tablespoons mustard oil

In a large bowl, combine the mangoes, salt, and turmeric. Cover and marinate for 1 hour.

In a small saucepan, toast the coriander seeds over medium-high heat for 5 minutes. Set aside to cool, then crush them.

Using a spice grinder or mortar and pestle, combine the mustard and fenugreek seeds and grind into a powder.

To the bowl of mangoes, add the mustard-fenugreek powder, chili powder, fennel seeds, nigella seeds, and crushed coriander seeds. Stir in 1 cup (8 fl oz/250 ml) of mustard oil. Season with salt until it tastes very salty. Using a dish towel and saucepan lid, cover the bowl and refrigerate for 24 hours.

The next day, stir the mixture, then cover it again and refrigerate for another 24 hours.

On the third day, add the remaining 2 cups (17 fl oz/500 ml) of mustard oil, then cover and refrigerate for another 2 days.

On the fifth day, pack the achar into sterilized glass jars. Top each with a tablespoon of mustard oil. The pickles can be stored in the refrigerator for up to 6 months.

VIETNAMESE PICKLES

[V] [VG] [GF] [DF] [NF] [5]

Vietnamese pickles, *dồ chua* ("sour stuff"), almost always include carrot and daikon pickled in vinegar, salt, and sugar. Recipes can vary by the size of the cut (usually a matchstick) and by the extra brine ingredients, like chiles or garlic. These pickles play a significant role in Vietnam's famous Báhn Mì (page 142) and are a popular side dish for many Vietnamese barbecue dishes, such as Lemongrass Pork Chops (page 140).

PREPARATION TIME 5 minutes
COOKING TIME 10 minutes
SERVES 12

2 large carrots, cut into matchsticks
2 daikon radishes, cut into matchsticks
½ cup (1¾ oz/50 g) sugar
2 tablespoons salt
1 cup (8 fl oz/240 ml) rice wine vinegar

In a large bowl, combine the carrots, daikon, sugar, and salt. Massage the salt and sugar into the vegetables, until the crystals have dissolved. Pour in 2 cups (16 fl oz/475 ml) of water and the vinegar. Place the vegetables into a large jar or container, then pour in the brine.

The pickles can be stored in the refrigerator for up to 1 week.

PERSIAN PICKLES

[V] [VG] [GF] [DF] [NF]

Torshi makhloot, or Persian mixed pickles, accompany many main courses in Iran, especially grilled dishes, and are usually made with fresh vegetables and high-quality wine vinegar. The straightforward process requires 3 weeks of refrigeration and turns out wonderfully fragrant, slightly spicy pickles.

PREPARATION TIME 20 minutes,
plus 3 hours drying and 3 weeks pickling
SERVES 12

2 tablespoons tarragon
2 tablespoons mint
2 tablespoons basil
5 cloves garlic
3 large carrots, chopped
2 eggplants (aubergines), peeled and diced
2 large cucumbers, chopped
2 jalapeños, chopped
1 small head cauliflower, separated into small florets
1 head celery, cut in ½-inch/1-cm slices
2 tablespoons coriander seeds
1 tablespoon salt
¾ teaspoon ground turmeric
2–3 quarts/2–3L white vinegar

Let the herbs dry on a plate for 3 hours until they are brittle.

In a large bowl or container, combine all the ingredients and stir to mix. Using a wooden spoon, pack the pickles into sterilized glass jars, packing them in until full. Pour in more vinegar, if needed, to cover.

Store the pickles in the refrigerator for 3 weeks to pickle.

SMOKED EGGPLANT DIP

VG NF

Eggplants (aubergines) are one of the easiest vegetables to smoke, and if you're firing up a smoker for a Brisket (page 116) or Half Chicken (page 229), invite an eggplant to join the party. The smoky flesh—mixed with tahini, lemon juice, and spices—transforms the somewhat bitter nightshade into a delicious *mutabal*. Serve this dip with cut vegetables and pita.

PREPARATION TIME 5 minutes
COOKING TIME 2–3 hours
SERVES 4

1 large eggplant (aubergine), top and bottom trimmed and halved lengthwise

1 tablespoon olive oil, plus extra for brushing

2 cloves garlic, minced

2 teaspoons salt, plus extra to taste

1 teaspoon ground cumin

½ teaspoon red pepper flakes

4 tablespoons tahini

Juice of 1 lemon, plus extra to taste

4 tablespoons Greek yogurt

Pita bread, to serve

Oak, hickory, or cherry wood, for smoking

Preheat a smoker to 225°F/107°C.

Brush the inside of the eggplant (aubergine) halves with oil. Place the eggplant in the smoker, flesh side down, and smoke for 2–3 hours, until softened and browned. Transfer the eggplant to a cutting board, then set aside to cool. Peel off the skin or scoop out the flesh with a spoon.

In a food processor, combine the eggplant flesh, garlic, salt, cumin, red pepper flakes, tahini, lemon juice, and oil. Blend until smooth. Add the yogurt and blend again. Season to taste with salt and lemon juice. Transfer to a small serving bowl.

Serve with pita bread.

This recipe originated as a late-night treat after a long day tending to the smoker at Mighty Quinn's. Leftover caramelized burnt ends are loaded onto a heap of crispy, salty French fries, then topped with wing sauce and a handful of scallions (spring onions). Add an ice-cold beer, and this is a perfect dish for casual get-togethers, as well as a great use of leftovers.

PREPARATION TIME 15 minutes, plus at least 1 hour soaking
COOKING TIME 15 minutes
SERVES 4–6

2 lb/900 g russet potatoes, unpeeled,
cut into ¼-inch/5-mm batons
2–3 quarts/2–3 L canola oil
2 cups (16 fl oz/475 ml) Texas Table Sauce (page 335)
1 lb/450 g Burnt Ends (page 119)
1 cup (8 fl oz/240 ml) Chili-Lime Wing Sauce (page 335)
½ cup (3¼ oz/90 g) chopped red onions
½ cup (1¾ oz/50 g) sliced scallions (spring onions)
Salt

Cut the potatoes into skin-on ¼-inch/5-mm fries. Submerge the cut fries in cold water for at least 1 hour and up to overnight.

Drain the fries, then lay them on a baking sheet in a single layer to dry out.

Fill a deep-fryer or Dutch oven (casserole) a third full with oil and heat over medium-high heat to 350°F/180°C. Working in batches to avoid overcrowding, carefully lower the French fries into the hot oil. Deep-fry for 3–4 minutes, until golden. Using a slotted spoon, transfer the fries to a paper towel–lined plate to drain.

In a small saucepan, combine the Texas table sauce and burnt ends. Warm over medium heat.

In another small saucepan, warm the chili-lime wing sauce over medium heat.

Reheat the pan of oil to 375°F/190°C. Working in batches, refry the fries for about 3 minutes, until golden brown and crispy. Using a slotted spoon, transfer them to a large bowl. Season to taste with salt, then toss well.

To serve, place the fries in a serving dish, top with the burnt ends, drizzle with the chili-lime sauce, and sprinkle with the red onions and scallions (spring onions).

Hush puppies, or fried cornmeal nuggets, are a staple side dish at barbecues in the southern United States. The keys to great hush puppies are not overmixing the batter and frying at the right temperature. Mind those two rules and it's easy to make these fun, crispy treats.

PREPARATION TIME 10 minutes
COOKING TIME 15 minutes
SERVES 10–12

4¼ cups (34 fl oz/1 L) canola oil
1 cup (5 oz/150 g) all-purpose (plain) flour
1 cup (4 oz/115 g) cornmeal
½ teaspoon baking soda (bicarbonate of soda)
1 tablespoon salt, plus extra to taste
2 teaspoons black pepper
2 eggs
1 cup (8 fl oz/240 ml) buttermilk
1 large or 2 small onions, diced

Heat the oil in a deep-fryer or Dutch oven (casserole) over medium-high heat to 375°F/190°C.

In a large bowl, combine the flour, cornmeal, baking soda (bicarbonate of soda), salt, and pepper and whisk well.

In a small bowl, whisk the eggs and buttermilk. Stir the mixture into the flour mixture, until just combined. Fold in the onions.

Using a small ice-cream scoop or spoons, carefully lower the battered onions into the hot oil and fry for 3–5 minutes, until golden brown. Work in batches to avoid overcrowding. Using a slotted spoon, transfer the hush puppies to a paper towel–lined plate. Season with salt. Repeat with the remaining batches.

Serve immediately.

This elevated take on Hush Puppies (page 305) turns out crisp, light, airy fritters packed with sweet corn. The easily shareable side pairs well with almost any smoked meat. You can also serve them dipped in hot honey as a pre-barbecue snack.

PREPARATION TIME 10 minutes
COOKING TIME 15 minutes
SERVES 8–10

FOR THE HOT HONEY

2 cups (16 fl oz/480 ml) honey	
3 tablespoons Calabrian chiles	

FOR THE FRITTERS

1 cup (5 oz/150 g) all-purpose (plain) flour	
2 tablespoons sugar	
1½ teaspoons baking powder	
3 eggs	
1½ tablespoons salt, plus extra to taste	
1 tablespoon Pork and Poultry Rub (page 358)	
¾ cup (6 fl oz/175 ml) whole (full-fat) milk	
5–6 ears of corn, kernels removed	
4¼ cups (34 fl oz/1 L) canola oil	

FOR THE HOT HONEY Combine the honey and chiles in a food processor or blender and blend until smooth. Pour into a small bowl, then set aside.

FOR THE FRITTERS In a large bowl, combine the flour, sugar, and baking powder and mix well. Add the eggs, salt, pork rub, and milk and mix until just combined. Fold in the corn.

Heat the oil in a deep-fryer or Dutch oven (casserole) over medium-high heat to 375°F/190°C. Using a small ice-cream scoop or spoons, carefully lower the batter into the hot oil and fry for 3–5 minutes, until golden brown. Work in batches to avoid overcrowding. Using a slotted spoon, transfer the corn fritters to a paper towel–lined plate. Season with salt. Repeat with the remaining batches.

Serve immediately with the hot honey.

Plantains are a staple of Cuban cuisine and require different preparation, depending on their degree of ripeness. Very ripe plantains (with black skin) are usually grilled with sugar or cane syrup, as they are in this recipe. These can be served as a side, but they are sweet enough to eat as dessert.

PREPARATION TIME 5 minutes
COOKING TIME 20 minutes
SERVES 4

4 tablespoons butter

4 tablespoons dark cane syrup

½ teaspoon ground cinnamon

4 very ripe (black) plantains, unpeeled,
ends trimmed, and sliced lengthwise

4 tablespoons brown sugar, plus extra as needed

Preheat a grill to high heat.

Melt the butter in a small saucepan over medium heat. Stir in the cane syrup and cinnamon and bring to a boil. Boil for 5–10 minutes, until the glaze thickens.

Brush the plantains with the glaze, then sprinkle over the brown sugar. Place the plantains on the grill, cut sides down, and grill for 1½ minutes.

Rotate 90 degrees and grill for another 1½ minutes to create crosshatch grill marks. Turn the plantains over and brush with the glaze. Cook for another 3 minutes, repeating the same grill pattern on the other side.

Transfer the plantains to a serving dish and top with the remaining glaze. Serve warm.

GRILLED HALLOUMI

Halloumi, a firm, brined cheese that originated in Cyprus, and is served in homes and restaurants throughout Greece, can withstand the heat. When this salty cheese hits the grill, it becomes firm, even charred, on the outside, while remaining creamy and soft (but not melted) inside. Traditionally, halloumi is made with a mixture of goat's and sheep's milk, though cow's milk halloumi is also available.

PREPARATION TIME 5 minutes
COOKING TIME 5 minutes
SERVES 4

12 oz/350 g halloumi, cut into 8–12 slices
4 tablespoons olive oil
Juice of 1 lemon
4 tablespoons chopped thyme

Preheat a grill to high heat.

Brush the halloumi with the oil. Place the halloumi on the grill and grill for 2½ minutes, or until grill marks are visible and the exterior of the cheese gives when pushed. Flip over and grill for another 2½ minutes. Transfer the cheese to a serving dish, then sprinkle over lemon juice and herbs.

Serve warm.

GRILLED PROVOLONE

Provoleta is a provolone-like cheese found in Argentina and cooked over coals until bubbling but not quite melted. It's typically served as an appetizer but makes a great side or snack. This recipe adapts the dish by using the easier-to-find provolone.

PREPARATION TIME 10 minutes
COOKING TIME 5–10 minutes
SERVES 2–4

8 oz/225 g provolone cheese,
cut into 1-inch/2.5-cm-thick slices

1 teaspoon dried oregano

½ teaspoon red pepper flakes

FOR SERVING

1 baguette, sliced in ½-inch/1-cm circles

Chimichurri (page 340)

Preheat a grill to medium-high heat and set a medium cast-iron skillet (frying pan) or grill pan on top of the grill.

When the skillet is hot, pile on the cheese slices. Add ½ teaspoon of oregano and ¼ teaspoon of red pepper flakes. Cook for 2 minutes, then flip and grill for another 2–3 minutes, until browned.

Transfer the cheese to a plate, then sprinkle over with the remaining ½ teaspoon of oregano and ¼ teaspoon of red pepper flakes.

Serve immediately with the baguette and a side of chimichurri.

Elote is the quintessential Mexican street food. Grilled corn is slathered with a rich, tangy white sauce and sprinkled with cheese and chili powder, transforming the simple cob into a portable, handheld treat.

PREPARATION TIME 10 minutes
COOKING TIME 20 minutes
SERVES 8

1 cup (3¾ oz/110 g) cotija cheese, plus extra to serve
½ cup (4 fl oz/120 ml) mayonnaise
½ cup (4¼ oz/125 g) sour cream
½ cup (1 oz/30 g) finely chopped cilantro (coriander)
1 teaspoon chili powder, plus extra to serve
2 cloves garlic, minced
8 ears of corn, shucked
2 limes, cut into wedges, to serve

Preheat a grill to medium-high heat for direct grilling.

In a large bowl, combine the cheese, mayonnaise, sour cream, cilantro (coriander), chili powder, and garlic. Place the corn on the grill and cook for 10–15 minutes, until charred in spots.

Remove the corn from the grill, then coat it in the cheese mixture. Sprinkle with extra cheese and chili powder, and serve with lime wedges.

One of barbecue's most beloved side dishes can trace its American roots to James Hemings, the French-trained Black chef who was enslaved by Thomas Jefferson. This version uses four cheeses for depth of flavor and supreme melt. The breadcrumb topping adds texture, while the smoked paprika brings a sweet note that complements smoked or grilled meat dishes.

PREPARATION TIME 15 minutes
COOKING TIME 50 minutes
SERVES 8–10

FOR THE PASTA

1 lb/450 g short pasta, such as shells or macaroni

FOR THE CHEESE SAUCE

2 cups (8 oz/225 g) shredded white American cheese

2 cups (8 oz/225 g) shredded white cheddar cheese

1 cup (3 oz/85 g) grated Parmesan

1 cup (4¼ oz/120 g) shredded Gruyère

½ cup (2¼ oz/60 g) butter

½ cup (2¼ oz/60 g) all-purpose (plain) flour

2 cups (16 fl oz/475 ml) whole (full-fat) milk

2 cups (16 fl oz/475 ml) heavy (double) cream

1½ tablespoons salt

1 tablespoon black pepper

1 teaspoon smoked paprika

FOR THE TOPPING

4 tablespoons butter

5 cloves garlic, minced

2 cups (3½ oz/100 g) panko breadcrumbs

1 tablespoon salt

2 sprigs rosemary, chopped (optional)

Preheat an oven to 350°F/180°C/Gas Mark 4.

FOR THE PASTA Bring a large pot of salted water to a boil. Add the pasta and cook to al dente according to the manufacturer's directions. (Don't overcook the pasta as it will continue to cook in the oven.) Drain.

FOR THE CHEESE SAUCE Combine the cheeses in a medium bowl. Reserve 1 cup (4 oz/120 g) of this mixture for the topping.

Melt the butter in a medium saucepan over medium heat, until just beginning to brown. Stir in the flour and whisk the roux until golden brown. While whisking, slowly pour in the milk and cream. Cook for 5–10 minutes, until the sauce is thick enough to coat the back of a wooden spoon. Remove the sauce from the heat and whisk in the cheese mixture until melted. Season with salt, pepper, and smoked paprika. Stir in the drained pasta. Transfer to a baking dish.

FOR THE TOPPING Melt the butter in a small saucepan over medium heat. Add the garlic and sauté for 1–2 minutes, until fragrant. Remove from the heat.

In a medium bowl, combine the garlic, breadcrumbs, salt, rosemary (if using), and the reserved cheese mixture.

Spread the topping evenly over the top of the mac and cheese. Bake on the middle rack for 30 minutes, or until golden brown and bubbling. Set aside for 10–15 minutes, then serve.

VG

This dish is basically Thanksgiving in a bowl. While this casserole makes a great holiday side, it also works well with a platter of smoked meats. The recipe comes from North Carolina, but sweet potato casserole was once popular in New England, according to Amelia Simmons's *American Cookery*, published in 1796.

PREPARATION TIME 15 minutes
COOKING TIME 1½–2¼ hours
SERVES 6–8

FOR THE CASSEROLE

6 sweet potatoes
1 cup (7 oz/200 g) sugar
2 teaspoons salt
½ cup (4 fl oz/120 ml) whole (full-fat) milk
4 tablespoons melted butter
2 tablespoons vanilla paste
3 eggs

FOR THE TOPPING

1½ cups (11½ oz/325 g) dark brown sugar
½ cup (2¾ oz/80 g) all-purpose (plain) flour
6 tablespoons butter, softened
1 cup (4¼ oz/120 g) chopped pecans

Preheat an oven to 425°F/220°C/Gas Mark 7.

FOR THE CASSEROLE Place the sweet potatoes on a baking sheet and roast for 1–1½ hours, until they can be easily pierced with a fork. Set aside until cool enough to handle. Reduce the oven temperature to 350°F/180°C/Gas Mark 4. Peel the sweet potatoes, then place them into a large bowl. Add the sugar, salt, milk, butter, and vanilla and mix to incorporate. Add the eggs and mix until smooth. Transfer the mixture into a baking dish.

FOR THE TOPPING Combine all the ingredients in a medium bowl. Spread the topping evenly over the sweet potato mixture.

Bake the casserole for 30–45 minutes, until the topping is golden and the sweet potatoes are cooked through.

Serve warm.

The official dish of Texas likely originated in Mexico City, where it was historically made by women (unlike smoked meats, which were typically made by men). This outstanding chili is often served as a side dish for smoked meat, but it also makes a satisfying appetizer or main dish.

PREPARATION TIME 30 minutes
COOKING TIME 2½–3 hours
SERVES 10–12

7 ancho chiles
2 dried New Mexico chiles
2 guajillo chiles
4 jalapeños, deveined and seeded
1 head garlic, cloves separated and peeled
1 (28-oz/294-g) can crushed tomatoes
1 tablespoon ground cumin
1 tablespoon cumin seeds
1 tablespoon ancho chili powder
1 teaspoon red pepper flakes
3 tablespoons canola oil
3 lb/1.3 kg beef stew meat, cut into 1-inch/2.5-cm cubes
1 lb/450 g ground (minced) pork
4 Spanish onions, chopped
2 oz/55 g semisweet chocolate
1 teaspoon sugar
2 cups (16 fl oz/475 ml) beer
½ cup (2 oz/55 g) masa
Salt and black pepper

Place the ancho, New Mexico, and guajillo chiles in a saucepan. Add enough cold water to cover. Bring to a boil, then reduce the heat to medium and cook for 10–15 minutes, until the chiles have softened. Set aside to cool.

Meanwhile, in a blender or food processor, combine the jalapeños, garlic, tomatoes, cumin, chili powder, and red pepper flakes and blend until smooth.

When the chiles have cooled enough to handle, remove them from the saucepan. Remove the stems and seeds, then add them to the food processor. Blend again until smooth.

Heat the oil in a large Dutch oven (casserole) over medium-high heat. Working in batches to avoid overcrowding, add the beef and sear all over. Transfer to a plate.

Add the pork and brown. Transfer to a plate.

Add the onions and sauté for 7 minutes, or until softened and translucent. Add the beef, pork, tomato mixture, chocolate, sugar, and beer. Simmer, uncovered, for 2–2½ hours, until the beef is tender. If needed, add water to loosen the chili.

In a small bowl, combine the masa and enough water to make a slurry or thin paste. Stir the mixture into the chili, then simmer for another 20–30 minutes and stir frequently. Season to taste with salt and pepper.

Serve warm.

This recipe evolved from a New Year's Day black-eyed pea (bean) dish from Hugh Mangum III. The additions of creamy, absorbent white beans and rich, smoky brisket trimmings transformed the peas into a revelation. Feel free to substitute dried beans for canned. This dish can be made a day in advance—beans soak up flavor and often taste better the next day.

PREPARATION TIME 20 minutes
COOKING TIME 1 hour 15 minutes
SERVES 6–8

16 thick slices (rashers) bacon, chopped
2 onions, chopped
1 head garlic, cloves separated and minced
2 (14-oz/400-g) cans black-eyed peas (beans), drained
2 (14-oz/400-g) cans great northern beans, drained
1 cup (8 fl oz/240 ml) ketchup
½ cup (3¾ oz/110 g) dark brown sugar
4 tablespoons Worcestershire sauce
4 tablespoons maple syrup
1–2 chipotles in adobo sauce, finely chopped
Smoked meat trimmings
Salt and black pepper, to taste

Cook the bacon in a Dutch oven (casserole) over medium heat for 10–12 minutes, until the bacon has rendered. Using a slotted spoon, transfer the bacon to a paper towel–lined plate to drain. Leave 2–3 tablespoons of the rendered bacon fat in the pan.

Add the onions and sauté over medium-high heat for 8–10 minutes, until translucent. Add the garlic and sauté for 2–3 minutes, until fragrant.

Then add the beans, ketchup, brown sugar, Worcestershire sauce, and maple syrup and stir well. Stir in a chipotle (reserving the other one, if using, for later).

Cover the pan, reduce the heat to low, and simmer for 30 minutes. Stir occasionally to prevent the beans from sticking or burning. Season to taste with salt and pepper and, if desired, add another chipotle. Stir in the reserved bacon and smoked meat trimmings. Leave uncovered and simmer for 15–20 minutes. Season again.

Serve immediately.

This rustic flatbread called *shrak*, ubiquitous at mealtimes in Jordan, is often dipped into oil and za'atar and used to scoop up sauces. *Shrak* is equal parts whole wheat (wholemeal) and white flour. It uses a cooking technique with a hot bowl, which achieves a soft, subtly nutty bread perfect as a side dish for a messy feast.

PREPARATION TIME 30 minutes,
plus 2 hours proofing (proving)
COOKING TIME 10–15 minutes
SERVES 4

1 cup (4¼ oz/120 g) plain (all-purpose) flour,
plus extra for dusting
1 cup (4 oz/115 g) whole wheat (wholemeal) flour
1 teaspoon salt
½ tablespoon instant (rapid rise) yeast
½ tablespoon honey
1 teaspoon salt
2 tablespoons olive oil, plus extra for greasing

In a large bowl or stand mixer fitted with a hook attachment, combine the flours, salt, yeast, and honey. Slowly add ¾ cup (6 fl oz/175 ml) of warm water, kneading until the dough comes together. Add the oil and knead for 15 minutes. (Alternatively, transfer the dough to a lightly floured surface and knead with your hands for 15 minutes, or until the dough is smooth.)

Transfer the dough to an oiled bowl, cover with a dish (tea) towel, and set aside to proof (prove) in a warm place for 1 hour, or until doubled in size. Transfer the dough to a lightly floured surface and divide it into 4 equal pieces. Return the dough to the bowl, cover with a dish towel, and proof for 1 hour.

Set a wok or large metal bowl, upside down, over a gas stove and turn on the flame. Heat the wok for 5 minutes until very hot.

On a clean surface generously dusted with flour, roll out a dough ball into a disk. Gently lay the dough over the hot wok and cook on one side for 2–3 minutes, until lightly brown and pliable but not crisp. Place the flatbread on a dish towel, covering it with the overhang to keep it warm. Repeat with the remaining dough balls.

V VG DF NF 5

Lepinja, a simple flatbread, accompanies barbecue dishes in Bosnia, Serbia, Croatia, and Slovenia. The fluffy flatbread is perfect for soaking up juicy meats and rich sauces.

PREPARATION TIME 40 minutes,
plus 55 minutes proofing (proving)
COOKING TIME 10 minutes
SERVES 6

4 cups (1 lb 5 oz/600 g) all-purpose (plain) flour, plus extra for dusting
1½ teaspoons active dry (fast-action) yeast
1½ teaspoons salt
2 tablespoons canola oil

Place the flour in a large bowl and form a well in the center. Add the yeast and 1½ cups (12 fl oz/350 ml) of lukewarm water, then set aside for 5–10 minutes.

Knead the mixture. Add the salt and knead for another 5 minutes. Add the oil and knead for another 4 minutes, or until smooth. Cover the bowl with a dish towel, then set aside in a warm place for 45 minutes to proof (prove), or until the dough has doubled in size.

On a lightly floured surface, roll the dough into a log. Divide it into 6 equal portions and roll each into a ball. Place the balls in a bowl, then cover and set aside to proof for 10 minutes.

Preheat an oven to 480°F/250°C/Gas Mark 9. Lightly dust a baking sheet with flour.

Flatten each ball into a disk, about 6 inches/15 cm in diameter. Place them on the prepared baking sheet, then set aside to rest for 10 minutes.

Using a knife, make a crisscross pattern on each disk. Bake the flatbreads for 8–10 minutes, until golden brown. Transfer the flatbreads to a wire rack, then sprinkle with water and cover with a dish towel.

Serve warm or at room temperature.

TURKISH LAMB FLATBREAD

Lahmacun, a popular street food in Turkey, is a meat-topped thin pizza or flatbread, often eaten on the go, rolled up, or cut into triangles. The name comes from the Arabic term *lahm bi ajeen*, which means "dough with meat." In Turkey, it's traditionally made with ground (minced) lamb, tomato paste (purée), and warm spices and cooked in a wood-fired oven.

PREPARATION TIME 35 minutes,
plus 1 hour proofing (proving)
COOKING TIME 20 minutes
SERVES 8

FOR THE DOUGH
3½ cups (27 fl oz/800 ml) milk

1 tablespoon active dry (fast-action) yeast

1 teaspoon sugar

5 cups (1 lb 10 oz/750 g) all-purpose (plain) flour

1 teaspoon salt

1 tablespoon canola oil

FOR THE TOPPING
½ red bell pepper, seeded, deveined, and cut into chunks

1 shallot, halved

2 cloves garlic

4 tablespoons chopped parsley

1 teaspoon smoked paprika

1 teaspoon ground allspice

½ teaspoon ground cumin

½ teaspoon Aleppo pepper

½ teaspoon ground cinnamon

½ teaspoon cayenne pepper

½ teaspoon salt

4 tablespoons tomato paste (purée)

2 tablespoons olive oil

7 oz/200 g ground (minced) lamb

FOR THE DOUGH In a large bowl, whisk the milk, yeast, and sugar together. Set aside for 10 minutes until frothy. In a stand mixer fitted with the hook attachment, combine the flour and salt. With the motor running, slowly pour in the yeast mixture and mix until the dough comes together. Knead for another 5 minutes, or until the dough becomes elastic. (Alternatively, mix in a large bowl and knead with your hands.) Cover with a dish towel, then set aside in a warm place to proof (prove) for 1 hour.

FOR THE TOPPING Meanwhile, in a food processor, combine all the ingredients except the lamb and pulse until the mixture is homogeneous but slightly chunky. Transfer this mixture into a large bowl and add the lamb. Using your hands, mix until combined.

Preheat a grill to medium-high heat.

Punch the dough, then divide it into 8 equal pieces. Roll each ball into a 12-inch/30-cm disk. Spread the meat mixture evenly over each disk, leaving a ½-inch/1-cm border.

Place half the flatbreads on the grill and cook for 5 minutes, turning once, until the edges are browned. Place the flatbreads on a dish towel, covering it with the overhang to keep it warm. Repeat with the remaining dough balls.

Cornbread, a cake-like bread leavened with baking powder, was first made by Native Americans and is a fixture in the southern United States. A good cornbread is moist with a bit of crumb (but not crumbly) and has some caramelization along the edges. This slightly sweet version gets texture from the corn kernels and pairs well with smoked meats, chili, and burnt-end baked beans.

PREPARATION TIME 15 minutes
COOKING TIME 30–45 minutes
SERVES 8–10

¼ cup (2¼ oz/60 g) melted salted butter, cooled to room temperature, plus extra for greasing
2 cups (8½ oz/240 g) all-purpose (plain) flour
1 cup (4 oz/115 g) cornmeal
1 cup (7 oz/200 g) sugar
1½ tablespoons baking powder
2 teaspoons salt
1½ cups (12 fl oz/350 ml) whole (full-fat) milk
½ cup (4 fl oz/120 ml) canola oil
2 eggs
1 cup (6 oz/175 g) fresh or frozen corn kernels

Preheat an oven to 350°F/180°C/Gas Mark 4. Butter a 10-inch/25-cm cast-iron skillet or a square baking pan. Place the skillet or baking pan in the oven to preheat. (This helps produce caramelization.)

In a large bowl, combine the flour, cornmeal, sugar, baking powder, and salt and mix well. In a medium bowl, combine the milk, butter, oil, and eggs. Whisk to combine. Mix the wet ingredients into the dry ingredients until just combined. Stir in the corn and fold until just combined.

Carefully remove the pan from the oven. Pour in the batter and bake for 30 minutes, or until a knife or toothpick (cocktail stick) inserted into the center comes out clean. If still wet, bake for up to another 15 minutes. Set aside to rest for 15 minutes.

Serve warm.

PARAGUAYAN CORNBREAD

This recipe combines the best parts of two traditional Paraguayan cornbreads: *sopa paraguaya*, which uses cornstarch (cornflour) or cornmeal, and *chipa guasú*, which uses corn kernels. The result is a lusciously rich and textured cornbread that makes a great side dish for any barbecue.

PREPARATION TIME 15 minutes
COOKING TIME 45 minutes–1 hour
SERVES 8

4 tablespoons butter, plus extra for greasing
1 onion, chopped
3 cups (12 oz/350 g) medium-ground cornmeal
1 tablespoon baking powder
2 teaspoons salt
2 cups (16 fl oz/475 ml) whole (full-fat) milk
1 cup (5¾ oz/170 g) cottage cheese
4 eggs
2⅔ cups (1 lb/450 g) frozen corn kernels, thawed
2 cups (9 oz/250 g) shredded Monterey Jack cheese
Black pepper, to taste

Preheat an oven to 375°F/190°C/Gas Mark 5. Butter a 9 ×11-inch/23 x 28-cm baking pan (tin).

Melt the butter in a small skillet over medium-high heat. Add the onion and sauté for 5–7 minutes, until soft and translucent. Set aside to cool.

In a large bowl, combine the cornmeal, baking powder, salt, and pepper. Mix in the milk, cottage cheese, and eggs. Add the onion, corn, and shredded cheese. Pour the batter into the prepared baking pan and bake for 45–60 minutes, until a toothpick (cocktail stick) inserted into the center comes out clean. Set aside to cool for 10 minutes.

Slice into squares, then serve.

This Indian bread comes together quickly and easily in a stand mixer, and it cooks in minutes on a hot grill. Brushed with melted butter, the pillowy flatbread is delectable.

PREPARATION TIME 15 minutes,
plus 4 hours proofing (proving)
COOKING TIME 20 minutes
MAKES 12

4 cups (1 lb 8 oz/675 g) bread flour, plus extra for dusting
2 tablespoons sugar
2½ teaspoons salt
2 teaspoons instant (rapid rise) yeast
1⅔ cups (12 oz/350 g) Greek yogurt
½ cup (4 oz/115 g) melted butter

In the bowl of a stand mixer fitted with a hook attachment, combine the flour, sugar, salt, and yeast. Whisk until combined. Add the yogurt and knead on low speed until it forms a smooth dough.

Transfer the dough onto a lightly floured surface and knead for 5 minutes. Place the dough back into the bowl and cover with plastic wrap (clingfilm). Set aside to rise in a warm place for 2 hours, or until doubled in size.

Divide the dough into 12 equal pieces and roll each into a ball. Place the balls on a baking sheet and cover with a dish towel. Set aside to rise in a warm place for 2 hours, or until doubled in size.

Preheat a grill to medium-high heat.

Using your hands or a rolling pin, stretch each ball into 6 x 10-inch/15 x 25-cm oval shapes. Working in 2–3 batches to avoid overcrowding, place the naan on the grill and cook for 3–5 minutes, until charred. Flip and cook for another 3–5 minutes, until both sides are charred.

Transfer the naan to a plate, then brush it with butter. Cover with a dish towel and grill the remaining naan.

BUTTERMILK BISCUITS

VG NF

Biscuits are ubiquitous in the American South. They are often served warm (ideally straight from the oven) with gravy, butter, or honey. To make them light, buttery, and flaky—as they should be—use very cold, grated butter. If the butter is overworked or too warm, the biscuits become what southerners call "lead sinkers."

PREPARATION TIME 10 minutes
COOKING TIME 15 minutes
SERVES 8–12

3 cups (1 lb/450 g) all-purpose (plain) flour,
plus extra for dusting
2 tablespoons sugar
1½ tablespoons baking powder
1 tablespoon salt
½ cup (4 oz/115 g) cold salted butter
1¼ cups (10 fl oz/300 ml) buttermilk

Preheat an oven to 425°F/220°C/Gas Mark 7. Line a baking sheet with parchment paper.

In a large bowl, combine the flour, sugar, baking powder, and salt and mix thoroughly.

Using a box grater, grate the cold butter into the flour mixture and, working gently, thoroughly combine. Pour in the buttermilk and gently fold the mixture together until just combined.

Transfer the biscuit dough to a well-floured work counter. Press on the dough gently but firmly enough to form a square. Fold the dough in half over itself and press down to form a square again. Repeat 2 more times. (This step helps give the biscuits their interior layers.) After the last fold, press down with your hands to create an even 1-inch/2.5-cm thick layer of dough.

Dust the dough lightly with flour. Using a 2–3-inch/ 5–7.5-cm ring mold or pastry cutter, cut the dough into circles. Once you have cut all the biscuits, re-roll the scraps to use again.

Place the cut biscuits onto the prepared baking sheet and bake for 15 minutes, or until just golden brown on top.

Serve warm.

CHEDDAR AND JALAPEÑO BISCUITS

 VG NF

These simple buttermilk biscuits are enriched with cheddar cheese and fresh jalapeños. Feel free to use a small can of diced hatch chiles in place of the jalapeños.

PREPARATION TIME 10 minutes
COOKING TIME 15 minutes
SERVES 8–12

2 jalapeños, seeded and chopped
3 cups (1 lb/450 g) all-purpose (plain) flour,
plus extra for dusting
2 cups (8½ oz/240 g) shredded mild cheddar cheese
2 tablespoons sugar
1½ tablespoons baking powder
1 tablespoon salt
½ cup (4 oz/115 g) cold salted butter
1¼ cups (10 fl oz/300 ml) buttermilk

Preheat an oven to 425°F/220°C/Gas Mark 7. Line a baking sheet with parchment paper.

In a large bowl, combine the jalapeños, flour, cheese, sugar, baking powder, and salt. Mix thoroughly. Using a box grater, grate the cold butter into the flour mixture and, working gently, thoroughly combine. Add the buttermilk and gently fold the mixture together until just combined.

Transfer the biscuit dough to a well-floured work surface. Press on the dough gently but firmly enough to form a square. Fold the dough in half over itself and press down to form a square again. Repeat twice more. (This step helps to give the biscuits their interior layers.) After the last fold, press down with your hands to create an even 1-inch/2.5-cm thick layer of dough.

Dust the dough lightly with flour. Using a 2–3-inch/ 5–7.5-cm ring mold or pastry cutter, cut the dough into circles. Once you have cut all the biscuits, re-roll the scraps to use again.

Place the cut biscuits onto the prepared baking sheet and bake for 15 minutes, or until just golden brown on top.

Serve warm.

SAUCES & RUBS

NORTH CAROLINA BARBECUE SAUCE

V | VG | GF | DF | NF

In North Carolina, pulled pork reigns supreme, and a Pulled Pork Sandwich (page 155) is one of the foundations of American barbecue. Whether it's from a whole hog, pork shoulder, or bone-in butt, pulled pork is almost always dressed with a vinegar-based sauce—a perfect foil for the smoky, fatty meat, and crisp skin. Use this sauce to mop (baste) the pork while it smokes, and/or mix it in with the pulled pork.

PREPARATION TIME 5 minutes
COOKING TIME 10 minutes
MAKES 5¼ cups (42 oz/1.25 kg)

1 (7-oz/200-g) can chipotles in adobo sauce
2½ cups (20 fl oz/600 ml) apple cider vinegar
1 cup (7¾ oz/220 g) dark brown sugar
2 tablespoons salt
2 tablespoons coarsely ground black pepper
1 tablespoon red pepper flakes
1 tablespoon garlic granules
1 tablespoon onion powder
1 tablespoon ground mustard
1 tablespoon paprika

Strain the adobo sauce into a saucepan and reserve the chipotles for another use.

Add the remaining ingredients to the pan, pour in 1 cup (8 fl oz/240 ml) of water and bring to a boil. Cook for 5 minutes, stirring, until the mixture is homogeneous. Set aside to cool.

The sauce can be stored in an airtight container in the refrigerator for up to 2 weeks.

SOUTH CAROLINA MUSTARD SAUCE

 P. 337

GF | DF | NF

Although most barbecue sauces are ketchup-based, this sauce from South Carolina has a distinct profile with mustard and honey flavors. It pairs especially well with poultry, pork, and French fries.

PREPARATION TIME 5 minutes
COOKING TIME 30 minutes
MAKES About 3½ cups (27 oz/800 g)

4 tablespoons dark brown sugar
2 tablespoons salt
1 tablespoon coarsely ground black pepper
1 teaspoon cayenne pepper
2 cups (16 fl oz/475 ml) yellow mustard
½ cup (4 fl oz/120 ml) apple cider vinegar
½ cup (4 fl oz/120 ml) honey
4 tablespoons ketchup
2 tablespoons Worcestershire sauce

Combine all the ingredients in a small saucepan. Bring to a boil, then reduce the heat to medium-low and simmer for 30 minutes. Set aside to cool.

The sauce can be stored in the refrigerator for up to 2 weeks.

CHILI-LIME WING SAUCE

VG GF NF 5

Use your favorite store-bought chili sauce to make this versatile marinade and dipping sauce. It's not overly spicy or sweet, and the lime nicely balances out the richness of this crowd-pleaser.

PREPARATION TIME 5 minutes
COOKING TIME 10 minutes
MAKES 3 cups (25 oz/750 g)

3 cups (25 fl oz/750 ml) chili sauce
3 cups (1½ lb/680 g) salted butter, cut into 1-inch/2.5-cm cubes
Zest and juice of 12 limes
1 tablespoon salt

Bring the chili sauce to a simmer in a large saucepan. Whisk in the butter, a piece at a time, until all of it has been incorporated. Remove the pan from the heat. Whisk in the lime zest, juice, and salt. Set aside to cool.

The sauce can be stored in an airtight container in the refrigerator for up to 2 weeks.

TEXAS TABLE SAUCE

GF DF NF

This all-purpose barbecue sauce has the requisite ketchup and vinegar base, but maple syrup and chipotle peppers add extra sweet and smoky notes. Plus, the mustard punch nicely complements rich, fatty meat.

Use it as a dip for Smoked Brisket slices (page 116), a dressing for Pulled Pork Sandwiches (page 155), and a finishing glaze for smoked chicken.

PREPARATION TIME 15 minutes
COOKING TIME 10 minutes
MAKES 2 quarts/2 L

1½ cups (12 fl oz/350 ml) apple cider vinegar
1–2 chipotles in adobo sauce, minced
6 tablespoons ground mustard
4 tablespoons dark brown sugar
2 tablespoons salt
1 tablespoon garlic granules
1 tablespoon onion powder
1 tablespoon black pepper
1 tablespoon paprika
1 cup (8½ oz/240 g) ketchup
½ cup (4 fl oz/120 ml) hot sauce
6 tablespoons Worcestershire sauce
2 tablespoons maple syrup
2 tablespoons molasses

In a large saucepan, combine the apple cider vinegar and 1½ cups (12 fl oz/350 ml) of water and warm over medium-low heat. Add the remaining ingredients and whisk until fully combined. Heat the sauce over medium-high heat for 5 minutes. Stir and set aside to cool.

The sauce can be stored in an airtight container in the refrigerator for up to 1 month.

VIETNAMESE DIPPING SAUCE

DF NF 5

The quintessential Vietnamese sauce *nuoc cham* transforms simple ingredients into a complex and versatile sauce. The recipe varies by region and family, but the sauce is generally thinner than most American dipping sauces. The slightly sweet, tangy, and funky flavors wildly enhance most grilled meats, and the sauce can be used as a marinade or vinaigrette.

PREPARATION TIME 10 minutes
MAKES 1 cup (8 oz/225 g)

4 tablespoons sugar
1 clove garlic, minced
1 red bird's eye chile, seeded and minced
4 tablespoons lime juice
3 tablespoons fish sauce

In a small bowl, whisk together the sugar and ½ cup (4 fl oz/120 ml) of hot water, until the sugar dissolves. Stir in the remaining ingredients.

The sauce can be stored in an airtight container in the refrigerator for up to 1 week.

AJÍ AMARILLO SAUCE AND PASTE

PERU

SAUCE VG GF DF NF   **PASTE** V VG GF DF NF

The feisty yellow amarillo pepper is six times as spicy as a jalapeño, wonderfully fruity, and easy to grow. This recipe turns the pepper into a handy paste, which can also be found in Latin stores, but is far more pungent and potent when made at home. The paste is used to make this tangy, creamy Peruvian dipping sauce, a perfect condiment for grilled meats.

PREPARATION TIME 5 minutes
SAUCE SERVES 6
PASTE MAKES 4 tablespoons

FOR THE SAUCE
2 jalapeños, coarsely chopped
2 cloves garlic, chopped
½ cup (1 oz/30 g) chopped cilantro (coriander)
½ cup (4 fl oz/120 ml) mayonnaise
4 tablespoons sour cream
1 tablespoon Ají Amarillo Paste (see below)
2 teaspoons lime juice
1 teaspoon white vinegar
2 tablespoons olive oil
Salt and black pepper

FOR THE PASTE
2 ají amarillo chiles, stemmed, seeded, and chopped
1 clove garlic, chopped
1 tablespoon chopped onion
1 tablespoon olive oil
½ teaspoon salt, plus extra to taste
Black pepper

FOR THE SAUCE In a blender or food processor, combine all the ingredients except the oil, salt, and pepper. Blend until smooth. Slowly drizzle in the oil and blend again. Season to taste with salt and pepper.

The sauce can be stored in an airtight container in the refrigerator for up to 1 week.

FOR THE PASTE In a food processor, combine all the ingredients and blend into a smooth paste. Season to taste with salt and pepper.

→ **CLOCKWISE, FROM LEFT**
VIETNAMESE DIPPING SAUCE, AJÍ AMARILLO SAUCE,
SOUTH CAROLINA MUSTARD SAUCE (PAGE 334)

THAI DIPPING SAUCE

DF	NF

Thai *nam jim* is a magical sauce that serves as a dip for dumplings, spring rolls, grilled meat, and fish, and can also season a bowl of noodles or even a salad. It's a typical Thai condiment that brings big flavor wherever it goes.

PREPARATION TIME 10 minutes, plus 1 hour standing
MAKES 2 cups (16 oz/475 g)

2 green bird's eye chiles, seeded and finely chopped
1 red bird's eye chile, seeded and finely chopped
1 shallot, minced
1 large clove garlic, minced
4 tablespoons finely chopped cilantro (coriander)
4 tablespoons brown sugar
4 tablespoons fish sauce
4 tablespoons lime juice

Combine all the ingredients in a bowl with 4 tablespoons of water and mix well. Set aside for 1 hour at room temperature to let the flavors combine.

The sauce can be stored in an airtight container in the refrigerator for up to 1 week.

GRILLED PINEAPPLE SALSA

V	VG	GF	DF	NF	

This unique salsa combines the fruity sweetness of pineapple with the serious heat of a habanero. Mixed with a garlicky paste and brightened with cilantro (coriander) and lime, the salsa pairs beautifully with grilled meats.

PREPARATION TIME 15 minutes
COOKING TIME 25 minutes
MAKES 4 cups (38 oz/1 kg)

3 cloves garlic
1 red onion, finely chopped
½ pineapple, peeled, cored, and cut into ¾-inch/2-cm-thick slices
1 tablespoon canola oil
2 tablespoons lime juice
2 habanero chiles, stemmed
4 tablespoons olive oil
2 large tomatoes, finely chopped
1 teaspoon salt, plus extra to taste
½ cup (1 oz/30 g) finely chopped cilantro (coriander)

Preheat a grill to high heat.

Place the garlic on a piece of aluminum foil and fold the foil over to create a sealed packet. Repeat with the onion and another piece of foil. Place them directly on the grill and cook for 15 minutes, turning occasionally.

Brush the pineapple with oil, then place it on the grill and cook for 3 minutes on each side. Add the chiles and grill for 6 minutes. Set aside to cool for 5 minutes. Chop the pineapple into ¼-inch/5-mm cubes.

In a large bowl, combine the pineapple, grilled onion, and lime juice.

In a food processor, combine the garlic, chiles, oil, tomatoes, and salt and blend into a smooth paste. Add to the pineapple-onion mixture. Stir in the cilantro (coriander), then season to taste with salt.

The salsa can be stored in an airtight container in the refrigerator for up to 1 week.

CHILEAN SALSA

V VG GF DF NF

Like Pico de Gallo (right) or Chimichurri (page 340), Chilean *pebre* is served alongside grilled meats throughout Latin and South America. In this recipe, the thick salsa gets its heat from jalapeños. If you prefer a hotter sauce, add the chile seeds.

PREPARATION TIME 15 minutes
COOKING TIME 10 minutes
MAKES 3 cups (25 oz/750 g)

Bunch of cilantro (coriander)
5 cloves garlic, minced
1–2 jalapeños, chopped
1 teaspoon salt, plus extra to taste
½ teaspoon black pepper
2 tomatoes, chopped
½–1 cup (4–8 fl oz/120–240 ml) olive oil
⅓ cup (2¾ fl oz/80 ml) red wine vinegar, plus extra to taste

In a food processor, combine the cilantro (coriander), garlic, jalapeños, salt, and pepper and pulse until coarsely chopped. Add the remaining ingredients and ⅓ cup (2¾ fl oz/80 ml) of cold water and process until smooth. Season to taste with more salt or vinegar.
The salsa can be stored in an airtight container in the refrigerator for up to 5 days.

PICO DE GALLO

V VG GF DF NF

Pico de gallo (meaning "beak of the rooster") gets its name from its vibrant red color. This condiment can turn up the volume on any grilled dish. Simple and light, it is made with chopped tomatoes and chiles and goes well with almost everything—especially a bowl of tortilla chips.

PREPARATION TIME 10 minutes, plus 15 minutes marinating
MAKES 4 cups (38 oz/1 kg)

4 tomatoes, chopped
2 serrano chiles, seeded, deveined, and chopped
1 small onion, chopped
2 tablespoons chopped cilantro (coriander) or parsley
3 tablespoons lime juice
Salt and black pepper, to taste

Combine all the ingredients in a large bowl. Cover and refrigerate for at least 15 minutes.
The salsa can be stored in an airtight container in the refrigerator for up to 3 days.

CHIMICHURRI

V | VG | GF | DF | NF

Although *chimichurri* originated in Argentina, many South American countries have their own version of this herbaceous condiment. This Uruguayan recipe combines red wine vinegar and Fresno chiles to create a lively, acidic sauce that instantly brightens grilled fish. It also makes the perfect companion for grilled steak.

PREPARATION TIME 15 minutes
MAKES 2½ cups (18 oz/550 g)

2 cups (4¼ oz/120 g) chopped parsley
7–10 cloves garlic, minced
4 red Fresno chiles, minced
½ cup (¼ oz/10 g) oregano leaves, chopped
½ cup (4 fl oz/120 ml) red wine vinegar
2 cups (16 fl oz/475 ml) extra-virgin olive oil
Salt and black pepper, to taste

Combine all the ingredients in a large bowl. Season to taste with salt and pepper.

The chimichurri can be stored in an airtight container in the refrigerator for 1 week.

CHARRED TOMATO SALSA

V | VG | GF | DF | NF

This Guatemalan salsa known as *chirmol* is popular throughout Latin America. The key is to char the tomatoes on the grill until they turn black yet remain slightly uncooked in the center. The salsa should be served at room temperature.

PREPARATION TIME 10 minutes
COOKING TIME 15 minutes
MAKES 2½ cups (18 oz/550 g)

6 Roma tomatoes
⅓ cup (2¼ oz/60 g) finely chopped white onion
1 cobanero or chiltepin chile, finely chopped
1 tablespoon finely chopped cilantro (coriander)
1 tablespoon finely chopped mint
1 teaspoon lime juice
½ teaspoon salt

Preheat a grill to medium-high heat.

Place the whole tomatoes on the grill and roast for 15 minutes, turning frequently, until the skin turns dark brown. Transfer the tomatoes to a cutting board, then set aside to cool. Coarsely chop.

In a medium bowl, combine all the ingredients. Mix gently and season to taste with salt.

The salsa can be stored in an airtight container in the refrigerator for up to 3 days.

→ **CLOCKWISE, FROM LEFT**
CHIMICHURRI, LEBANESE GARLIC SAUCE (PAGE 352), CHARRED TOMATO SALSA

RED PEPPER-EGGPLANT SAUCE

V VG GF DF NF ◖ ◎ ⊗

Ajvar, which originated in Serbia, became popular throughout the Balkan region after World War II. Often served with grilled meats, the mild condiment blends charred red bell peppers and grilled eggplant (aubergine) with garlic, oil, and vinegar. Many supermarkets now sell jars of *ajvar*, but this homemade version offers unparalleled sweetness and smoky depth.

PREPARATION TIME 20 minutes, plus 15 minutes standing
COOKING TIME 50–55 minutes
MAKES 2 cups (16 oz/475 g)

1 eggplant (aubergine)
5 red bell peppers (2 lb/900 g)
5 cloves garlic, minced
4 tablespoons sunflower or olive oil
1 tablespoon white vinegar
1 teaspoon salt, plus extra to taste
Black pepper

Preheat a grill to high heat for indirect grilling.

Prick the eggplant (aubergine) all over with a fork. Place the peppers on the hot side of the grill and the eggplant on the cooler side. Cover and cook for 10–15 minutes, turning occasionally, until the peppers are blackened all over. Transfer the peppers to a large bowl, cover with plastic wrap (clingfilm), and set aside for 15 minutes. Grill the eggplant for another 15 minutes, or until softened.

Remove the stem, skin, and seeds from the peppers. Transfer the eggplant to a cutting board. Cut off the top, then split lengthwise down the middle. Scoop out the flesh.

In a food processor, combine the peppers, eggplant, and garlic. Pulse until chopped. Add the oil, vinegar, and salt and pulse until smooth.

Transfer the sauce to a small saucepan and simmer over medium-low heat for 25 minutes. Season to taste with salt and pepper. Set aside to cool to room temperature.

The sauce can be stored in an airtight container in the refrigerator for up to 2 weeks.

RED OR GREEN MOJO

V VG GF DF NF

Mojo (meaning "sauce") likely originated in the Canary Islands, a Spanish archipelago off the coast of Africa. Popular in Latin American and Caribbean cuisines, this tangy, versatile sauce is made with a combination of garlic, olive oil, and vinegar—plus warm spices like cumin and paprika. The variations are red *mojo*, made with red chiles, and green *mojo*, prepared with green chiles and herbs.

PREPARATION TIME 10 minutes,
plus at least 30 minutes standing
MAKES 2 cups (16 oz/475 g)

FOR THE RED MOJO
½ head garlic, cloves separated and peeled
2–3 small red Thai chiles, stems removed (seeded for a milder sauce)
2 teaspoons salt
1 teaspoon ground cumin
1 teaspoon smoked or sweet paprika
½ teaspoon dried oregano
½ teaspoon red pepper flakes
½ cup (4 fl oz/120 ml) extra-virgin olive oil
4 tablespoons red wine vinegar

FOR THE GREEN MOJO
½ head garlic, cloves separated and peeled
1 jalapeño, chopped and seeded
2 cups (4¼ oz/120 g) coarsely chopped cilantro (coriander)
2 teaspoons salt
1 teaspoon ground cumin
1 teaspoon smoked or sweet paprika
½ teaspoon dried oregano
½ teaspoon red pepper flakes
½ cup (4 fl oz/120 ml) extra-virgin olive oil
4 tablespoons red wine vinegar

FOR EITHER MOJO Place the garlic in a food processor and blend until it forms a smooth paste. Add the remaining ingredients and blend until smooth. Set aside at room temperature for at least 30 minutes to allow the flavors to meld. Season to taste with more salt or vinegar.

The sauces can be stored in airtight containers in the refrigerator for up to 1 week.

→ **CLOCKWISE, FROM LEFT**
RED PEPPER EGGPLANT SAUCE, GREEN MOJO,
SAMBAL MATA (PAGE 346)

PICKAPEPPA SAUCE

V VG GF DF NF 5

This famous sauce, a revelatory accompaniment to grilled meats, gets its tangy sweetness from tamarind, fresh mango, and raisins. Ketchup, onions, and ancho chili add spice and depth. The sauce comes together quickly in a blender and pairs surprisingly well with Jerk Chicken (page 222). If you can't find ripe mango, substitute frozen chunks.

PREPARATION TIME 5 minutes
COOKING TIME 30 minutes
MAKES 3 cups (25 oz/750 g)

1 cup (8 fl oz/240 ml) apple cider vinegar
1 cup (8 fl oz/240 ml) ketchup
½ cup (3½ oz/100 g) raisins
¼ cup (1½ oz/40 g) diced onions
¼ cup (2 oz/60 g) dark brown sugar
¼ cup (2 oz/60 g) tamarind paste
½ ripe mango, chopped
1 tablespoon garlic granules
1 tablespoon ancho chili
1 teaspoon kosher salt
½ teaspoon cracked black pepper
¼ teaspoon cayenne pepper
¼ teaspoon ground cloves
¼ teaspoon dried thyme

Combine the ingredients in a large saucepan and simmer over medium-low heat for 10 minutes, or until the onions and raisins soften. Remove from the heat and let the sauce cool for 5–10 minutes. Purée the sauce in a blender until smooth.

Serve alongside grilled meats in a small bowl. Refrigerate for up to 1 week.

TOMATO KETCHUP

V VG GF DF NF 5

"Ketchup" was originally a Chinese fermented fish sauce introduced to the Western world by British and Dutch traders in the seventeenth century. In the early nineteenth century, after the sauce had evolved into several savory incarnations, Americans added tomatoes. In 1876, Henry J. Heinz famously manufactured his thicker, sweeter, and less vinegary version. The following tomato-based recipe is a tangy, earthy, sweet blend that makes a perfect partner for simply grilled meats.

PREPARATION TIME 10 minutes
COOKING TIME 90 minutes
MAKES 2 cups (16 oz/475 g)

2 lb (900 g) ripe tomatoes, chopped
1 small onion, finely chopped
2 cloves garlic, minced
½ cup (4 fl oz/120 ml) apple cider vinegar
½ cup (4 oz /120 g) brown sugar
1 teaspoon salt
½ teaspoon ground mustard
½ teaspoon ground cinnamon
¼ teaspoon ground cloves
¼ teaspoon allspice
¼ teaspoon cayenne pepper (optional)

In a large pot, combine the tomatoes, onion, garlic, and ¼ cup (2 fl oz/60 ml) water. Simmer over medium heat until the tomatoes break down and become soft, 20–25 minutes. Once the tomatoes have softened, use a blender to blend the mixture until it is smooth. Strain the purée through a fine sieve to remove seeds and skins, pressing to extract as much liquid as possible.

Return the strained tomato mixture to the pot and add the apple cider vinegar, brown sugar, salt, mustard, cinnamon, cloves, allspice, and cayenne pepper (if using). Stir well to combine.

Bring the mixture to a gentle simmer and cook over low heat, stirring occasionally, for about 45 minutes to 1 hour, until the ketchup thickens. Adjust seasonings to taste.

Allow the ketchup to cool, then transfer to an airtight container. Store in the refrigerator for up to 3 weeks.

ROUILLE

V VG GF DF NF 5

The name of this classic Provençal sauce (traditionally served with bouillabaisse) translates to "rust,"which refers to its reddish-orange color. *Rouille* was originally made with breadcrumbs, garlic, olive oil, and chile peppers, but evolved into a more refined emulsion that incorporated ingredients like saffron, tomatoes, and egg yolks. This garlicky version made with fire-roasted red peppers is a perfect accompaniment for grilled meats, seafood, and vegetables.

PREPARATION TIME 5 minutes
COOKING TIME 10 minutes
MAKES 2 cups (16 oz/475 g)

1 red bell pepper
3 large garlic cloves, crushed
2 egg yolks
1 tablespoon fresh lemon juice
1 teaspoon smoked paprika
Small pinch of saffron threads
1½–2 cups (12–16 fl oz/360–480 ml) extra-virgin olive oil
Salt and cracked black pepper, to taste

Preheat a grill to high heat.

Char the red pepper, turning often, until the skin has blackened. When cool enough to handle, peel and seed the pepper.

In a food processor, combine the peeled pepper, garlic, egg yolks, lemon juice, smoked paprika, and saffron. Blend to combine. With the food processor running, slowly add the olive oil until the sauce emulsifies. Season to taste with salt and pepper and serve immediately.

Store in the refrigerator for up to 1 week.

SAUCE VIERGE

V VG GF DF NF 5

This subtle, herbaceous sauce, which elegantly brightens grilled fish, chicken, and vegetables, is called *"vierge"* or "virgin" because it uses raw ingredients (tomatoes and herbs) and extra-virgin olive oil. It was popularized by French chef Michel Guérard, a pioneer of the "nouvelle cuisine" movement in the 1970s, which championed lighter sauces over the heavy, richness of classical French cooking.

PREPARATION TIME 10 minutes
COOKING TIME 5 minutes
MAKES 2 cups (16 oz/475 g)

2 medium ripe tomatoes, finely diced
1 small garlic clove, minced
1 tablespoon finely chopped fresh basil
1 tablespoon finely chopped fresh parsley
1 tablespoon finely chopped fresh tarragon (optional)
2 tablespoons extra-virgin olive oil
1 tablespoon lemon juice
Salt and pepper, to taste

In a medium bowl, combine all of the ingredients. Mix well and season to taste with salt and pepper. Let the sauce sit at room temperature for 30 minutes before using. Cover and store in the refrigerator for 1 week.

SAMBAL MATA

 P. 343　GF DF NF

This Balinese condiment, popular across Indonesia and Malaysia, has many variations, but is commonly made with lemongrass, chiles, shallots, garlic, lime, and coconut oil. Some chopping is involved—but the result is worth the effort. The crunchy, spicy, and rich sauce elevates everything it touches, especially grilled meats.

PREPARATION TIME: 10 minutes
COOKING TIME: 5 minutes
MAKES 2 cups (17 oz/480 g)

8 shallots, finely chopped
5 red bird's eye chiles, stemmed, seeded, and thinly sliced
1 mild red chile, stemmed, seeded, and thinly sliced
3 makrut lime leaves, middle vein discarded and chopped
3 cloves garlic, minced
2 stalks lemongrass, outer leaves removed and finely chopped
½ teaspoon shrimp paste
½ teaspoon salt
¼ teaspoon sugar
2 tablespoons lime juice
3 tablespoons coconut oil

In a medium bowl, combine the shallots, chiles, makrut lime leaves, garlic, lemongrass, and shrimp paste. Add the salt, sugar, and lime juice.

Heat the oil in a small skillet over medium heat. Pour the hot oil over the lemongrass mixture and stir to combine.

The sambal can be stored in an airtight container in the refrigerator for up to 1 week. To serve, briefly reheat the refrigerated sambal until the coconut oil has liquified.

INDONESIAN PEANUT SAUCE

 P. 349　GF DF 5

The creamy and nutty Indonesian *sambal kacang* sauce accompanies meat satays across the archipelago. After roasted peanuts are pulsed, the sauce comes together quickly.

PREPARATION TIME 10 minutes
COOKING TIME 5–10 minutes
MAKES 3½ cups (1 lb /450 g)

2⅓ cups (12 oz/350 g) roasted peanuts
1 tablespoon tamarind paste
4 tablespoons canola oil
2 tablespoons fish sauce
2 teaspoons sugar

In a food processor, pulse the peanuts into a coarse powder.

In a large skillet, combine the peanut powder and the remaining ingredients. Pour in 1 cup (8 fl oz/ 240 ml) of room-temperature water. Cook over medium heat for 5–10 minutes, until the mixture turns creamy. If needed, add a little more water to thin out the sauce.

The sauce can be stored in an airtight container in the refrigerator for up to 2 weeks.

KOREAN BARBECUE SAUCE

VG GF DF NF

The ubiquitous Korean barbecue sauce *ssamjang* (which means "wrapped thick sauce") combines the umami of *doenjang* (soybean paste) with the heat of *gochujang* (chili paste). Slather it on lettuce leaves, then wrap those leaves around grilled meat.

PREPARATION TIME: 10 minutes
MAKES scant ¾ cup (6 oz/180 g)

4 tablespoons *doenjang* (soybean paste)
2 tablespoons *gochujang* (Korean chili paste)
1 tablespoon honey
1 tablespoon toasted sesame oil
2 scallions (spring onions), thinly sliced
2 cloves garlic, minced
2 teaspoons toasted sesame seeds

Combine all the ingredients in a large bowl and mix well.

The sauce can be stored in an airtight container in the refrigerator for up to 3 days.

RED PEPPER SAUCE

GEORGIA

V VG GF DF NF

Ajika, a central flavoring in Georgian cuisine, is a sweet, slightly bitter sauce that hits many notes with a lingering heat. Although similar to Red Pepper-Eggplant Sauce (page 342), this recipe is far more complex, with unusual ingredients, including blue fenugreek and marigold powder.

PREPARATION TIME 15 minutes
MAKES 1 cup (8 oz/225 g)

2 red bell peppers, seeded and deveined
2–3 red Fresno chiles, seeded and deveined
6 cloves garlic, minced
4 tablespoons cilantro (coriander) leaves
3 tablespoons purple basil leaves
3 tablespoons chopped parsley
1 tablespoon salt, plus extra to taste
2 teaspoons blue fenugreek
1 teaspoon marigold powder
1 teaspoon ground coriander
2 tablespoons sunflower oil

In a food processor, combine the peppers, chiles, and garlic. Pulse a few times until finely chopped. Add the cilantro (coriander), purple basil, parsley, and salt. Pulse again until the herbs are finely chopped. Add the fenugreek, marigold, and coriander and pulse again just to combine.

With the motor running, slowly stream in the oil until it is emulsified.

Transfer the sauce to a fine-mesh sieve and strain until it is a thick paste. Season to taste; it should be very salty.

The sauce can be stored in an airtight container in the refrigerator for up to 2 weeks.

TZATZIKI

V | VG | GF | NF

Salted yogurt, cucumber, garlic, lemon juice, and herbs combine to make the ideal condiment for spicy grilled meats and sausages. Although authentic Greek *tzatziki* is often made with yogurt from sheep's or goat's milk, any strained yogurt will work.

PREPARATION TIME 5 minutes
MAKES 1 cup (8 oz/225 g)

1 clove garlic, grated
½ English cucumber, shredded and blotted dry
1 tablespoon dried dill
½ teaspoon salt, plus extra to taste
¼ teaspoon black pepper, plus extra to taste
½ cup (3½ oz/100 g) Greek yogurt
½ cup (4¼ oz/125 g) sour cream

Combine all the ingredients in a medium bowl. Season to taste with more salt and pepper.

Store in an airtight container in the refrigerator for up to 1 week.

PIRI-PIRI SAUCE

V | VG | GF | DF | NF | 5

Piri-piri (or *peri-peri*) sauce owes its roots to the Portuguese who settled in Mozambique and planted bird's eye chiles *(Capsicum frutescens)*, the basis for this fruity hot sauce. While there are now infinite variations of *piri-piri* sauce (named after the Swahili word for "hot chiles"), most combine sun-baked chiles with citrus and oil. When possible, use African bird's eye chiles, but Fresno, Thai bird's eye, red jalapeño, or any fresh hot red chiles will work. Adjust the number of chiles according to their potency.

PREPARATION TIME 10 minutes
MAKES 1 cup (8 oz/225 g)

2–5 red chiles, seeded, stemmed, and coarsely chopped
2 cloves garlic, chopped
1 roasted red bell pepper, peeled, seeded, and coarsely chopped
2 teaspoons salt
½ cup (4 fl oz/120 ml) extra-virgin olive oil, plus extra if needed

In a blender, combine all the ingredients and purée for 2–3 minutes until smooth. If needed, add more oil to taste.

The sauce can be stored in an airtight glass jar in the refrigerator for up to 1 month.

→ **CLOCKWISE, FROM LEFT**
TZATZIKI, PIRI PIRI SAUCE,
INDONESIAN PEANUT SAUCE (PAGE 346)

ADOBO SAUCE

V VG GF DF NF S

Adobo sauce is a fiery Mexican condiment, and this version, which originated with Mighty Quinn's executive chef Alex Stanko, gets its complexity from beer, brown sugar, Worcestershire sauce, and cumin. It is delicious as a dipping sauce or as a glaze for Baby Back Ribs (page 150). It also makes a wonderful companion to spareribs and pulled pork.

PREPARATION TIME 20 minutes
COOKING TIME 30 minutes
MAKES 1½ quarts/1.5 L

4 dried ancho chiles
2 tablespoons canola oil
3–4 medium Spanish onions, diced
12 cloves garlic, chopped
2 cups (16 fl oz/480 ml) beer (ale or lager)
2 cups (16 fl oz/480 ml) ketchup
3 tablespoons apple cider vinegar
3 tablespoons dark brown sugar
2 tablespoons Worcestershire sauce
1 tablespoon ground cumin
2 chipotles in adobo
(from a can of chipotles in adobo), chopped
Salt and black pepper, to taste

Place the dried ancho chiles in a small saucepan and cover with water. Bring the water to a boil and then remove the pan from heat. Once the water has cooled down enough to touch, drain the ancho chiles, then stem, seed, and chop them.

Place a medium saucepan over medium heat. When hot, add the oil and the onions and sauté for 2–3 minutes. Add the garlic and sauté until fragrant, about 1–2 minutes. Add the ancho chiles, beer, ketchup, apple cider vinegar, dark brown sugar, Worcestershire sauce, cumin, and chipotle peppers. Bring the sauce to a boil, then reduce to a simmer for 15–20 minutes. Let the sauce cool for 5 minutes.

Working in batches, blend the sauce in a blender or food processor until smooth. Taste for seasoning and add more salt and pepper if needed. Store in the refrigerator for up to 1 week.

SOUTH AFRICAN RELISH

V VG GF DF NF

This chunky, colorful vegetable relish known as *chakalaka* is a staple at any South African *braai*, and multiple variations include baked beans. The slightly sweet yet versatile sauce gets a kick from the chiles.

PREPARATION TIME 15 minutes
COOKING TIME 20–30 minutes
MAKES 4 cups (38 oz/1 kg)

2 tablespoons canola oil
1 onion, chopped
2 cloves garlic, minced
2 green bird's eye chiles, seeded, deveined, and chopped
2 carrots, grated
1 green bell pepper, seeded, deveined, and chopped
1 red bell pepper, seeded, deveined, and chopped
1 teaspoon grated fresh ginger or ginger paste
1 teaspoon ground cumin
1 teaspoon ground coriander
1 teaspoon ground turmeric
1 teaspoon paprika
1 (14.5-oz/411-g) can chopped tomatoes
1 (14.5-oz/411-g) can baked beans
Salt and black pepper, to taste

Heat the oil in a large saucepan over medium heat. Add the onion, garlic, chiles, and a pinch of salt. Sauté for 5 minutes, or until the onion is translucent.

Add the carrots, peppers, and ginger and sauté for 5–7 minutes, until the vegetables are tender. Add the cumin, coriander, turmeric, and paprika and stir to combine. Add the tomatoes and baked beans to the saucepan and mix well. Bring to a boil, then reduce the heat to low and simmer for 15–20 minutes, stirring occasionally. Season to taste with salt and pepper. Set aside to cool to room temperature.

The relish can be stored in an airtight container in the refrigerator for up to 1 week.

CHERMOULA

V VG GF DF NF

Similar to Chimichurri (page 340), *chermoula* is a bright, herb-based condiment often served with grilled meats or as a dip for bread in African and Middle Eastern cuisines.

If you don't have a blender or food processor, finely chop the herbs by hand and mix all the ingredients in a large bowl.

PREPARATION TIME 10 minutes, plus 1 hour refrigeration
MAKES 1 cup (8 oz/225 g)

2 cloves garlic, minced
½ cup (1 oz/30 g) chopped cilantro (coriander) leaves
½ cup (1 oz/30 g) chopped parsley leaves
1 tablespoon paprika
1 teaspoon ground cumin
1 teaspoon ground coriander
¼ teaspoon cayenne pepper
Juice of 1 lemon
Juice of ½ lime
½ cup (4 fl oz/120 ml) extra-virgin olive oil
Salt and black pepper, to taste

In a blender or food processor, combine the garlic, cilantro (coriander), parsley, paprika, cumin, coriander, and cayenne pepper. Pulse until the herbs are finely chopped.

Add the lemon juice, lime juice, and oil and pulse until well combined. Season to taste with salt and pepper. Transfer the sauce to a small bowl, cover, and refrigerate for at least 1 hour.

The sauce can be stored in an airtight container in the refrigerator for up to 3 weeks.

PEPPER-GARLIC PASTE

V VG GF DF NF

Pilpelchuma, which translates to "pepper-garlic" in Hebrew, is a red chili paste that originated with Libyan Jews and is now a popular condiment throughout Africa and the Middle East. Traditionally made with dried red peppers, garlic, caraway and cumin seeds, it is used to make marinades, sauces, and spreads. To increase the heat, replace the chipotle with a hotter chile like guajillo.

PREPARATION TIME 10 minutes, plus 15 minutes soaking
COOKING TIME 5 minutes
MAKES 1½ cups (15 oz/430 g)

15 dried chipotle peppers, chopped
½ tablespoon caraway seeds
½ tablespoon cumin seeds
15 cloves garlic
⅓ cup (2¾ fl oz/80 ml) canola oil
1 tablespoon Aleppo pepper
½ teaspoon salt
½ teaspoon sugar
3 tablespoons lemon juice

Soak the chopped chipotle peppers in hot water for 15 minutes.

In a small skillet over medium heat, heat the caraway and cumin seeds for 2 minutes, or until nutty and fragrant. Set aside to cool for 2 minutes, then grind in a spice grinder.

Drain the soaked chiles, then rinse thoroughly. Remove the seeds.

In a food processor, combine the garlic and half of the oil and blend for a minute. Add the chiles, ground caraway and cumin, Aleppo pepper, salt, sugar, and lemon juice and process to a fine paste. Transfer the sauce into a small jar and top with a layer of the remaining oil.

The chili paste can be stored in an airtight container in the refrigerator for up to 2 weeks.

LEBANESE GARLIC SAUCE

LEBANON

 P. 341

V | VG | GF | DF | NF | 5

This rich yet airy white sauce called *toum* accompanies many traditional Lebanese dishes like Lebanese Chicken Skewers (page 55). Be sure to use fresh garlic and drizzle in the oil very slowly.

PREPARATION TIME 10 minutes
COOKING TIME 10 minutes
MAKES 2 cups (16 oz/475 g)

½ cup (2½ oz/70 g) cloves garlic
1 teaspoon salt
2 tablespoons lemon juice
1 cup (8 fl oz/240 ml) canola oil

Combine the garlic and the salt in a food processor and pulse until combined. Add 1 tablespoon of lemon juice and blend until it forms a paste.

With the motor running, slowly trickle in 4 tablespoons oil and ½ tablespoon of lemon juice. Repeat with another 4 tablespoons of oil and the remaining ½ tablespoon of lemon juice. Add 4 tablespoons oil and 1 tablespoon of ice water. Then add the remaining oil and blend until the sauce is emulsified.

The sauce can be stored in an airtight glass container in the refrigerator for up to 2 weeks.

INDIAN YOGURT SAUCE

INDIA

VG | GF | NF

This cooling condiment, or *raita*, is always made from yogurt but can include a variety of vegetables, herbs, and spices. It is an integral part of many meals in India, especially barbecue, where it's a welcome relief from spicy dishes.

PREPARATION TIME 10 minutes, plus 15 minutes standing
COOKING TIME 10 minutes
MAKES 1½ cups (15 oz/430 g)

1 large English cucumber, peeled
1 teaspoon salt, plus extra to taste
1 cup (7 oz/200 g) Greek yogurt
½ teaspoon garam masala
⅛ teaspoon cayenne pepper
2 tablespoons chopped cilantro (coriander)
1 small serrano chile, minced

Grate the cucumber into a colander. Add the salt, toss, and set aside in the sink for 15 minutes. Rinse the cucumber, then squeeze dry with a towel. Transfer it to a medium bowl.

In a small bowl, combine the yogurt, garam masala, and the cayenne pepper. Add the yogurt mixture to the bowl of cucumbers. Stir in the cilantro (coriander) and chile. Season to taste. Refrigerate until ready to serve.

The sauce can be stored in an airtight container in the refrigerator for up to 3 days. Stir before serving.

LAMB SAUCE

VG GF NF

This tangy sauce, which balances tart yogurt with lime, sweet honey, and warm spices, pairs exceptionally well with lamb—especially fattier cuts like shoulder or neck. It's also a perfect complement to grilled leg of lamb.

PREPARATION TIME 5 minutes
MAKES 2½ cups (18 oz/550 g)

2 cloves garlic, minced
1 tablespoon ground cumin
2 teaspoons ground coriander
1 teaspoon red pepper flakes
1 teaspoon smoked paprika
1 teaspoon salt, to taste
2 cups (14 oz/400 g) Greek yogurt
2 tablespoons honey
Zest and juice of 2 limes
Black pepper, to taste

Combine all the ingredients in a medium bowl. Season to taste with salt and pepper.

The sauce can be stored in an airtight container in the refrigerator for up to 2 weeks.

ALABAMA WHITE SAUCE

GF DF NF

In the early 1920s, Big Bob Gibson from Decatur, Alabama, would cook for large gatherings in his backyard. He smoked pork shoulders with an eastern North Carolina mop-style sauce and dipped chicken into a mayonnaise-vinegar sauce that kept the meat moist. When Bob opened his first barbecue restaurant in 1925, that tangy, peppery white sauce—a great complement to smoked chicken (page 237)—was on the menu and has since become one of the most popular barbecue sauces in the country.

PREPARATION TIME 5 minutes
MAKES: 3½ cups (27 oz/800 g)

5 tablespoons sugar
2 tablespoons black pepper, plus extra to taste
1 tablespoon salt, plus extra to taste
1 tablespoon garlic granules
2 cups (16 fl oz/475 ml) mayonnaise
¾ cup (6 fl oz/175 ml) apple cider vinegar
1 tablespoon Worcestershire sauce
1 tablespoon hot sauce

Combine all the ingredients in a medium bowl. Season to taste with salt and pepper.

The sauce can be stored in an airtight container in the refrigerator for up to 2 weeks.

SERBIAN CHEESE SPREAD

SERBIA

Kajmak, a traditional Balkan condiment often served with grilled sausages and bread, is a cheese spread made from unpasteurized, unhomogenized milk. Similar in texture to clotted cream, it is fluffy with a strong cheesy flavor. Traditional Serbian *kajmak* matures for months in wooden vessels called *čabrica*. This recipe makes a younger *kajmak* that doesn't need aging.

PREPARATION TIME 5 minutes, plus at least 12 hours cooling
COOKING TIME 20 minutes
MAKES 2 cups (15 oz/440 g)

2 quarts/1.9 L raw cow's milk or sheep's milk
1 teaspoon salt

Bring the milk to a boil in a medium saucepan. Turn off the heat, then set aside for 4 hours to cool completely. Do not stir.

Use a spoon to skim the cream off the surface. Place the cream into a bowl, then refrigerate. Repeat the boiling and cooling process 3–4 times, skimming off the cream and adding it to the bowl in the refrigerator each time. Season with salt and mix well.

The cheese spread can be stored in an airtight container in the refrigerator for up to 2 weeks.

BARBECUE SPREAD

UNITED STATES VIRGIN ISLANDS

This cooling, creamy spread, beloved at barbecues in St. Croix and other parts of the United States Virgin Islands, pairs well with Bahamian Grilled Chicken (page 220), pork, fish, and burgers. Serve it as a sauce or scoop it up with Grilled Plantains (page 308) or tortilla chips.

PREPARATION TIME 5 minutes
SERVES 4–6

1–2 avocados, mashed
2 tablespoons chopped onion
2 tablespoons chopped green bell pepper
4 tablespoons mayonnaise
2 tablespoons ketchup
Tabasco sauce, to taste
Salt and black pepper, to taste

In a small bowl, combine all the ingredients. Season to taste with Tabasco sauce, salt, and pepper.

The spread can be stored in an airtight container in the refrigerator for up to 1 week.

LIVER SAUCE

DF NF

This tangy liver-based sauce (often called *Mang Tomas* after a popular *lechón* shop in Manila) is the go-to sauce for Spit-Roasted Pig or *lechón* (page 179), although Filipinos also serve it with fried chicken and dumplings. You can find it in Asian markets in a bottle labeled "All-Purpose Sauce," but the homemade version is even tastier.

PREPARATION TIME 10 minutes
COOKING TIME 10 minutes
SERVES 12

4 oz/115 g fresh pork liver or chicken liver
2 tablespoons canola oil
1 small yellow onion, finely chopped
5 cloves garlic, finely chopped
⅓ cup (2¾ fl oz/80 ml) white vinegar
4 tablespoons brown sugar
⅓ cup (1½ oz/40 g) breadcrumbs
Salt and black pepper

Pulse the liver in a food processor until it forms a paste. (Don't wash the processor bowl yet; it will be used again.)

Heat the oil in a medium saucepan over medium-high heat. Add the onion and sauté for 5 minutes, or until softened. Add the garlic and sauté for another 30 seconds, or until fragrant. Add the liver paste, vinegar, and brown sugar and stir to combine. Pour in 1½ cups (12 fl oz/350 ml) of water and bring to a boil. Add the breadcrumbs, then reduce the heat and cook for another 5 minutes.

Pour the sauce back into the food processor and blend until smooth. Season to taste with salt and pepper. Set aside to cool to room temperature.

The sauce can be stored in an airtight container in the refrigerator for up to 2 weeks.

BELGIAN BEER MARINADE

VG DF NF

Beer, the drink of choice for many American barbecue aficionados, is an ideal base for meat marinades. Stronger beers will result in stronger flavors, so choose according to your tastes. This marinade gets a malty sweetness and earthy bitterness from Belgian beer and becomes a powerful flavor-maker with the addition of honey, mustard, fresh ginger, and paprika.

PREPARATION TIME 10 minutes
MAKES 4 cups (32 oz/960 g)

2 cups (16 fl oz/475 ml) Belgian beer
½ cup (4 fl oz/120 ml) honey
½ cup (4 fl oz/120 ml) mustard
4 tablespoons canola oil
4 scallions (spring onions), chopped
4 cloves garlic, crushed
2 slices fresh ginger, crushed
1 onion, thinly sliced
½ red bell pepper, seeded, deveined, and finely chopped
1 teaspoon salt
1 teaspoon black pepper
1 tablespoon pickling spices
1 tablespoon paprika

In a large bowl, whisk together the beer, honey, mustard, and oil. Add the remaining ingredients and stir well.

The marinade can be stored in an airtight container in the refrigerator for up to 3 days.

SOUTH AFRICAN SPICE RUB

V | VG | GF | DF | NF

Braai is the Afrikaans word for both a barbecue or cookout event and the actual grill, which is usually an open outdoor grill.

This fragrant dry rub, called *braai* rub, is fantastic on any cut of steak, but it has special meaning when used on a T-bone—which Archbishop Desmond Tutu, while campaigning to unite South Africans around the *braai*, said mimics the shape of Africa itself.

PREPARATION TIME 10 minutes
MAKES 1¼ cups (10 oz/280 g)

½ cup (2½ oz/70 g) salt
4 tablespoons brown sugar
4 tablespoons coriander seeds
2 tablespoons black peppercorns
2 tablespoons paprika
1 tablespoon dried thyme
1 tablespoon onion powder
2 teaspoons garlic granules

In a spice grinder, combine all the ingredients and blend until it becomes a fine powder.

The rub can be stored in an airtight glass jar for up to 4 weeks.

WEST AFRICAN SPICE RUB

 P. 359

V | VG | GF | DF

Known as *tsire* in northern Africa and *suya* in the south, this West African spice rub has a base of dry-roasted peanuts. It is traditionally used in northern Cameroon, Nigeria, Niger, and some parts of Sudan as a rub for grilled meats, but its earthy, nutty flavor makes it a unique garnish for soups, salads, and eggs.

PREPARATION TIME 10 minutes
MAKES 1½ cups (9 oz/250 g)

1½ cups (7¾ oz/220 g) dry-roasted peanuts
1½ teaspoons chili powder
1½ teaspoons ground ginger
½ teaspoon ground nutmeg
½ teaspoon ground cloves
½ teaspoon ground cinnamon

Pulse the peanuts in a food processor until crumbly. Add the remaining ingredients and pulse until just combined.

The rub can be stored in an airtight glass jar for up to 1 month.

SYRIAN SPICE RUB

V | VG | GF | DF | NF

Many variations of this Middle Eastern spice blend, *baharat*, are used in marinades and sauces for grilled meats and fish, as well as in rice dishes. It allegedly originated in Syria, and most variations include cumin, coriander, cinnamon, cardamom, and cloves.

PREPARATION TIME 15 minutes
COOKING TIME 5 minutes
MAKES ⅓ cup (2¾ oz/75 g)

1½ tablespoons paprika
1 tablespoon black peppercorns
1 tablespoon cumin seeds
2 teaspoons coriander seeds
1 teaspoon cloves
1 teaspoon ground cinnamon
½ teaspoon cardamom pods
¼ teaspoon ground nutmeg

Dry-roast all the ingredients in a small skillet over medium-high heat until fragrant. Set aside to cool. In a spice grinder, grind all the cooled ingredients to a fine powder.

The rub can be stored in an airtight glass jar for up to 2 weeks.

ADOBO RUB

V | VG | GF | DF | NF

Adobo (from the Spanish word *adobado*, meaning "marinated") is a versatile seasoning popular in many of the countries that were under Spanish and Portuguese rule, especially the Philippines, much of South America, and Spanish-speaking parts of the Caribbean. Each country has its own twist on the spice blend, but most variations work beautifully with chicken and pork, like the Adobo Baby Back Ribs (page 150).

PREPARATION TIME 5 minutes
MAKES 4 cups (1 lb 4 oz/570 g)

1 cup (4¼ oz/120 g) paprika
1 cup (5 oz/140 g) salt
½ cup (3½ oz/100 g) black pepper
½ cup (3 oz/85 g) garlic powder
½ cup (3 oz/85 g) onion powder
4 tablespoons ground cumin
4 tablespoons dried oregano

Combine all the ingredients in a bowl and mix well.

The rub can be stored in an airtight container for up to 1 month.

CAJUN RUB

[V] [VG] [GF] [DF] [NF]

Despite the infinite variations, Cajun rubs generally include black pepper, onion powder, garlic powder, cayenne pepper, and paprika. Some cooks add cumin, herbs, or celery seeds. Creole rubs, also from Louisiana, typically add herbs like oregano and thyme to the basic Cajun blend. Use this bold seasoning to rub meat, season stews, or sprinkle on vegetables.

PREPARATION TIME 5 minutes
MAKES 1 cup (5½ oz/150 g)

5 tablespoons smoked paprika
4 tablespoons salt
4 tablespoons garlic powder
2 tablespoons black pepper
2 tablespoons onion powder
2 tablespoons cayenne pepper
1 tablespoon red pepper flakes

Combine all the ingredients in a bowl and mix well.
 The rub can be stored in an airtight container for up to 1 month.

PORK AND POULTRY RUB

[V] [VG] [GF] [DF] [NF]

This all-purpose rub has just enough heat to temper the white sugar (brown sugar tends to clump). It is ideal for seasoning almost any cut of pork or chicken before grilling or smoking.

PREPARATION TIME 5 minutes
MAKES 4½ cups (1 lb 8 oz/675 g)

1 cup (1¾ oz/120 g) paprika
½ cup (2½ oz/70 g) salt
½ cup (3½ oz/100 g) sugar
½ cup (1¾ oz/50 g) chili powder
½ cup (2¼ oz/60 g) black pepper
½ cup (2½ oz/70 g) ground cumin
½ cup (3 oz/85 g) garlic granules
4 tablespoons ground mustard
4 tablespoons ancho chili powder
1 teaspoon cayenne pepper

Combine all the ingredients in a bowl and mix well.
 The rub can be stored in an airtight container for up to 3 months.

→ **CLOCKWISE, FROM LEFT**
CAJUN RUB, PORK AND POULTRY RUB,
WEST AFRICAN SPICE RUB (PAGE 356)

LAMB RUB

V | VG | GF | DF | NF

This simple rub is a quick fix for lamb shoulder, belly, shanks, and neck. The sugar helps to create a sturdy, flavorful bark while balancing the rub's savory flavors.

PREPARATION TIME 5 minutes
MAKES 3¾ cups (1 lb 8 oz/675 g)

2 cups (10 oz/280 g) salt
1 cup (6¾ oz/190 g) black pepper
4 tablespoons sugar
4 tablespoons garlic granules
3 tablespoons ground cumin
2 tablespoons ground coriander

Combine all the ingredients in a bowl and mix well.
   The rub can be stored in an airtight container at room temperature for 1 month.

BEEF RUB

V | VG | GF | DF | NF | 5

Although beef benefits from even a simple salt and pepper rub, this Texas-born combination of paprika, garlic, and cayenne pepper adds another dimension of flavor to ribs, steaks, and even burgers.

PREPARATION TIME 5 minutes
MAKES 3¼ cups (1 lb/350 g)

1 cup (4¼ oz/120 g) paprika
1 cup (5 oz/140 g) salt
1 cup (5 oz/140 g) coarsely ground black pepper
1 teaspoon cayenne pepper
2 tablespoons garlic granules

Combine all the ingredients in a bowl and mix well.
   The rub can be stored in an airtight container at room temperature for 3 months.

CREOLE RUB

V VG GF DF NF

This versatile spice mixture, which blends French, Spanish, African, and Caribbean flavors, originated in Louisiana, where it became a hallmark of Creole cuisine. The slightly spicy, smoky blend of paprika, garlic, thyme, oregano, and cayenne is often used to season chicken, shrimp (prawns), and catfish for grilling or blackening—a technique made famous by Chef Paul Prudhomme in the 1980s.

PREPARATION TIME 5 minutes
COOKING TIME 5 minutes
MAKES 1 cup (8 oz/225 g)

4 tablespoons paprika
2 tablespoons garlic powder
2 tablespoons onion powder
2 tablespoons dried oregano
2 tablespoons dried thyme
2 tablespoons black pepper
2 tablespoons white pepper
2 tablespoons salt
1 tablespoon cayenne pepper
2 teaspoons ground cumin

Combine all the ingredients in a small bowl and mix well. Store in an airtight container in a cool, dry place for up to 2 weeks.

JERK RUB

V VG GF DF NF

This Jamaican rub gets its name from the word "jerking," which is the method of poking holes in meat for better penetration of the seasoning. The jerk spice blend became associated with this process, and the name stuck. It is traditionally used to season chicken, but it works well on pork, fish, and even vegetables.

PREPARATION TIME 10 minutes
MAKES 1 cup (5½ oz/150 g)

2 tablespoons onion powder
2 tablespoons garlic powder
4 teaspoons brown sugar
4 teaspoons dried thyme
4 teaspoons salt
4 teaspoons black pepper
2 teaspoons cayenne pepper
2 teaspoons ground allspice
2 teaspoons dried parsley
2 teaspoons paprika
2 teaspoons red pepper flakes
1 teaspoon ground cinnamon
1 teaspoon ground nutmeg
½ teaspoon ground cloves
½ teaspoon ground cumin

Combine all the ingredients in a bowl and mix well.
  The rub can be stored in an airtight container for up to 1 month.

DESSERTS

GRILLED PINEAPPLE

Grilled pineapple, flavored with coconut and palm sugar, is a simple and refreshing dessert served in roadside shops and restaurants all over Thailand. To ensure maximum sweetness, use a ripe pineapple; a pineapple is ripe if you can easily remove one of the leaves.

PREPARATION TIME 15 minutes
COOKING TIME 10–20 minutes
SERVES 8

1 pineapple
1 (14-fl oz/400-ml) can coconut milk
½ cup (3¾ oz/110 g) loosely packed brown sugar
¼ teaspoon salt
1 tablespoon canola oil

Preheat a grill to medium heat.

Cut off the top, bottom, and skin of the pineapple, then slice it lengthwise into quarters. Cut out the core of each quarter, then slice each section in half to create 8 pieces.

Warm the coconut milk in a small saucepan over medium heat. Add the brown sugar and salt and stir until the sugar has dissolved. Set aside.

In a large bowl, combine the pineapple and half of the coconut mixture. Pour the other half into a dipping bowl and refrigerate until ready to eat.

Thread the pineapple onto skewers, then brush them with the oil. Place them on the grill and cook for 5–10 minutes on each side, until the pineapple turns bright yellow and has grill marks. Transfer to a serving dish.

Serve with the chilled dipping sauce.

CHARRED PEACHES WITH LABNEH

This simple dessert combines grilled peaches with *labneh*, a thick strained yogurt popular in the Middle East and the Mediterranean. The fruit, caramelized from the heat, pairs beautifully with the creamy labneh, honey, and vanilla.

PREPARATION TIME 10 minutes
COOKING TIME 5 minutes
SERVES 4

2 peaches, halved and pitted (stoned)
1 tablespoon grapeseed oil
½ cup (3½ oz/100 g) labneh or Greek yogurt
1 vanilla bean, scraped
1 teaspoon honey
1 tablespoon pomegranate seeds
4 tablespoons chopped mint

Preheat a grill to high heat.

Brush the peaches with the oil. Place them on the grill, cut side down, and cook for 3–4 minutes, until charred.

In a small bowl, whisk together the labneh or yogurt, vanilla, and honey.

Spread the labneh on a serving dish and top with the peaches, pomegranate seeds, and mint.

GRILLED SUMMER PEACHES WITH SMOKED VANILLA BEAN ICE CREAM

Sweet grilled summer peaches pair perfectly with this transformative ice cream, which gets a toasty, spiced flavor from the smoked vanilla bean.

PREPARATION TIME 10 minutes, plus at least 4 hours chilling and 30 minutes churning
COOKING TIME 1 hour
SERVES 6

FOR THE ICE CREAM

3 vanilla beans
2 cups (16 fl oz/475 ml) heavy (double) cream
1 cup (8 fl oz/240 ml) whole (full-fat) milk
¾ cup (5 oz/140 g) sugar
½ teaspoon salt
7 egg yolks

FOR THE PEACHES

6 ripe peaches
1–2 tablespoons light brown sugar
1 teaspoon flaky sea salt

FOR THE ICE CREAM Preheat a smoker to low heat (225°F/107°C).

Place the vanilla beans on the smoker and smoke them for 30–45 minutes. Set aside. When cool enough to handle, split and scrape the smoked vanilla beans into a small bowl.

In a small saucepan, combine the heavy (double) cream, milk, sugar, salt, and smoked vanilla beans. Simmer over medium heat for 5 minutes, or until the sugar is completely dissolved. Set aside.

In a separate bowl, whisk the egg yolks. Slowly whisk a third of the hot cream into the yolks, then whisk the yolk mixture back into the saucepan with the remaining cream. Gently cook over medium-low heat for 5–10 minutes, until the mixture is thick enough to coat the back of a spoon (about 170°F/76°C on an instant-read thermometer).

Strain the mixture through a fine-mesh sieve into a bowl, then set aside to cool to room temperature. Cover and refrigerate for at least 4 hours but, preferably, overnight.

Once chilled, churn the mixture in an ice-cream machine for about 20–30 minutes, or according to the manufacturer's directions. Store the ice cream in a freezer until needed.

FOR THE PEACHES Preheat a grill over medium-high heat.

Slice the peaches in half from the top to the bottom, then pit (stone). Place the peaches on the grill, cut side down, and cook for 2–4 minutes, until their natural sugars caramelize. Flip the peaches and grill for another 1–2 minutes. Sprinkle the peaches with light brown sugar and a few flakes of sea salt. Transfer the peaches to individual serving dishes or bowls.

Serve warm with the smoked vanilla bean ice cream.

GRILLED BANANAS FOSTER

Bananas Foster, bananas flambéed in a caramel rum sauce and topped with vanilla ice cream, originated in 1950s New Orleans at chef Owen Brennan's restaurant, Vieux Carré. The dish was named after Brennan's friend Richard Foster, the chairman of the New Orleans Crime Commission. This flashy, delicious dessert is easy to prepare on a grill.

PREPARATION TIME 10 minutes
COOKING TIME 30 minutes
SERVES 6

½ cup (4 oz/115 g) salted butter
1 cup (7¾ oz/220 g) dark brown sugar
1 tablespoon vanilla paste
1 teaspoon salt
1 teaspoon ground cinnamon
¼ teaspoon ground cloves
¼ teaspoon ground allspice
½ cup (4 fl oz/120 ml) dark rum or bourbon
6 firm, ripe bananas
Vanilla ice cream, to serve

Preheat a grill to high heat.

Melt the butter in a small saucepan over medium-low heat, until it starts to turn brown and smell nutty. Add the brown sugar, vanilla, salt, cinnamon, cloves, and allspice and whisk to combine. Stir in the rum or bourbon, then increase the heat to medium-high. Cook for 3–5 minutes, until the sauce is thick enough to coat the back of a spoon.

Split the bananas in half lengthwise. Brush them with the sauce, then place them on the grill and cook for 5–10 minutes, until caramelized. Brush again, then flip and cook for another 5–10 minutes, until caramelized on the other side. Carefully transfer the bananas to individual plates.

Drizzle with the warm sauce, then top with a scoop of vanilla ice cream. Serve immediately.

A warm fruit cobbler served à la mode is summer in a bowl. The golden buttery crust cradles warm fruit that is just sweet enough. Topped with ice cream or whipped cream, this dessert is always a winner. This recipe uses a pan on the grill and offers a choice of filling—peach or blueberry and peach—but feel free to substitute either option with your preferred fruit.

PREPARATION TIME 15 minutes, plus 15 minutes macerating
COOKING TIME 45 minutes–1 hour
SERVES 8–12

FOR THE PEACH FILLING
6 peaches, cut into ½-inch/1-cm slices
½ cup (3¾ oz/110 g) light brown sugar
1 tablespoon vanilla paste
2 teaspoons salt
1 teaspoon ground cinnamon
½ teaspoon ground fresh ginger

FOR THE BLUEBERRY-PEACH FILLING
4 peaches, cut into ½-inch/1-cm slices
3 cups (1 lb/450 g) blueberries
½ cup (3¾ oz/110 g) light brown sugar
1 tablespoon vanilla paste
2 teaspoons salt
½ teaspoon ground ginger

FOR THE TOPPING
1¼ cups (6¾ oz/190 g) all-purpose (plain) flour
1 cup (7 oz/200 g) sugar
2 teaspoons baking powder
1½ teaspoons salt
1 cup (8 fl oz/240 ml) whole (full-fat) milk
8 tablespoons (4 oz/115 g) salted butter, cubed

FOR SERVING
Fresh whipped cream or vanilla ice cream

Preheat a grill to medium heat for indirect grilling.

FOR THE FILLING Combine all the ingredients in a large mixing bowl. Set aside for 15 minutes to macerate.

FOR THE TOPPING In a large bowl, combine the flour, sugar, baking powder, and salt. Pour in the milk and mix again.

Place a 10-inch/25-cm cast-iron skillet on the hot part of the grill. Add the butter and cook until slightly browned. Add the topping mix and spread it evenly to cover the bottom of the pan. Spoon the fruit on top, then move the pan away from direct heat. Close the grill lid and cook for 45–60 minutes, until the fruit topping is golden brown. Set aside for 15–20 minutes.

Serve warm with fresh whipped cream or a scoop of vanilla ice cream.

BLUEBERRY-PINEAPPLE UPSIDE-DOWN SKILLET CAKE

This is a spin on the classic pineapple upside-down cake, which originated in 1925 when the Dole company held a pineapple recipe contest won by Mrs. Robert Davis from Norfolk, Virginia. This version is made in a cast-iron skillet on the grill. The fruit on the bottom becomes the top, which keeps the cake extraordinarily moist. It is a perfect final act for a barbecue feast.

PREPARATION TIME 20 minutes
COOKING TIME 40–45 minutes
SERVES 6–8

FOR THE CAKE

½ cup (4 oz/115 g) salted butter, softened
1 cup (7 oz/200 g) sugar
2 eggs
1 tablespoon vanilla paste
1½ cups (8 oz/225 g) all-purpose (plain) flour
1½ teaspoons baking powder
1 teaspoon salt
½ cup (4 fl oz/120 ml) whole (full-fat) milk

FOR THE FRUIT

4 tablespoons salted butter
½ cup (3¾ oz/110 g) packed brown sugar
1 pineapple, peeled, cored, and cut into ¼-inch/5-mm-thick rings
1 cup (5½ oz/150 g) fresh or frozen blueberries

FOR SERVING

Fresh whipped cream or vanilla ice cream

FOR THE CAKE In a large bowl or stand mixer, cream the butter and sugar. Add the eggs and vanilla and beat until thoroughly combined.

In a separate medium bowl, whisk together the flour, baking powder, and salt. Gently add the flour mixture to the butter-sugar mixture. Using a rubber spatula, fold in the milk.

FOR THE FRUIT Preheat a grill to medium heat. Place a cast-iron skillet on the grill and warm up for 10 minutes. Carefully remove the skillet from the grill.

Melt the butter in the skillet, then tilt the pan to coat the bottom and sides. Sprinkle the brown sugar evenly across the bottom of the pan. Arrange the pineapple rings, then scatter the blueberries evenly on top.

Pour the batter over the fruit mixture, then return the pan to the grill. Close the lid and grill for 30 minutes. Check on the color: If it has no color, grill for another 10–15 minutes, uncovered. If the cake is beginning to brown, loosely cover it with aluminum foil while it's grilling. The cake is done when a toothpick (cocktail stick) inserted into the center comes out clean. Set aside for 10–20 minutes.

Carefully invert the cake onto a serving dish. Top with whipped cream or vanilla ice cream and serve immediately.

A beloved treat in the United States, this delicious and easy take on the childhood classic uses vanilla paste, sea salt, and brown butter (butter cooked in a pan until it starts to brown).

PREPARATION TIME 5 minutes, plus 45–60 minutes cooling
COOKING TIME 10 minutes
SERVES 8–12

½ cup (2 oz/55 g) butter, plus extra for greasing
8 cups (12½ oz/360 g) mini marshmallows
1 tablespoon vanilla paste
1½ teaspoons flaky sea salt
6 cups (15½ oz/150 g) puffed rice cereal

Butter a baking pan, then line it with parchment paper.

Melt the butter in a large saucepan over medium heat until it begins to brown and smells nutty. Add 6 cups (9¾ oz/275 g) of marshmallows, then reduce the heat to low and stir until the marshmallows have melted. Remove from the heat, then stir in the vanilla paste and salt. Add the cereal and the remaining 2 cups (3¼ oz/90 g) of marshmallows and mix well.

Transfer the mixture to the prepared baking pan and cover with plastic wrap (clingfilm). Set aside at room temperature for 45–60 minutes to cool. Invert the pan onto a cutting board. Remove the parchment paper, then cut into squares.

APPLE OR BLUEBERRY CRISP

A fruit crisp gives you the warm, fruity crumble of a pie with far less effort. This version, which can be made with apples or blueberries, uses earthy spices and sugary oats to create a crowd-pleasing dessert that makes a great finale for any barbecue.

PREPARATION TIME 20 minutes
COOKING TIME 45 minutes
SERVES 6–8

FOR THE FILLING
8 apples, peeled, cored, and cut into ¼-inch/5-mm slices, or 10 cups (3 lb 5 oz/1.5 kg) fresh or frozen blueberries
2 tablespoons sugar
2 tablespoons brown sugar
1 tablespoon vanilla paste
1 teaspoon ground cinnamon
1 teaspoon ground ginger
1 teaspoon salt

FOR THE CRUMB TOPPING
1½ cups (5¾ oz/170 g) cold butter, plus extra for greasing
1½ cups (11½ oz/325 g) brown sugar
1 cup (3½ oz/100 g) rolled oats
1 cup (5 oz/150 g) all-purpose (plain) flour
1 teaspoon ground cinnamon
1 teaspoon salt

FOR SERVING
Vanilla ice cream

Preheat an oven to 350°F/180°C/Gas Mark 4. Grease a cake pan or cast-iron skillet.

FOR THE FILLING Combine all the ingredients in a large bowl. Transfer the filling to the prepared pan.

FOR THE CRUMB TOPPING In a large bowl, combine all the ingredients except the butter. Using a box grater, grate the cold butter into the bowl and mix well. Spread the oat mixture evenly over the fruit filling. Bake for 45 minutes, or until bubbling and golden brown. Set aside for 15–20 minutes.

Serve warm with vanilla ice cream.

SMOKED SKYR CHEESECAKE WITH BLUEBERRIES

In Iceland, skyr yogurt has been cherished for centuries for its extraordinary creaminess. This cheesecake combines skyr with cream cheese, then uses the grill (or smoker) to infuse the cake with a deep smokiness. Topped with a sweet and tart blueberry compote, this dessert is worthy of any celebration.

PREPARATION TIME 30 minutes
COOKING TIME 1½–2 hours
SERVES 8–12

FOR THE BLUEBERRY TOPPING

2 cups (11 oz/315 g) fresh or frozen blueberries
4 tablespoons sugar
1 tablespoon cornstarch (cornflour)
1 tablespoon lemon juice
1 teaspoon vanilla extract

FOR THE CHEESECAKE

10 oz/290 g cinnamon cookies (biscuits)
6 tablespoons melted butter
2 cups (1 lb/450 g) cream cheese
1 cup (7 oz/200 g) Icelandic yogurt
½ cup (3½ oz/100 g) sugar
2 eggs
Zest of 1 lemon
2 teaspoons vanilla extract

FOR THE BLUEBERRY TOPPING In a small saucepan, combine the blueberries, sugar, and cornstarch (cornflour). Pour in ½ cup (4 fl oz/120 ml) of water and stir over medium heat until the blueberries burst and the mixture thickens. Set aside, then stir in the lemon juice and vanilla.

FOR THE CHEESECAKE Preheat a grill or smoker to low heat (300°F/150°C) for indirect grilling. (If smoking, use a water pan.)

Add the cookies (biscuits) to a food processor and pulse until crumbled. Add the melted butter and pulse until it resembles wet sand. Press the crumb into a 10-inch/25-cm springform pan and smooth the surface with a measuring cup until it's even. Wrap the outside of the pan with aluminum foil.

In a stand mixer fitted with the whisk attachment, combine the cream cheese, yogurt, and sugar and mix on medium speed. Add the eggs, one at a time, beating on low speed until combined. Stir in the lemon zest and vanilla. Pour the batter into the pan, then place it on the grill and cook for 1½–2 hours, until the top is golden brown and the internal temperature is 145°F/63°C.

Serve warm or at room temperature, topped with the blueberries.

VG

Kürtőskalács, also known as "chimney cake," is one of Hungary's most popular desserts. Originally from the Transylvanian region of Romania, the cake has a cylindrical shape created by wrapping dough around a wooden spit and cooking it over hot coals. Like doughnuts, these mini-cakes come in different flavors and are topped with glaze or sugar. In this version, the dough is wrapped around foil-covered, empty soda cans, baked, and topped with cinnamon and walnuts.

PREPARATION TIME 30 minutes,
plus at least 30 minutes proofing (proving)
COOKING TIME 20–25 minutes
MAKES 8 cakes

FOR THE DOUGH

⅔ cup (5½ fl oz/160 ml) lukewarm milk
½ cup (3½ oz/100 g) sugar
1 tablespoon instant (rapid rise) yeast
½ cup (4 oz/115 g) butter, softened
4 eggs
2 teaspoons vanilla extract
½ teaspoon salt
6½ cups (12 lb 2 oz/950 g) all-purpose (plain) flour, plus extra for dusting
1 tablespoon canola oil, for greasing

FOR THE TOPPING

1 egg, for brushing
2 tablespoons milk, for brushing
1½ cups (10½ oz/300 g) sugar
1 tablespoon ground cinnamon
½ cup (1¾ oz/50 g) chopped walnuts (optional)

FOR THE DOUGH In a stand mixer fitted with the paddle attachment, combine the milk, 4 tablespoons of sugar, and the yeast. Set aside for 5 minutes, or until the mixture becomes foamy. Add the remaining 4 tablespoons of sugar, the butter, eggs, vanilla, and salt. Mix for a few minutes to combine. Slowly add the flour and mix until a dough forms.

Using the dough attachment, knead the dough on low speed for 4–5 minutes. Increase to medium speed and knead for another 4–5 minutes.

Meanwhile, grease a large bowl with oil. Place the dough into it, then cover with plastic wrap (clingfilm) and proof (prove) at room temperature for 30–60 minutes, until doubled in size.

Preheat an oven to 350°F/180°C/Gas Mark 4.

On a lightly floured work surface, roll the dough into a 20- x 16-inch/50- x 40-cm rectangle, about 1 inch/2.5 cm thick. Using a sharp knife, cut 8 strips lengthwise.

Cover an empty soda (drink) can with aluminum foil and coil a dough strip around the can without any overlap. (Keep the remaining dough covered with plastic wrap.) Roll the can on a clean work surface, applying light pressure to flatten the dough and make the strips stick together. Repeat for the remaining chimney cakes.

FOR THE TOPPING In a small bowl, combine the egg and the milk. Using a pastry brush, coat each chimney cake with egg wash.

On a large plate, combine the sugar, cinnamon, and walnuts (if using). Roll the cakes in the mixture, gently pressing down for the mixture to adhere onto the cakes. Ensure all sides are evenly covered. Place the cans with chimney cakes on top of a baking sheet and bake for 20–25 minutes, rotating once, until golden. Slide the cakes off the cans.

Serve warm.

SKILLET BOURBON BREAD PUDDING
WITH SALTED CARAMEL

Bread pudding can be traced back to eleventh-century Britain when cooks would repurpose leftover or stale bread into what was known as "poor man's pudding." At that time, the bread was softened and flavored with boiling water and spices. These days, the versatile bread pudding is usually made with cream or milk, eggs, and spices like nutmeg and cinnamon. This decadent version uses the grill to cook the bourbon-infused pudding, which is topped with a salted caramel sauce.

PREPARATION TIME 20 minutes
COOKING TIME 30–45 minutes
SERVES 8

FOR THE BREAD PUDDING

4 tablespoons salted butter
1 cup (8 fl oz/240 ml) heavy (double) cream
1 cup (8 fl oz/240 ml) whole (full-fat) milk
1 cup (7¾ oz/220 g) dark brown sugar
2 tablespoons bourbon
1 tablespoon vanilla paste
1 teaspoon salt
4¼ cups (34 oz/1 kg) cubed brioche or challah

FOR THE SALTED CARAMEL

½ cup (4 oz/115 g) salted butter
2 cups (16 fl oz/475 ml) heavy (double) cream
½ cup (3¾ oz/110 g) dark brown sugar
1 teaspoon sea salt

FOR SERVING

Fresh whipped cream

Preheat a grill to medium heat for indirect grilling.

FOR THE BREAD PUDDING Heat the butter in a small saucepan over medium heat until it begins to brown. Set aside to cool.

In a large mixing bowl, combine the cream, milk, brown sugar, bourbon, vanilla paste, and salt and whisk until well combined. Whisk in the butter. Add the brioche or challah and gently mix until the bread cubes are evenly coated and saturated.

Place the mixture into a cast-iron skillet. Add the skillet to the coolest side of the grill, then close the lid and bake for 30 minutes, or until the center has set. If needed, bake for another 10–15 minutes. Set aside.

FOR THE SALTED CARAMEL Meanwhile, melt the butter in a saucepan over medium heat. Whisk in the cream, then the brown sugar and salt. Whisk for another 5–10 minutes, until it thickens and begins to bubble. Remove from the heat.

Serve the bread pudding with the caramel and a dollop of whipped cream.

SKILLET MOCHA BROWNIES

VG GF NF

These decadent brownies are made in a cast-iron skillet on the grill and served warm straight from the pan. The addition of coffee ratchets up the chocolate intensity, which also gets a boost from several handfuls of semisweet (dark) chocolate chips (coated in flour so they suspend in the batter instead of falling to the bottom of the pan). Every brownie bite is full of chunky chocolate that begs for a hit of vanilla ice cream.

PREPARATION TIME 15 minutes
COOKING TIME 35–40 minutes
SERVES 8–10

1 cup (8 oz/225 g) butter, plus extra for greasing
3 cups (1 lb 2 oz/500 g) semisweet (dark) chocolate chips
3 eggs
1 cup (7 oz/200 g) sugar
1½ tablespoons instant espresso or strong coffee
1½ tablespoons vanilla paste
½ cup (2¾ oz/80 g) all-purpose (plain) flour
1½ teaspoons baking powder
1 teaspoon salt
1 cup (5¾ oz/170 g) semisweet (dark) chocolate chips
2 tablespoons all-purpose (plain) flour, plus extra for dusting

FOR SERVING
Vanilla ice cream

Preheat a grill to 350°F/180°C.

In a small saucepan, combine the butter and 2 cups (12 oz/350 g) of chocolate chips over medium heat until melted. Stir, then set aside to cool.

In a large bowl, combine the eggs, sugar, coffee, and vanilla paste. Add the melted chocolate mixture and whisk again. Add the flour, baking powder, and salt and stir to combine.

In a small bowl, combine the remaining 1 cup (5¾ oz/170 g) of semisweet (dark) chocolate chips and flour. Fold this into the brownie mixture.

Butter and flour a 10-inch/25-cm cast-iron skillet, shaking off any excess flour. Pour the brownie mixture into the pan and place it on the grill, away from direct heat. Close the lid, then bake for 20 minutes. Open the grill and carefully bang the pan once or twice on a flat surface to distribute the batter. Bake for another 15–20 minutes.

Serve warm with vanilla ice cream.

GUEST CHEFS

MAKSUT AŞKAR

Born in Iskenderun and raised in Antakya, Maksut Aşkar studied tourism and hotel management in Istanbul, while simultaneously working in restaurants and bars. This sparked a passion for food design, which led to "edible art" endeavors at museums, galleries, and events, and consultancy projects for major food and beverage brands. His journey as a chef began in 2007. Maksut owned three restaurants before opening Neolokal in 2014, within the cultural institution SALT Galata. Inspired by his multicultural upbringing and the flavors of his childhood, he modernizes classic Anatolian recipes, to ensure their future relevance and to safeguard traditions. In 2023 and 2024 Neolokal received a Michelin star and a Green Michelin star. Maksut is also the co-founder of Foxy, a Michelin Bib Gourmand-awarded bistro featuring local, natural wines.

SERVES 8

FOR THE MEATBALLS
3½ oz/100 g green bell pepper, seeded, deveined, and roughly chopped
1 oz/25 g scallions (spring onions), roughly chopped
3 oz/80 g onion, roughly chopped
1 lb 5 oz/600 g ground (minced) leg of lamb
7 oz/200 g ground (minced) lamb belly
¾ oz/20 g parsley, finely chopped
1 egg, plus 1 egg yolk
½ teaspoon ground black pepper
Pinch of ground cumin
1¼ oz/35 g dried breadcrumbs
2 teaspoons salt

FOR THE LAVASH
5 cups (1 lb 10 oz/750 g) all-purpose (plain) flour
3 tablespoons extra-virgin olive oil
2 teaspoons salt
1½ cups (11 fl oz/325 ml) water

FOR THE PIYAZ SAUCE
1 clove garlic
7 oz/200 g boiled white beans
scant ½ cup (3½ fl oz/100 ml) extra-virgin olive oil
1¾ oz/50 g egg yolk
Splash of vinegar (optional)
1½ teaspoons salt
Pinch of ground white pepper
1 tablespoon plus 1 teaspoon lemon juice
3 tablespoons tahini
1 oz/25 g onion
5 tablespoons vegetable stock

FOR THE ONION SALAD
1 red onion, sliced
Pinch of sumac
1 tablespoon chopped parsley
Salt

FOR THE MEATBALLS Add the green bell pepper, scallions (spring onions), and onion to a blender, and blend to a purée. Strain the juices from the purée and discard. Put the purée and all the remaining ingredients in a bowl and knead by hand until they bind together. Refrigerate for 1 hour.

Divide the meatball mixture into 1½ oz/40 g pieces and roll into a uniform ball shape. Skewer 3 meatballs per skewer, and grill on a charcoal grill until evenly seared, making sure the inside is cooked through.

FOR THE LAVASH Put all the ingredients and scant 1½ cups (11 fl oz/325 ml) water in the bowl of a stand mixer with a dough hook and mix until kneadable. Then gently knead by hand until the dough is smooth. Put the dough in a bowl, cover, and let it rest for 30 minutes.

Divide the dough into 8 even balls. Using a rolling pin, press the dough to form rounds about 3 mm thick. Grill the dough over a fire for 2–3 minutes each side.

FOR THE PIYAZ SAUCE Blanch the garlic clove in boiling water for 1 minute, then transfer to a blender with the beans and olive oil and blend to a purée.

Pasteurize the egg yolk in a sous vide water bath, in a vacuum pack, for 5 minutes at 136°F/58°C; alternatively, poach an egg in boiling water with a splash of vinegar, then separate the yolk.

Add the yolk and all the remaining ingredients to the blender and mix at 75 percent power for 5 minutes. Strain the sauce for a smooth texture.

FOR THE ONION SALAD Combine the onion with the sumac, parsley, and a pinch of salt.

TO SERVE Arrange 3 meatballs on a piece of lavash, drizzle with piyaz sauce, and top with onion salad.

MAY CHOW

Renowned Chef May Chow revolutionized the Hong Kong dining scene with her iconic restaurants Little Bao and Happy Paradise. Before she became the youngest recipient of Asia's Best Female Chef award and was featured on Anthony Bourdain's *Parts Unknown*, Chow was a highly energetic child, who could always be found making something (and setting fires) in her mom's Shanghainese home kitchen. Anyone who has seen her—as a finale judge on *Top Chef Masters* or on *Today with Hoda and Jenna*—knows her personality is as bold and authentic as her flavors. Her personal and innovative approach to modern Chinese cuisine has poised her to redefine the Chinese culinary experience globally.

SERVES 4

FOR THE MARINADE

1¾ cups (12 oz/350 g) sugar
¾ oz/20 g red yeast rice, blended into a powder
½ cup (5 oz/140 g) hoisin sauce
½ cup (5 oz/140 g) oyster sauce
½ cup (5 oz/140 g) sesame paste
1½ oz/40 g light soy sauce
1½ oz/40 g dark soy sauce
¾ oz/20 g garlic powder
1¼ oz/35 g rose wine (we use Mei Kuei Lu Chiew from Golden Star)

FOR THE PORK

3 lb /1.4 kg pork collar (we use Kurobuta pork collar for a leaner texture, but you can go for Boston butt or Iberico; choose a well-marbled piece)

FOR THE MARINADE Combine all the ingredients in a large mixing bowl and mix thoroughly with a hand blender.

FOR THE PORK Using a sharp knife, carefully trim any excess fat from the pork. While a little fat is good for the flavor, removing excess fat will prevent flare-ups and ensure even cooking. Cut the pork collar with the grain into strips about 1.5 inches/4 cm thick. They should have a good balance of fat and meat.

Place the pork into a zip-top bag and pour in the marinade. Seal the bag and work the marinade into the meat until every piece is evenly coated, then leave to marinate for 1–2 hours.

Set your precision cooker to 145°F/63°C for sliceable but tender pork. When the bath is at temperature, add the sealed bag and cover with foil or plastic wrap (cling film). Allow to cook for 2–3 hours.

Remove the pork from the bag and carefully blot dry with paper towels. Discard the juices.

Brush the meat with enough of the char siu marinade to coat.

Preheat your grill, making sure it's extremely hot. You want a nice sear on the meat to seal in the juices before you turn it, but try not to get it too crispy on one side. You will be turning the meat often during the cooking process to prevent burning, and to make sure the marinade gets nice and caramelized. On the hot grill, you should be cooking it for about 1–2 minutes before flipping it. You can also use a blow torch for more caramelization.

Check the pork with a meat thermometer to be sure it's done—it should be 145°F/63°C—and remove it from the grill to let it rest for 5 minutes before slicing.

Slice the char siu about ½ inch/1 cm thick, or to your desired thickness.

Serve with a sunny-side-up egg and bowl of rice.

ROSS DOBSON

GF DF NF ◑ ◎ ⊗

Ross Dobson is from Warialda ("place of wild honey") in the north west of New South Wales, Australia. He lives in western Sydney, in Dharug country, where he has owned and operated several cafés and restaurants, including a tapas restaurant, a pop-up yum cha café, and an award-winning café in the heritage gardens of the Penrith Regional Gallery. He has authored more than twenty cookbooks, including *Australia: The Cookbook* (Phaidon, 2021), as well as several on barbecuing and fire-pit cooking.

SERVES 4 (as an appetizer)

2 teaspoons ground cumin
2 teaspoons hot paprika
1 lb 2 oz/500 g fillet steak, cut into 1-inch/2–3 cm cubes
2 brown onions, coarsely grated
2 teaspoons sea salt, plus extra to serve
2 tablespoons lemon juice
2 tablespoons finely chopped flat-leaf parsley
2 tablespoons finely chopped cilantro (coriander)
Lemon wedges, to serve

Put the cumin in a small frying pan. Cook on medium heat for 1–2 minutes, shaking the pan, so the cumin cooks evenly and is fragrant. Remove the pan from the heat as the cumin starts to smoke and before it starts to burn. Tip into a bowl and add the paprika.

Add the beef cubes and toss to coat in the spices.

Put the grated onions and salt in another bowl. Leave for 10 minutes, so the salt extracts the liquid from the onions. Put a fine sieve over the bowl with the beef. Tip the onions into the sieve and press all the liquid into the bowl below. Discard the grated onions. Add the lemon juice and herbs to the beef, and stir to combine. Leave for 15–20 minutes for the flavors to develop.

Preheat a grill to high heat.

Thread the marinated meat cubes onto 4 metal skewers. Place them on the grill and cook for 4 minutes, without turning or moving. Turn the kebabs over and cook for a further 3 minutes. Transfer to a serving plate. Serve with lemon wedges on the side to squeeze over. Sprinkle with extra sea salt to taste.

MOUSTAFA ELREFAEY

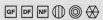

Moustafa Elrefaey is the executive chef and cofounder of the restaurant chain Zööba, bringing Egyptian street food to the world. Since 2012, Zööba has opened sixteen branches in five different countries on three continents. It was named on MENA's 50 Best Restaurants list in 2022; and in 2023 it was the best restaurant in Egypt, while Elrefaey received MENA's 50 Best Chefs' Choice Award. Chef Elrefaey is a strong advocate for preserving Egyptian food heritage. He has held the roles of Egyptian Ambassador at the Cultural Culinary Heritage Committee of the World Association of Chefs Society; Technical Chef of the E.U. Mediterranean Diet Project; and Egyptian Ambassador at the World Chefs Without Borders. He also recently co-founded Nakoll, offering a solution to the high cost and lack of accessibility to professional culinary education for young people in Egypt.

SERVES 8

3½ oz/100 g grated onion pulp (squeeze it after you grate it and set the liquid aside)
⅓ oz/10 g chopped hot peppers
¾ oz/18 g sea salt
Pinch of ground black pepper
Pinch of allspice
1 tablespoon chopped flat-leaf parsley
2 lb 3 oz/1 kg ground (minced) beef
2 sheets caul fat (also known as lace fat or fat netting, it is the thin membrane that surrounds sheep organs)

In a stainless steel bowl, combine the grated onions, peppers, salt, pepper, allspice, and parsley. Add the ground beef and mix in gently (make sure you don't overwork the ground/minced beef) to make the kofta. Cover and store in the refrigerator for 2 hours.

Place the caul fat on your kitchen counter.

Divide the kofta mix into 3 oz/80 g balls and roll them into cylinder shapes around 5 inches/12 cm long. Place the kofta fingers on the caul fat, and cut around it enough to wrap each kofta individually in a single layer of caul fat.

Thread them on to steel (not stainless steel) skewers, with a little room between each one.

Brush the leftover liquid from the onions over each piece (it will add another layer of flavor).

Use a hot charcoal grill to grill the kofta for 8–10 minutes, turning occasionally, until cooked through.

Serve hot with tahini sauce, pita bread, and haty salad (tomato, onion, and parsley).

MONIQUE FISO

GF DF NF ◖ ◎ ⊗

Monique Fiso is a chef, writer, and entrepreneur. She is known for her contribution to the revitalization of Māori and Pasifika cuisine, and for breaking down barriers in the culinary world. Her first book, *Hiakai*, is considered one of the most important cookbooks written in Aotearoa (the Māori-language name for New Zealand). Fiso's career has taken her all across the world. She has spent time cooking and living in the United States, Mexico, Australia, and Aotearoa. With over two decades of experience, Monique continues to elevate her craft. She is fiercely passionate about cooking with fire, foraging, food sovereignty, and the preservation of Indigenous knowledge.

SERVES 6

FOR THE KŌURA

2 whole kōura, 1 lb 9 oz–1 lb 12 oz/700-800 g each (kōura are saltwater crayfish found throughout the coastal waters of Aotearoa/New Zealand; substitute with lobster, marron, or jumbo shrimp, if needed)

FOR THE TOMATO AND HOROPITO SAUCE

Olive oil, for drizzling

4 ripe tomatoes, cut in half

1 red onion, peeled and cut into eighths

1 whole red chili, split lengthwise and deseeded

½ cup (4 fl oz/120 ml) dry white wine

3 large cloves garlic, peeled and sliced

2 Italian parsley stalks, leaves finely chopped

2 thyme sprigs

2 bay leaves

2 teaspoons dried horopito flakes (horopito is a bush pepper tree endemic to Aotearoa/New Zealand; ground black pepper or ground sichuan pepper are suitable replacements, if needed)

½ teaspoon ground coriander seeds

½ teaspoon ground fennel seeds

1 kombu sheet

2 tablespoons honey

Zest and juice of 1 lemon

Flaky sea salt

FOR THE KŌURA Rinse the kōura under cold water to remove any sand or sediment. With a large chef's knife, split the kōura in half lengthwise. Kōura have spiky shells, so take care when doing this. Running along the length of the tail will be a dark-colored vein, which is part of the digestive tract and should be removed. Carefully lift it out, using the tip of a small knife or toothpick. Place the kōura onto a tray and refrigerate until required.

FOR THE TOMATO AND HOROPITO SAUCE Heat a grill to a medium-high heat. Drizzle 3 tablespoons of olive oil over the tomatoes, red onion, and chili. Lightly season with sea salt and place the ingredients onto the hot grill. Char the vegetables until they become slightly blackened and have grill marks.

Remove the vegetables from the grill and place them into a saucepan over a medium heat and cook for 5 minutes, stirring occasionally. The tomatoes and onions should break up a little. Add the white wine, garlic, parsley stalks, thyme, bay leaves, dried horopito flakes, ground coriander, and ground fennel. Continue cooking at a medium heat for a further 2 minutes, or until the wine has almost completely reduced.

Add 4 cups (34 fl oz/1 L) water, the kombu, honey, and lemon zest and juice. Bring to a boil, then lower the heat to a simmer. Gently reduce the sauce by half, or until it coats the back of a spoon. Stir regularly. You can set your saucepan on the corner of your barbecue, to tick away slowly and enhance the smokiness.

When the sauce has reached the desired consistency, remove it from the heat. Using tongs or tweezers, take the chili, parsley stalks, thyme, bay leaves, and kombu out of the sauce and discard.

Finish the sauce by seasoning with flaky sea salt. The sauce can be served warm or chilled. You can also adjust the sauce to taste with additional honey, lemon, or chili.

Drizzle a small amount of olive oil over the prepared kōura and season with flaky sea salt.

Ensure that the grill is hot. Place the kōura, meat side down, onto the grill and cook for 4–5 minutes until the meat is lightly charred with grill marks and the shells have begun to turn bright red.

Flip the kōura over and cook for a further 5–6 minutes.

Remove the kōura from the grill and place onto a serving dish. Generously spoon the tomato and horopito sauce over the kōura. Sprinkle the finely chopped parsley leaves over the top and serve immediately.

OSSO SHORT RIBS WITH CONFIT POTATOES

RENZO GARIBALDI

Renzo Garibaldi is Peruvian-born and -raised, a meat and fire lover, butcher-chef, and creator of Osso Carniceria y Salumeria, which opened its doors in 2013 in Lima, Peru. It started as a butcher's shop specializing in dry aging and whole butchery, with a private table for special dining events. It turned into a restaurant dedicated to a fire style of cooking, always looking to get the best of the products through fire, smoke, and time. Osso is also a meat brand that sells products throughout Peru. Osso is now present in Lima, Peru; Sao Paulo, Brazil; Bogota, Colombia; and Miami, United States.

SERVES 4

Short ribs (ask your butcher for a cut of 2½ inches/ 6 cm of short rib)

FOR THE BRINE

Scant ¼ cup (3 oz/80 g) sea salt
Scant ¼ cup (1½ oz/40 g) sugar
1 oz/30 g honey
5 bay leaves

FOR THE COMPOUND BUTTER

2 teaspoons fennel seeds
¾ oz/20 g pink peppercorns
⅓ oz/10 g allspice
¾ oz/20 g garlic powder
⅕ cup (2¼ oz/60 g) sea salt
7 oz/200 g clarified butter, at room temperature
7 oz/200 g bone marrow, cut into small pieces, at room temperature

FOR THE CONFIT POTATOES

10½ oz (300 g) potatoes, cut into 1 x 1-inch/ 2.5 x 2.5cm cubes
1 oz/30 g cloves garlic, lightly crushed but whole
⅓ oz/10 g rosemary, finely chopped
1 teaspoon paprika
¾ oz/20 g salt
Scant 1 cup (6 oz/180 g) lard
1½ oz/40 g clarified butter

FOR THE SAUCE

2¼ oz/60 g red onion, julienned
½ oz/15 g cloves garlic, lightly crushed but whole
½ cup (4 fl oz/120 ml) olive oil
1¼ oz/35 g white vinegar
½ cup (4 oz/120 g) soy sauce
¾ oz/20 g oyster sauce
1¼ cups (10 fl oz/300 ml) beef stock
3½ oz/100 g mushrooms, sliced
¾ oz/20 g spinach, finely chopped
¾ oz/20 g tomatoes, finely chopped

FOR THE BRINE Heat all the brine ingredients with 8 cups (68 fl oz/2 L) water in a large pot until the sugar and salt are dissolved, then bring to the boil. Remove from the heat and add ice to help bring the temperature down.

Put the brine in a container with enough space to hold the meat, add the ribs, then put the container in the refrigerator for 24 hours.

FOR THE COMPOUND BUTTER In a skillet over low heat, toast the fennel seeds, moving the pan and trying not to burn the seeds. Grind the seeds in a coffee grinder or blender. Add the pink peppercorns and allspice and grind together briefly, then do the same with the garlic powder. Finally, add the salt and grind for a few seconds until mixed together.

Take the clarified butter and bone marrow from the fridge and let them come to room temperature. In a large bowl, combine both with the rub.

Using a spatula, spread the mix on a tray lined with parchment paper, in a layer about ½ inch/1 cm thick, and freeze for 12 hours before using in 1 x 2-inch/3 x 6-cm pieces.

FOR THE CONFIT POTATOES Combine the potatoes with the garlic, rosemary, paprika, salt, and lard in an oven tray. Over a medium-high grill, place the potatoes in a cast-iron skillet with some clarified butter and sear every side. Then continue to cook over a low heat until crispy and cooked through; alternatively, cook in the oven at 284°F/140°C, turning every 20 minutes, until fully cooked. Remove the garlic.

FOR THE SAUCE Cook the onion and garlic in the olive oil. Add the vinegar and cook until it evaporates. Then add the soy sauce, oyster sauce, and beef stock. Reduce until halved in quantity, then add the mushrooms, spinach, and tomato.

Cook the ribs on the grill at medium heat, adding a sheet of compound butter on top every 30 minutes, until the internal temperature of the ribs reaches 201°F/94°C.

BEER-CAN CHICKEN WITH ROASTED GARLIC AND SHALLOT JAM

ELIZABETH KARMEL

North Carolina native Elizabeth Karmel—a.k.a. Grill Girl—is a nationally respected authority on grilling, barbecue, and Southern food. She is also a food and beverage consultant, writes for the Associated Press and *Forbes*, and co-writes the weekly What's 4 Dinner Substack newsletter. The author of four acclaimed cookbooks, her latest is *Steak and Cake*. She is the founding Executive Chef of the Hill Country Barbecue Market in New York City and Washington D.C.; and Hill Country Chicken, also in New York. Karmel created GirlsattheGrill.com in 2002.

SERVES 4; Jam makes 1½ cups (11 oz/320 g)

FOR THE JAM

1 lb (16 oz/450 g) shallots, peeled

Olive oil

Kosher salt

3 oz/80g peeled cloves garlic (about 15–20)

½ cup (4 oz/110 g) raw cane sugar

⅛ cup (1 oz/30g) honey

½ cup (4 fl oz/120 ml) spring water

1 cup (8 fl oz/240 ml) red wine vinegar

1 tablespoon distilled white vinegar

1 tablespoon Cognac

1 teaspoon dried thyme or 2 sprigs fresh thyme

FOR THE CHICKEN

1 whole small roasting chicken, about 4 lb/1.8 kg

Olive oil

1 tablespoon favorite dry rub or kosher salt and freshly ground black pepper

1 (12 fl oz/340 ml) can favorite beer

FOR THE JAM Preheat the oven or grill to 400°F/200°C. Coat the shallots in olive oil and sprinkle generously with salt. Lay on a sheet pan (baking tray) fitted with a cooling rack.

Place the garlic cloves in a double layer of aluminum foil; drizzle with oil and sprinkle with salt, tossing to make sure each clove is oiled and seasoned—you may need to make two foil packets.

Place both the shallots and garlic in the oven (or on the grill) and roast for 30-45 minutes, checking occasionally. You want them to be caramelized but not completely mushy since you will be cooking again.

Meanwhile, mix the sugar, honey, water, red wine vinegar, white vinegar, Cognac, 1 teaspoon salt, and the thyme in a large heavy-bottomed, non-reactive saucepan set over medium heat. Stir to make sure the salt and sugar are dissolved. Add the shallots and garlic and stir gently.

Bring to a boil, then reduce the heat and simmer for 2 hours, stirring occasionally, until the shallots are translucent and soft enough to smash and spread. Taste and adjust the seasoning if necessary with a splash of vinegar. Remove from the heat and cool before serving. The jam will keep in a clean glass jar fitted with a lid for about 2 weeks.

FOR THE CHICKEN When you are ready to cook the chicken, remove the neck and giblets, and pat dry with paper towels. Coat the chicken lightly with olive oil and season with the dry rub or salt and pepper. Set aside.

Preheat your grill to 350°F/180°C. Open a beer can, drink or pour out about ¼ cup (2 fl oz/60 ml) of the beer, and make an extra hole in the top of the can with a church key can opener.

Place the beer can on a quarter sheet tray or cake pan (tin). Place or "sit" the chicken on top of the beer can by slipping the cavity of the chicken over the can. The chicken will appear to be sitting. Make sure the legs of the chicken are in front of the beer can, to support the chicken as it cooks.

Pick up the chicken and beer can together and place carefully in the center of the cooking grate over indirect medium heat. Again, make sure the legs of the chicken are in front of the beer can to support the chicken as it cooks.

Cover the grill and cook the chicken for 1–1½ hours, depending on size, or until the internal temperature registers 165°F/74°C in the breast area and 180°F/82°C in the thigh. The smaller the chicken, the less time it will take to cook, so look at the total weight before unwrapping.

When removing the chicken from the grill grate, be careful not to spill the contents, as it will be very hot. Remove it carefully to a platter, holding the beer can with tongs and a clean, dry kitchen towel to keep the chicken from toppling over.

Let it rest for 10 minutes before carving and serving with the jam alongside.

SPICED PORK SHOULDER CHOP WITH BEAN SALSA AND CHARRED LETTUCE

VUSUMUZI NDLOVU

Vusi Ndlovu was born in Zimbabwe and raised in South Africa. He is the chef and co-owner of EDGE, which loves to celebrate the bounty of Africa around a fire. He made a name for himself working in some of the best restaurants in South Africa and Europe. He also ranked among the top seven chefs at the S.Pellegrino Young Chef Academy Competition finale in 2018. Ndlovu is one of the founding members of the African Culinary Library, a resource dedicated to preserving and promoting African food culture and cuisine.

SERVES 4

FOR THE BILTONG SPICE
¾ oz/25 g salt
2 tablespoons ground black pepper
1 tablespoon plus 1 teaspoon ground coriander
⅓ oz/10 g brown sugar
1 teaspoon chilli flakes

FOR THE PORK
4 pork shoulder chops (ask your butcher to cut these ¾ inch/2 cm thick)
4 tablespoons canola oil
4¼ oz/120 g Biltong spice (see above)

FOR THE BEAN SALSA
2 red bell peppers diced
2 green bell peppers diced
2 yellow bell peppers diced
3 shallots sliced
Generous ¾ cup (6¾ fl oz/200 ml) canola oil
1 oz/30 g fresh oregano, chopped
4 cloves garlic, minced
3 small fresh red chilis, finely chopped
Zest and juice of 2 limes
420 g/15 oz baked beans
Salt, to taste

FOR THE CHARRED LETTUCE
2 heads baby gem lettuce (washed)
3 tablespoons canola oil
Salt, to taste

FOR THE BILTONG SPICE Place all the ingredients in a pestle and mortar and crush to a powder, then reserve in an airtight container until required. The recipe should make more than you need, so keep some for future use.

FOR THE PORK Rub the chops with oil. Season with the prepared spice and allow to sit at room temperature for 30 minutes.

FOR THE BEAN SALSA In a mixing bowl, add all the prepared vegetables. Mix well and allow to sit in a warm place for about 30 minutes. Add the remaining ingredients and season accordingly. Reserve at room temperature until required.

FOR THE CHARRED LETTUCE Cut the baby gem lettuce in half. Season with oil and salt, then reserve until it's time to grill.

TO ASSEMBLE When your coals come to temperature, grill your pork steak, turning every minute to prevent the spice from burning. Cook for a total of 8 minutes, then allow to rest in a warm place for 10 minutes.

While the pork is resting, fan the coals to make sure they are super hot. Grill the prepared lettuce until well charred; once placed on the grill do not move as that will affect the char.

Slice the pork into bite-size pieces, arrange on a large plate, and dress the plate with bean salsa. Separate the leaves from the baby gem lettuce and arrange around the plate.

SU KYOUNG PARK

Located in Seoul's bustling Sindang-dong neighborhood, Gold Pig Restaurant, founded by Su Kyoung Park, is celebrated for its mastery of pork barbecue. Park also oversees three specialized barbecue restaurants across Seoul and Jeju: Geumdwaeji Sikdang for pork barbecue, Yeongdong Jangeo for grilled eel, and Geobu Galbi for Jeju beef barbecue. Under her leadership, Geumdwaeji Sikdang has earned the recognition of the Michelin Guide for six consecutive years, solidifying its reputation as a top destination for barbecue enthusiasts. Park's commitment to promoting Korean barbecue culture is evident in her integration of local ingredients and traditional dishes, fostering culinary innovation.

SERVES 3-4

FOR THE PORK BACK RIBS

4 lb/1.8 kg pork back ribs, bone in (in the traditional Korean butchering system, the best cut to use is from the 5th rib to the 15th, which yields about 1 lb 5 oz–1 lb 9 oz/600–700 g per rib given a 12 x 4 inch/30 x 10 cm length; this recipe uses about 3 ribs at this measurement)

FOR THE MARINADE

1¾ cups (12 oz/350 g) brown sugar

1½ cups (12 oz/350 g) jin ganjang (Korean soy sauce)

1 teaspoon ground black pepper

2 tablespoons soybean oil

2 tablespoons sesame oil

3oz/80 g minced garlic

2¼ oz/60 g minced ginger

3 oz/80 g daepa (Korean large green onion), white part only sliced into ¾ inch/2 cm thick slices

3 oz/80 g onion, roughly chopped

FOR THE PORK BACK RIBS Wash the pork back ribs in cold running water and dry with a dry cloth or kitchen towel. Make long cuts alongside the bone between each joint, while leaving the entire rib intact. The rib will open up while grilling, ensuring the seasoning is evenly penetrated throughout.

FOR THE MARINADE In a large mixing bowl, combine 4 cups (34 fl oz/1 L) with the brown sugar and mix until fully dissolved. Once dissolved, add the jin ganjang, black pepper, soybean oil, sesame oil, minced garlic, and ginger, and stir until combined.

Add the daepa and onion to the marinade mixture.

In a large container, combine the prepared ribs and the marinade and submerge. Cover and let marinate for a minimum of 12 hours and maximum of 24 hours in the refrigerator.

Preheat the oven to 350°F/180°C/Gas Mark 4. Place the ribs onto a roasting pan (tin) with an elevated rack, to allow excess fat to drip and allow even cooking on all sides. Roast on the first side for 15 minutes, then flip and roast for 10 minutes.

Alternatively, if using an air fryer, preheat to 400°F/200°C and air fry on the first side for 15 minutes, then turn after 10 minutes.

This recipe can also be made over an open fire, and on a traditional grill if the grill allows for proper drainage of oil.

Remove the ribs from the heat using tongs, and plate and serve immediately on a large platter.

TOMOS PARRY

Tomos Parry was born in Anglesey, North Wales. Having trained under the mentoring scheme of Grady Atkins at Le Gallois, Tomos began his professional career at The River Café, followed by Michelin-starred Kitchen Table in Fitzrovia, before progressing to Head Chef at Climpson's Arch in Hackney. From there, he went on to open Kitty Fisher's in Mayfair and was instrumental in its success.

In March 2018, Tomos opened his first restaurant, Brat, in Shoreditch, which was awarded a Michelin star in October 2018 and named London's best restaurant at the 2019 National Restaurant Awards. In the summer of 2020, Brat announced its residency at Climpson's Arch, and in summer 2023, Tomos opened his third London restaurant, Mountain, on Soho's Beak Street, which was awarded its first Michelin star in February 2024.

SERVES 4–6

1 oz/30 g crushed walnuts
1 clove garlic
1½ cups (6 fl oz/360 ml) olive oil
2 lb 3 oz–3lb 5 oz/1–1.5 kg beef (bavette steak works very well)
15 scallions (spring onions)
4 tablespoons sherry vinegar
1 tablespoon chopped gherkins
5 cherry tomatoes
1 tablespoon capers
Pinch of chili flakes
1 tablespoon finely chopped parsley
½ teaspoon chopped thyme leaves
Pinch of sugar
Salt and black pepper

If using an outdoor grill, it's important to get it fired up early, to allow the fire to settle so you are left with the embers. If using a griddle pan, warm over medium–high heat and preheat the oven to 350°F/180°C/Gas Mark 4.

Toast the crushed walnuts on a baking tray in the oven for 8–10 minutes, turning once until golden brown. Transfer to a mixing bowl, grate the garlic clove over the warm walnuts, and toss with 5 tablespoons of olive oil.

Season the beef with salt and a small amount of oil (no pepper at this stage, as it will burn). Cook on the grill/griddle pan, turning occasionally, until the middle/thickest part of the steak is 130–140°F/55–60°C (medium rare). Once at this stage, remove and place on a board to rest.

Using the same grill/griddle pan, carefully wipe out and place the scallions (spring onions) and tomatoes on the griddle, turning until softened. Once soft and with a nice charred color, transfer to a chopping board and chop, combining with the vinegar, gherkins, tomatoes, capers, chili flakes, parsley, thyme, walnuts, sugar, salt, and pepper and the remaining olive oil.

Slice the beef, season with some fresh black pepper, then spoon over the scallion sauce.

SALTED BEEF FAT CARAMEL PIE WITH BITTER CHOCOLATE GANACHE

JESS PRYLES

Jess Pryles is an Australian-born food personality who is widely known for her expertise in barbecue, meat science, and grilling techniques. She is the founder of the Hardcore Carnivore brand, and she has authored a cookbook of the same name. Pryles is also the host of her own TV show on Outdoor Channel, having also made appearances on Food Network, Hulu, and the *Today Show*, and she has been featured in *Forbes*, *Southern Living*, *Men's Journal*, and *Food & Wine*, among other publications.

MAKES One 9-inch/23-cm pie

FOR THE SMOKED BEEF TALLOW
2 lb/900 g beef fat trimmings (to get 2¼ oz/60 g smoked beef tallow)

FOR THE PIE CRUST
⅔ stick (2½ oz/70 g) salted butter
2 cups (17 oz/480 g) graham cracker crumbs

FOR THE BEEF FAT CARAMEL FILLING
½ cup (3 oz/85g) brown sugar
1 (14 oz/400 g) can condensed milk
2 teaspoons vanilla extract

FOR THE GANACHE
1 cup (6 oz/170 g) dark or bittersweet chocolate chips
½ cup (4 fl oz/120 ml) whipping cream

TO SERVE
1 teaspoon flaky salt
1 cup (8 oz/240 g) crème fraîche

TO MAKE THE SMOKED BEEF TALLOW Cut the beef fat into large chunks, and place into a foil pan or other suitable container for the smoker. Set a smoker to 225°F/107°C, and place the tallow inside. Smoke for 3 hours, stirring occasionally. Lower the temperature to 200°F/93°C, and continue to cook until the fat is completely melted, about 2–4 hours. There may still be small bits of meat present. Strain the rendered fat through a cheesecloth into a sterilized jar.

You only need 2¼ oz/60 g of the smoked tallow for this recipe. The rest can be stored in a jar and used in place of other oils when cooking.

FOR THE PIE CRUST Preheat the oven to 350°F/180°C/Gas Mark 4.

Melt the butter for the crust, then combine with the cracker crumbs until the mixture has the texture of wet sand. Press into the bottom and up the sides of a 9-inch/23-cm round pie pan (tin). Use the base of a flat cup to help flatten and compress the crumb.

Bake for 10 minutes to set the crust, which should be approximately ½–¾ inch/1.25–1.5 cm thick. Set aside to cool before filling.

FOR THE BEEF FAT CARAMEL FILLING Preheat the oven to 320°F/160°C/Gas Mark 3.

In a saucepan over low heat, melt the brown sugar with a touch of water, and once melted add the smoked tallow (adding tallow at the same time may cause the sugar to seize). Once the sugar has just started to bubble, add the condensed milk, then raise the temperature to medium and whisk constantly. Initially, the tallow will separate to the top, but it will eventually emulsify. Cook over medium heat, whisking constantly until thickened, about 5 minutes.

Pour into the waiting pie crust, and place into the preheated oven for 12–14 minutes. The pie must be removed once the edges of the filling begin to bubble. Allow to cool completely.

FOR THE GANACHE Place the chocolate chips into a bowl. Heat the whipping cream in a a pan over medium heat until nearly boiling, then pour over the chocolate, stirring constantly. The heat of the cream will melt the chocolate. Pour the ganache over the finished pie, spreading out evenly with a spatula. Allow to cool and set completely.

TO SERVE Sprinkle the pie with some flaky salt, then cut into slices. Serve each slice with 1 generous tablespoon of crème fraîche on the side.

WESTERN AUSTRALIAN MARRON, TOBIKU, AND KOMBU BEURRE BLANC

DAVE PYNT

Dave Pynt was born in Perth, Western Australia. He studied at the TAFE West Coast Institute of Training, before traveling overseas to cook alongside and learn from some of the world's best chefs. He is now chef-owner of Burnt Ends Hospitality Group, which manages Burnt Ends, a one-Michelin-starred barbecue restaurant in Singapore's Dempsey Hill that serves modern Australian barbecue. Since 2013, the restaurant has established itself as an integral part of Singapore's new food order, with its open-concept kitchen, new daily menus, and the belief that there is a magic that comes from cooking with wood. Pynt was the winner of Asia's 50 Best Restaurants Chefs' Choice Award 2017.

SERVES 4

FOR THE BEURRE BLANC

2 shallots, sliced

Scant ½ cup (3½ oz/100 g) white wine

1 oz/30 g heavy (double) cream

Scant ½ cup (3½ oz/100 g) smoked butter, cold

1 teaspoon tobiko

1 teaspoon shio kombu, chopped

1 teaspoon lemon juice

FOR THE MARRON

5 whole live marron (large freshwater crayfish)

4 cups (34 fl oz/1 L) vegetable oil

1 teaspoon freshly cut chives, to garnish

FOR THE BEURRE BLANC Add the shallots and white wine to a pot over medium heat and reduce by half. Add the cream and reduce by half again. Slowly add the cold, smoked butter until it forms a nice thick consistency. Season with tobiko and shio kombu and finish with lemon juice.

FOR THE MARRON Cut the live marron in half and remove the guts. Put the claws into a hot oven for 5–7 minutes until cooked.

Preheat the vegetable oil until the temperature reaches 350°F/180°C.

Place the half marron, shell side down, and grill over high heat until the internal temperature reaches 95°F/35°C.

Remove the half marron and place in a shallow 2-inch/5-cm-lipped baking tray. Pour the hot vegetable oil over the marron to finish the cooking.

Drain off the excess oil and arrange beautifully on a plate. Remove the claws from the oven and reconstruct the marron. Top the marron with the beurre blanc sauce and garnish with fresh chives.

JESSICA ROSVAL

Jessica Rosval was born and raised in Montreal, Canada, and is head chef of Casa Maria Luigia and Al Gatto Verde in Modena, Italy. She is the culinary director and co-founder of Roots and The Association for the Integration of Women.

MAKES 10

FOR THE HAY-SMOKED MILK ICE CREAM

Scant ½ cup (3 oz/90 g) granulated sugar

6 egg yolks

1 cup (8 fl oz/240 ml) milk (we are lucky enough to receive fresh milk every morning from the heritage white cows of Modena: La Bianca Modenese)

2 cups (16 oz/460 g) heavy (double) cream

1 teaspoon salt

3½ oz/100 g dried alfalfa hay

FOR THE CAKES

3 sticks (12 oz/340 g) butter

1½ cups (1 lb 2 oz /500 g) dulce de leche

6 whole eggs

6 egg yolks

Generous ¾ cup (3½ oz/100 g) all-purpose (plain) flour

2 teaspoons salt

FOR THE HAY-SMOKED MILK ICE CREAM Combine all the ingredients (except the hay) in a saucepan and heat to 176°F/80°C, stirring constantly. Pour the mixture into a shallow tray and place the tray in an offset smoker or cold smoker. Add the dried alfalfa hay to the firebox, and let it smoke at a temperature no higher than 140°F/60°C for 40 minutes.

Pour into a storage container and let rest in the refrigerator for 24 hours.

When ready, pour into your ice cream maker, ready to serve alongside the dulce de leche cakes.

FOR THE CAKES Set a woodburning oven to 400°F/200°C with no live flame. You will rely completely on the radiant heat from the oak ember bed for this.

Melt the butter and dulce de leche together in a saucepan. Add the eggs and egg yolks, and mix well using a rubber spatula. Finally, add the flour and the salt and continue to mix.

Grease ten 4 x 5-inch/10 x 14-cm cast-iron cake pans (tins), and fill with 3½ oz/100 g of cake filling.

Bake in the oven for approximately 6 minutes, or until the top is golden brown, but there is still a slight wiggle in the center.

Serve immediately with the ice cream alongside.

SEAN SHERMAN

Chef Sean Sherman, a member of the Oglala Lakota tribe, grew up on the Pine Ridge Reservation in South Dakota, Turtle Island (an Indigenous name for North America). He has become a leading advocate for Indigenous food sovereignty, focusing on revitalizing and promoting traditional Native foods. In 2015, in an effort to make Indigenous foods more accessible, he founded the nonprofit NATIFS (North American Traditional Indigenous Food Systems) and the Indigenous Food Lab, a professional kitchen and training center in Minneapolis, Minnesota. Sherman authored the award-winning *The Sioux Chef's Indigenous Kitchen* in 2017 and opened Owamni by The Sioux Chef in 2021, Minnesota's first full-service Indigenous restaurant. His work has earned him widespread recognition for his innovative approach to reclaiming and celebrating Indigenous culinary traditions.

SERVES 4

FOR THE CHOKECHERRY PULP
6 cups (2 lb 3 oz/1 kg) chokecherries

FOR THE MAPLE/PINE RUB
½ cup (2¾ oz/75 g) maple sugar
4 tablespoons fresh red or white pine needle powder (powder fresh pine needles in a blender)
3 tablespoons kosher salt
2 tablespoons dried wild ramp powder (use onion powder as a substitute, if needed)
2 tablespoons dried garlic
4 tablespoons ancho chile powder
2 tablespoons chipotle chile powder
2 tablespoons dried wild bergamot (use dried oregano as a substitute, if needed)
1 teaspoon crushed juniper berries

FOR THE SMOKED RIBS
2 racks bison back ribs

FOR THE BLUEBERRY BARBECUE SAUCE
1 cup (8 oz/240 g) agave syrup
3 cups (360 g) Chokecherry Pulp (see above)
1 cup /8 fl oz/240 ml) apple cider
½ cup (4 fl oz/120 ml) apple cider vinegar
4 tablespoons ancho chile powder
4 tablespoons dried wild bergamot (use dried oregano as a substitute, if needed)
2 tablespoons dried wild ramp powder (use onion powder as a substitute, if needed)
1 tablespoon kosher salt

FOR THE CHOKECHERRY PULP Add the choke cherries and 4 cups (34 fl oz/1 L) water to a pot and simmer for 2 hours.
Mash occasionally with a potato masher to separate the seeds.
Using a strainer with larger holes, strain the liquid and try to save as much pulp as possible while separating the seeds.
Cool until ready for use.

FOR THE MAPLE/PINE RUB Combine the ingredients for the dry rub.

FOR THE SMOKED RIBS Heat the smoker to 250°F/121°C.
Trim the fat membrane from the ribs. Gently massage the rub over both racks and chill in the refrigerator for a minimum of 30 minutes.
Place the ribs in the smoker and smoke until the internal temperature reaches 170°F/77°C.
Wrap in foil and continue to smoke until the meat reaches at least 200°F/93°C.

FOR THE BLUEBERRY BARBECUE SAUCE While the ribs are smoking, mix all the ingredients together in a bowl. Bring to a boil, then simmer on low heat for 20–30 minutes until reduced. Use an immersion blender to blend until smooth.
When the ribs are at least 200°F/93°C, remove the foil and brush the ribs with sauce.
Place the ribs back in the smoker for at least another 10 minutes, basting with sauce as needed.

MARSIA TAHA MOHAMED SALAS

Marsia Taha Mohamed Salas was born in Sofia, Bulgaria, of Bolivian nationality on her mother's side and Palestinian on her father's side. She has lived in La Paz, Bolivia, since she was five years old and this is the culture that has most influenced her life and career. She has seventeen years of gastronomic training, including restaurants in Denmark and Spain, and she has been the head chef of Gustu restaurant since 2013. For five consecutive years it was named the best restaurant in Bolivia and one of the 50 Best Restaurants in Latin America, according to World's 50 Best Restaurants. Her cuisine has always been inspired by Bolivian culture, identity, biodiversity, and products, and reflects all these elements.

SERVES 4

You will need: 5 bamboo trunks/shoots (tacuara), cleaned

2 g aji gusanito chili
1¼ cups (10½ oz/300 g) copoazu pulp (an Amazon fruit)
¾ oz/20g cherry tomatoes
3½ oz/100 g Amazonian nuts
1 lb 2 oz/500 g pirarucu fish, cleaned and cut into ⅔ inch/1.5 cm cubes
3½ oz/100 g fresh ginger, grated
5½ oz/150 g fresh palmito, cut into ½ inch/1 cm cubes
1 oz/30 g cilantro (coriander) stems, finely chopped
1 lb 2 oz/500 g mandioca roots (cassava), peeled and cut into small pieces
4 cups (34 fl oz/1 L) oil
Salt

Using a pestle and mortar, mash the aji gusanito with the copoazu pulp.

Char the cherry tomatoes over a flame just until the skin is burned. Once cool, peel away the skin.

Blend the Amazonian nuts with 1¼ cups (10 fl oz/300 ml) cold water, until you have a smooth texture.

In a bowl, mix the pirarucu fish with the ginger, aji gusanito and copoazu pulp, the palmito, cilantro (coriander) stems, and finally the peeled tomatoes.

Mix well, then use the mixture to fill the bamboo trunks and close up with tin foil. On top of an open fire, place the tacuara straight into the fire, and cook until the fish reaches 122°F/50°C.

Poach the mandioca roots in water until they get very, very soft, almost falling apart. Dry out the mandioca, let them cool down, then deep-fry in very hot oil (375°F/190°C) until they are super crunchy.

When ready, open the tacuara and add straight into a dish with the cassava fries.

SPICY TAMARIND BARBECUED FROG LEGS

RAWLSTON WILLIAMS

Chef Rawlston Williams was born on the Caribbean island nation of St. Vincent and the Grenadines, raised in Brooklyn, New York, and trained at the French Culinary Institute. He offers an elevated, forward-thinking take on Caribbean classics, a unique approach influenced by his worldly background and free-spirited life experiences. Chef Williams is constantly experimenting with new flavor combinations, always with bold and beautiful presentations, aiming to nourish and please.

SERVES 4

1 lb (450 g) frog legs (use chicken thighs as a substitute, if needed)

FOR THE MARINADE

1 scotch bonnet pepper, finely chopped

1 tablespoon finely chopped broad leaf thyme (Cuban oregano)

1 tablespoon finely chopped thyme

2 cloves garlic, minced

1 tablespoon finely chopped fresh culantro

2 tablespoons lime juice

1 teaspoon fresh ginger, grated

½ teaspoon salt

½ teaspoon ground black pepper

FOR THE BARBECUE SAUCE

2 tablespoons coconut oil

¼ cup (2 fl oz/60 ml) tangerine juice

½ teaspoon ground mace

¼ cup (2 oz/60 g) molasses

1 tablespoon brown sugar

¼ cup (2 oz/60 g) fresh tamarind pulp

¼ cup (2 oz/60 g) tomato paste

¼ cup (2 fl oz/60 ml) dark rum, optional

FOR THE MARINADE Combine the scotch bonnet pepper, broad leaf thyme (Cuban oregano), thyme, garlic, culantro, lime juice, ginger, salt, and black pepper in a large bowl. Alternatively, combine them in a blender or food processor.

Add the frog legs to the marinade and refrigerate for a minimum of 2 hours, or ideally overnight.

FOR THE BARBECUE SAUCE In a small heavy-bottomed saucepan, combine the coconut oil, tangerine juice, mace, molasses, brown sugar, tamarind pulp, tomato paste, and dark rum. Cook over medium to low heat until the sauce begins to thicken, whisking occasionally. Remove from the heat, strain, and set aside.

Remove the frog legs from the marinade and place on a wood-fired grill at medium heat. Cook for 3 minutes on each side or until fully cooked. Start basting the frog legs with the tamarind barbecue sauce after 90 seconds for each side. The aim is to allow the sugars and protein to develop a wonderful char.

Serve with additional barbecue sauce on the side and charred fruit such as pineapples.

INDEX

Hugh Mangum

Born to a father from Texas and a mother from the Bronx, in New York City, chef Hugh Mangum grew up appreciating the diverse food culture of Los Angeles. However, he always found the best barbeque, prepared by his father, in his backyard. In his twenties, Mangum toured as a professional musician drumming for bands including Maypole and Enemy. He eventually enrolled at the French Culinary Institute in New York, honoring an inheritance he received from his father.

In 2001, Mangum joined acclaimed chef Greg Brainin in New York at Jean George's Nougatine, where he found a natural knack for the meat station. Mangum worked for chefs in New York City and Philadelphia, before he and his wife Laura Malone converted an old general store in Carversville, Pennsylvania, into a specialty café serving prepared foods. The general store also served as Mangum's first incarnation of preparing smoked meats for customers.

In 2008, Mangum became the executive chef and pit master of Smoking Lil's restaurant in Doylestown, Pennsylvania. He then became executive chef and chief creative officer for Jules Thin Crust, an innovative pizza chain.

In 2011, Mangum introduced his slow-smoked barbecue creations to Smorgasburg, an outdoor food market in Brooklyn. Mighty Quinn's Barbeque, named after his eldest son Quinn, was an instant success and led to a flagship eatery in Manhattan's East Village. It received glowing reviews, most notably from Pete Wells of *The New York Times*, who gave it two stars, the highest rating for a barbecue restaurant in New York City. Since then, Mighty Quinn's has expanded throughout the United States.

Many know Mangum from his television appearances, including *Cook Like an Iron Chef* with Michael Symon, *Unique Eats*, and *Beat Bobby Flay*. He is a *Chopped* champion and appeared in the critically acclaimed movie, *Julie & Julia*. Mangum was the runner-up in season 5 of the Food Network show, *BBQ Brawl*.

In 2020, Mangum. with his wife and business partner Laura Malone, opened Rise Doughnuts in Wilton, Connecticut, which was named "Best Doughnuts in Connecticut" by *Connecticut Magazine* and was featured on *Good Morning America*.

Mangum currently lives in Connecticut with his wife and three children.

Shana Liebman

Shana Liebman is an award-winning writer and editor with a BA from Brown University, an MFA in fiction writing from Columbia University, and a culinary degree from the Institute of Culinary Education. She has a passion for food, culture, and storytelling and aspires to combine her literary pursuits with her love of cooking.

Her articles and essays have been featured in publications such as *New York Magazine*, *Salon*, *The New York Observer*, and *The Independent*, and she has explored a wide range of topics—from the sex lives of stay-at-home-moms to the rental-chicken industry; from New York street food to Jewish Elvis impersonators to ketamine clinics. She writes about travel—from guesthouses in Vieques to fine dining in the Algarve—for magazines, including *Endless Vacation*, *Travel & Leisure*, and *Budget Travel*. Shana is also the restaurant critic for *The Hudson Independent* and develops recipes for cookbooks and websites, including FOOD52.

As the Arts Editor of *Heeb Magazine*, she produced the acclaimed Heeb Storytelling series at Joe's Pub in New York City, which led to her book, *Sex, Drugs & Gefilte Fish* (an anthology of stories told by leading writers, comedians, and other Jewish superstars), published by Hachette in 2009. More recently, as the Chair of the Irvington Theater, she produces popular events, including documentary screenings, filmmaking classes for teens, and an annual short film festival.

Shana lives in New York with her husband and two sons, where she is an avid home cook—and, now more than ever, a die-hard barbecue aficionado.

ACKNOWLEDGMENTS
Hugh Mangum

I would like to start by thanking Keith Fox for humoring my request to have a conversation about writing this book and for giving me the opportunity to see that conversation come to fruition. Your trust in me has not been taken lightly. I am forever grateful.

To Emily Takoudes, thank you for your guidance, patience, and trust. Embarking on this journey was both exciting and daunting, and you have been so supportive and available. When I told my manager that we were working together, without hesitation he said, "Emily is the best there is... period." It is my great fortune that I have only ever worked with the best.

Rachel Malig & Ellie Smith... Shana and I are incredibly grateful for your guidance and ability to keep us on track while still imparting levity in the whole process. Here's to the next one!

To Nico Schinco, Katie Wayne, and Nikki Jessup... from the first "test shoot" day you all felt like old, close friends. Your enthusiasm and attention to detail were so appreciated. I am blessed that you were the team chosen to shoot and essentially cook this book. If I am so fortunate to do this again, I truly hope you all will join me. Thank you all so very much.

To Adam Johnson, this whole life in BBQ really took off after receiving a call from you back in 2010. Your spirit and your ability to always be pushing for the next thing is what guided me to Smorgasburg, where MQ was born in earnest. You are a believer in the good in people, you are a connecter, always looking to help out your people, and I am forever in debt to your belief in me. The world most definitely needs more Adam Johnsons in it.

To Alex Stanko, so much of what is in this book was born of our friendship and collaborating. For many years we spent more time together than with our families... countless long days and late nights playing with ideas and passion. You always supported me and had my back. Cooking with you will always be one of the greatest joys of my life and I could not have tackled this book without the work we put in together. It was, indeed, worth it.

John Criswell... you have taught me about loyalty and, outside of my family, you were the one who pushed me to dive into the BBQ deep end. You have always believed in me, and I am eternally grateful for our friendship.

To Kelli Solomon, thank you for converting, crunching, and organizing. Your attention to detail has been such a tremendous help. Shana and I are both so thankful for your assistance on this project.

Scott Feldman and Sarah Jane Coolahan, thank you both for always trying to make it happen. For advocating for me. For taking me on all those years ago. For negotiating, for advising, and for believing in me, even when I haven't.

To Micheal Symon and Bobby Flay, you have been my mentors since before we were friends. I've looked up to you both since 2000 while I was attending culinary school. Then as luck would have it we became friends. Your insight, opinions, and support have meant more to me than you will ever know. Thank you both for treating me like family.

To Michael Voltaggio, thank you for your friendship and for mentoring me. Thanks for your collaborative spirit and for your eagerness to share your knowledge. I am forever grateful to you.

To Shana Liebman, this book does not happen without you. Putting together a book of this size is an incredibly large undertaking, and you have worked tirelessly and passionately from the beginning. In what was quite a chaotic year of multiple projects for me, you have been my rock. You have been patient, insightful, and masterful in your gathering of information. Your collaborative spirit has been unmatched, and I cannot express enough my gratitude to have been able to work with you. My only hope is that this is only the first book we get to work on together. Thank you is simply not enough. Thank you too to Robin Hom for connecting us.

Kathy and Andy, thank you for your enthusiastic support and belief in me. You have always cheered me on with excitement, and it means the world to me that you are in my corner. I am forever grateful.

Mom, thanks for setting an example of hard work, tenaciousness, and entrepreneurial spirit. You never took no for an answer, and I'm happy that that part of you is alive and well in me. Thank you mom.

Dad, your enthusiasm towards delicious food was infectious and stoked an excitement in me since I was little. There seemed to be no place that wasn't worth a road trip if you had heard that they were serving something special. This book is a love letter to you. It is inspired by you; by your travels all over the world; by your birthplace in Texas and my attempt to cook the way you did, with all your heart and soul. It is inspired by all of the stories I eagerly listened to about food and meals past; by all of the conversations we had while eating delicious food... that is truly my most fond memory. I miss your voice so very much. Thank you for planting the seed and cultivating my passion in food that has become my North Star. You have been with me every step of the way. I love you. I hope I've made you proud.

To my wife Laura and kids Quinn, Lucas, and Henry, you are my world and the reason I exist. Thank you all for putting up with my kind of crazy; for dealing with my schedule these past twenty years, and for laughing at my jokes... sometimes. I can only say that I love you all with every fiber of my being, and making you all proud is what motivates me.

Laura, thank you for being the ultimate collaborator. Your prowess as a chef is only overshadowed by the incredible mother you are. I am forever in awe of you.

ACKNOWLEDGMENTS
Shana Liebman

First and foremost, I want to thank Hugh Mangum for the tremendous opportunity to join him on this journey. When we met, he reassured me that he was "not one of those asshole chefs." In fact, he is one of the most gracious, talented, and big-hearted people I know. I look forward to continuing our weekly chats, even when we are not debating direct vs. indirect heat. Also, I am so grateful to Robin Hom for connecting us.

Thank you, Emily Takoudes, for masterfully guiding us through the initial darkness and for trusting us to make a great book. Your eagle eye is unparalleled. Rachel Malig and Ellie Smith—thank you for all your thoughtful edits and needed encouragement. This book also benefited immensely from the great Kelli Solomon's editorial and culinary knowledge.

I could not have taken such a deep dive into global barbecue without my well-traveled, barbecue-savvy friends, Nick Diamond, Mike Didovic, Dave Herman, Bobby Kaufman, Jeremy Toeman, and Alexander Rus, who taught me all about backyard smokers, the difference between *mici* and *ćevapi*, and how to turn a plant pot into a tandoori oven. To Nicole Davis, my culinary partner in crime and beloved friend.

Thank you to my ICE instructors, Chef Celine (Beitchman) and Chef Jay (Weinstein), for your patience, wisdom, and for kicking my butt.

I am grateful for my loving parents' devotion to exceptional food, specifically my dad's inspirational passion for adventurous dining and my mom's enduring cleverness and curiosity in the kitchen (and for helping me organize hundreds of recipes in one crazy spreadsheet).

Finally, SO much love to Michael and my boys, Nate and Mack, for helping me eat my way around New York City (*méchoui* in Harlem, *inihaw na liempo* in Sunset Park, *char siu* in Flushing, jerk in the South Bronx, *esquites* on the Lower East Side). And for never doubting that I could write a book about barbecue. You guys are my everything.

RECIPE NOTES

Butter should always be unsalted, unless otherwise specified.

All herbs are fresh, unless otherwise specified.

Eggs are large (UK medium) unless otherwise specified.

Individual vegetables and fruits, such as onions and apples, are assumed to be medium, unless otherwise specified.

All milk is whole (3% fat), homogenized, and lightly pasteurized, unless otherwise specified.

Salt is always kosher salt, unless otherwise specified.

Exercise a high level of caution when following recipes involving any potentially hazardous activity, including the use of high temperatures, open flames, and when deep-frying. In particular, when deep-frying add food carefully to avoid splashing, wear long sleeves, and never leave the pan unattended.

Cooking times are for guidance only. If using a fan (convection) oven, follow the manufacturer's instructions concerning the oven temperatures.

All herbs, shoots, flowers, and leaves should be picked fresh from a clean source. Do exercise caution when foraging for ingredients, which should only be eaten if an expert has deemed them safe to eat. In particular, do not gather wild mushrooms yourself before seeking the advice of an expert who has confirmed their suitability for human consumption. As some species of mushrooms have been known to cause allergic reaction and illness, do take extra care when cooking and eating mushrooms and do seek immediate medical help if you experience a reaction after preparing or eating them.

Exercise caution when making fermented products, ensuring all equipment is spotlessly clean, and seek expert advice if in any doubt.

When no quantity is specified, for example of oils, salts, and herbs used for finishing dishes, quantities are discretionary and flexible.

All spoon and cup measurements are level, unless otherwise stated. 1 teaspoon = 5 ml; 1 tablespoon = 15 ml. Australian standard tablespoons are 20 ml, so Australian readers are advised to use 3 teaspoons in place of 1 tablespoon when measuring small quantities.

Cup, metric, and imperial measurements are used in this book. Follow one set of measurements throughout, not a mixture, as they are not interchangeable.

Grills can be either gas or charcoal.

A grill on high is 450°F/230°C or higher; medium is 350°F/180°C; low is 300°F/150°C.

Indirect heat means one side of the grill or smoker is hot, and the other side is cool. Unless indicated, heat the grill to direct heat (all burners on).

Phaidon Press Limited
2 Cooperage Yard
London E15 2QR

Phaidon Press Inc.
111 Broadway
New York, NY 10006

phaidon.com

First published 2025
©2025 Phaidon Press Limited

ISBN 978 1 83866 936 2

A CIP catalogue record for this book is available from the British Library and the Library of Congress.

Commissioning Editor: Emily Takoudes
Project Editor: Rachel Malig
Design: Evi-O.Studio | Evi O
Typesetting: Evi-O.Studio | Katherine Zhang
Production Controller: Andie Trainer
Photography: Nico Schinco
Food styling: Kaitlin Wayne
Food styling assistants: Nikki Jessop, Brett Statman, Nik McLeod, Max Bruno

Printed in China

The publisher and authors would like to thank Vanessa Bird, Cristina Lago, Michelle Meade, João Mota, Ellie Smith, Tracey Smith, and Kathy Steer for their contributions to the book.

And with special thanks to the guest chefs for their generous contributions: Maksut Askar, May Chow, Ross Dobson, Moustafa Elrefaey, Monique Fiso, Renzo Garibaldi, Elizabeth Karmel, Vusumuzi Ndlovu, Su Kyoung Park, Tomos Parry, Jess Pryles, Dave Pynt, Jessica Rosval, Sean Sherman, Marsia Taha Mohamed Salas, and Rawlston Williams.